UNDER THE WEATHER

Tom Fort was educated at Eton and Balliol College, Oxford, and spent more than twenty [obscured] as a journalist for BBC Radio News in Londo[n] [obscured] *Greener*, a social history of law[obscured] *of Eels*, a study of the fr[obscured] Oxfordshire, and is now wo[rking] [obscured].

Praise for *Under the Weather*

'A great little book about the British obsession with the climate, it's full of fruitful parcels of meteorological lore'
Conde Nast Traveller

'A delightfully discursive book' *Daily Mail*

'An enjoyable book' *Sunday Times*

'*Under the Weather* is a capacious book … a worthy addition to that long-lived conversation, and a reminder of how compelling it is' *Guardian*

'Fort has an appealing enthusiasm for his subject'
Financial Times

'He has written an entertaining survey of the history of man's ceaseless struggle to answer the big question: do I need to take my mac?' *Independent*

Also available by Tom Fort

The Grass is Greener
The Far From Compleat Angler
The Book of Eels

TOM FORT

UNDER THE WEATHER

arrow books

Published in the United Kingdom by Arrow Books in 2007

1 3 5 7 9 10 8 6 4 2

Copyright © Tom Fort 2006

Tom Fort has asserted his right under the Copyright, Designs
and Patents Act, 1988 to be identified as the author of this work.

This book is sold subject to the condition that it shall not, by way of
trade or otherwise, be lent, resold, hired out, or otherwise circulated without the
publisher's prior consent in any form of binding or cover other than that in
which it is published and without a similar condition, including this
condition, being imposed on the subsequent purchaser

First published in the United Kingdom in 2006 by Century

Arrow Books
The Random House Group Limited
20 Vauxhall Bridge Road, London, SW1V 2SA

Addresses for companies within The Random House Group Limited
can be found at: www.randomhouse.co.uk

The Random House Group Limited Reg. No. 954009

A CIP catalogue record for this book
is available from the British Library

ISBN 9780099461241

The Random House Group Limited makes every effort to ensure
that the papers used in its books are made from trees that have been
legally sourced from well-managed and credibly certified forests. Our paper
procurement policy can be found at: www.randomhouse.co.uk/paper.htm

Typeset by Palimpsest Book Production Limited, Grangemouth, Stirlingshire
Printed and bound in Great Britain by
Bookmarque Ltd, Croydon, Surrey

To my children,
Hugh, Ellie, Ed, Rosie and Katie

Acknowledgements and Credits

I am enormously grateful to Philip Eden for having taken the trouble to read my original draft and to make many suggestions to improve it. Any errors and heretical opinions that survive are entirely my responsibility and not his. I am also deeply appreciative of the efforts of my agent, Caroline Dawnay, who never gave up and never stopped encouraging me; and of the perceptiveness of Mark Booth at Century for commissioning the book. My thanks also go to John Yealland at the Clock Workshop in Caversham, Tony Kitto at Towneley Hall, Steve Jebson at the Met Office in Exeter, Edward Conant at Lyndon Hall, Halla Beloff, David Uttley, Sinclair Ross, Charles Briscoe, Adam Clark-Williams, Stephen Taylor and Matt Morris. Above all, I thank my wife, Helen, because without her the book would certainly not have been written.

I am also grateful to the following authors and publishers for permission to use quotations: Sinclair Ross, *The Culbin Sands: Fact and Fiction*; David Uttley, *The Anatomy of the Helm Wind*; Jane Brown, *The Pursuit of Happiness*; Nicholas Goodison, *English Barometers 1680–1860*; Charles Nevin, *Lancashire: Where Women Die of Love*; Cambridge University Press, William Burroughs, *Climate Change*;

Cicerone Press, Norman Nicholson, *The Lakers*; HarperCollins, Gordon Manley, *Climate and the British Scene*.

Where I have been unable to secure the relevant permission, I offer apologies and undertake to make any necessary corrections in future editions.

Contents

'It [meteorology] is a science of the pure air and of the bright heaven' — John Ruskin

Chapter 1

Weatherwise and Otherwise

THE BAROMETER HANGS AGAINST THE WALL IN THE KITCHEN. THE DARK, soft glow of the mahogany veneer, set off by the white of the paintwork, draws the eye to it. It is long and slender, elegant, quiet, intriguing. At the top, framed in the arched pediment, gleams a little brass finial. Below, the door of the register plate has moulded edges and is decorated with chequered stringing. The plate itself is made of brass and has been silvered by being rubbed with silver nitrate. Two of the legends – FAIR and RAIN – are engraved in Roman capitals; the others – *very dry, set fair, change, much rain, stormy* – in italics. Below the register descends the slim body of the instrument, the tube of mercury, winking and gleaming, held against the lustre of the wood by a brass bracket. At the bottom, concealing the ball of mercury, is a circle of wood, inlaid at its centre in ivory and ebony.

The name engraved along the top of the register plate is SOMALVICO JOSH, with the address 67 LEATHER LANE. Thereby hangs a story, but it is one that has been lost, since the Somalvicos – who were once numerous and prosperous – have vanished. So, too, have the little shops they ran, although the addresses survive.

The Italian instrument-makers came originally from around

Lake Como in Lombardy. They belonged to families of sub-sistence farmers, and sought to supplement meagre earnings by making and selling items to ornament the home: picture frames, looking glasses, bird cages and the like. They were clever with their hands, expert at carving, gilding and glass-blowing. But there was precious little in the way of a market for their skills among the impoverished peasants of the northern Italian plain, so they took to travelling north to peddle their artefacts. They went by mule and cart along the ancient trade route over the Alps into France. Some took the boat across Lake Constance and down the Rhine towards Holland. Some kept going until they reached England.

The first of the Somalvicos, Joseph – or Giuseppe, as the priest must have named him in whichever little church in whichever little village he was baptised – arrived in London around 1780. By then a small Italian community of craftsmen was already established in Holborn. Rents were low there, and employment could be found in one or other of the many workshops where the clocks, watches and precision instruments of which the English were so fond were made. The Italians were versatile, highly skilled and hard-working. Little by little they prospered and set up their own businesses. Then the word would go back to the family home in the village near the lake: come, there is a better life here.

England in the second half of the eighteenth century was the most prosperous country in Europe. It was also the most stable, the least troubled by currents and undercurrents of strife and revolution. There was the occasional upheaval, of which the Gordon Riots of 1780 was the most notable. But by and large the aristocracy and the waxing mercantile classes were able to organise matters for their own benefit and pleasure without much in the way of threat from below. The wealth flowing into the country from distant colonial conquests and from the booming manufacturing industry funded opulence and high living. Mansions sprouted in all parts of the land in parks laid out by Capability Brown or one of his imitators, and London was rebuilt to accommodate the aspirations of the ruling classes.

These country seats and town houses were decked out in the neo-classical style popularised by Robert Adam, and filled with paintings by Gainsborough and Reynolds, crockery by Wedgwood, chairs and sofas by Hepplewhite and Sheraton. Adam himself employed numerous Italian artists and craftsmen to carve and decorate the obligatory bas reliefs, stuccoed arabesques, wall panels and painted ceilings. But the rage for ornamentation went far beyond scenes from history and mythology, swag-draped chimneypieces, Corinthian pilasters, bacchic wreaths and the rest. The commissioning elite wanted the most ornate looking-glasses, the most intricately carved and gilded picture frames, the most interesting bird cages; and they wished to indulge their scientific enthusiasm by having the most elegant and instructive barometers to bend over and peer at and tap.

The Italian craftsmen in Holborn flourished. Joseph Somalvico opened a shop at 67 Leather Lane and sent for his sons Giacomo and Carlo, who became James and Charles. There were soon Somalvico premises in Brook Street, Hatton Garden, Kirby Street and at various addresses in Charles Street. A partnership was formed between Joseph Somalvico and Domenick (Domenico) Leone, and they made barometers at Holborn Hill and, subsequently, Brook Street.

Other Italians were arriving all the time, drawn by the stories of the money to be made from the English passion for the best craftsmanship. By 1840 they had percolated through the British Isles and dominated the trade in glass-blowing, spectacle-making, picture-framing, gilding, jewellery, music boxes and other decorative items, as well as clocks, watches, thermometers, telescopes and barometers. Some English instrument-makers even adopted bogus Italian names to share in the high reputation.

The Somalvicos do not seem to have strayed outside London. The multiplicity of addresses at which various members of the family traded at different times – Nicholas Goodison lists more than twenty in his standard reference book *English Barometers* – and the dearth of information about individuals make the dating of individual instruments difficult. Goodison places Joshua Somalvico at 67 Leather Lane as well as at 16 Charles Street and two addresses in Holborn, but with no dates, although he does suggest that the Leather Lane branch was still doing business after 1869. The style of my barometer, however, is of the early nineteenth century.

I inherited it from my grandmother. By then its mercury had long since perished, its tube had been broken and pieces had either fallen off and been lost, or been damaged. In this derelict state it accompanied me to various houses, to which it added a touch of distinction without serving any useful purpose. When I started working on this book, my wife decided that my labours would be encouraged if the Somalvico were restored. It so happens that a few miles from our home is a workshop which specialises in the restoration of clocks and precision instruments. The barometer was taken there; a year later it came back, its missing pieces replaced, its damaged pieces repaired, its register cleaned and re-engraved, its point and purpose restored. Now the shining glass tube containing the mercury rises unbroken from its hidden bowl, 32 inches in height, its top of the quicksilver column creeping up and down between its old friends Set Fair, Fair, Change and Rain.

I have no idea which Englishman (I assume it was a man) came out of 67 Leather Lane a couple of centuries ago with my Somalvico held carefully upright to keep the mercury in its place. Nor do I know who, over the intervening years, has stooped before it to stare at the glass and then out of the window, to check on the correspondence between liquid metal and the weather. All I do know is that they, whoever they were, and I are united in this one matter: which is that the instrument, and the elements outside, repay the trouble of study.

Everyone of my generation (I was born in 1951) remembers the freeze of '63, the heat wave of '76, the storm of October '87. For me, those weather events stand among the milestones along my life's path, marking boyhood, young manhood and respectable maturity. I say I remember them. But what do I remember?

I was eleven and a half when the most savage winter since 1740 announced itself with heavy snowfalls across much of the country on Boxing Day 1962. The freeze persisted until early the following March, with most of Britain under thick snow and suffering persistent sub-zero temperatures for at least sixty days. Transport was largely paralysed. Wildlife perished wholesale, including 90 per cent of the total population of wrens. Villages were cut off for days on end, and a family living in a remote farmhouse on Dartmoor saw no other human beings for more than two months. In Leicestershire a woman carrying bread was attacked and knocked to the ground by pigeons, while in the New Forest a woman who appeared outside her front door with a loaf was set upon by starving ponies.

But I remember none of this, not even looking out of the

window at the silent marvel of falling snow. I remember only short, finger-numbed days flying down an icy white slope on toboggans which could be directed with a steering mechanism at the front, so that at the bottom we – my elder brothers and I – veered left, shot over a frozen hummock, and landed on the ice of an old moat, slewing this way and that until we thumped against the bank at the far side. And being told that the Thames at Windsor was frozen, and that some of the boys at Eton College had been sent home because the pipes had burst, and wondering resentfully why the pipes at my prep school wouldn't do the same.

In May 1976, aged twenty-five, I left my job as a reporter on a weekly newspaper in Slough to take a rest after four years' work. In the middle of that June a high-pressure system of exceptional persistence settled over the British Isles. By the time it dispersed, amid torrential downpours, at the end of August, England and Wales had panted through the most severe drought for a thousand years. For two months on end there was a daily average of more than ten hours of sunshine. Trees shed their leaves early, rivers dried up, reservoirs were emptied. In Wales, more than a million people got their water from standpipes for nearly three months. As the heat wave proceeded, people wearied of it and became increasingly tetchy. But not me. I went to the Test match at Trent Bridge, Nottingham, where it was too hot to sit in my seat; and spent four days at the Oval in August watching the West Indies humble England on a ground burned biscuit-brown but for the valiant square of green in the middle. I played and watched cricket and went fishing in the early mornings before the sun came up, and in the evenings when it went down. I hung around in pub gardens, and one day roused myself to walk from Streatley on the Thames up on to the Ridgeway to Wantage, taking in three pints of bitter at the Bell at Aldworth, which did me no good at all under the scorching afternoon sun.

On 16 October 1987, by now a married man with two children and a third about to arrive, I was due at Broadcasting House in London for an eight o'clock start to my shift in the BBC's radio newsroom. As it turned out, I made it shortly after ten, and was the first of the day workers to get through. I was greeted with a ragged cheer by the night shift, who for twelve hours had been keeping the nation informed about the most destructive storm to strike Britain since the hurricane of November 1703, in which eight thousand lives were lost and which Queen Anne identified as 'a token of divine displeasure'. At the time, the havoc and devastation inflicted that October night – and in particular the spectacle on television and in the newspapers of great swathes of woodland splintered and flattened – were reported and interpreted in equally apocalyptic terms, as if a mortal blow had been struck at us and our heritage, as if things would never be the same again. In the event, the three million damaged houses were mostly repaired, and the fifteen million uprooted trees were cleared away and replaced in time by new, vigorous growth. The nation shrugged off the storm of '87 and went back to its business.

I remember the events, but not much of what happened. To find out the facts – the depth of the snow cover in '63, the temperatures in '76, the strength of the winds and the drop in barometric pressure in October '87 – I have to consult the records, compiled by those who have made the weather their profession or their passion, or both. I am not, and never have been, among them. I have never maintained a meteorological journal, nor ever thought of doing so. Yet I have always been, and always will be, attentive to the weather, aware of it, alive to it. I listen to the forecasts on the radio two or three times most days, and I like to linger over the weather charts and predictions in the newspapers. I even wonder, occasionally, why it is that the weather maps in my preferred daily paper, the *Guardian*, should be so inferior to those in *The Times* and the *Daily Telegraph*; the fact that I wouldn't consider changing on those grounds, however, indicates the limits of my commitment.

I like to think that I have a weather eye. My passion, as a recreation, is fishing, and all fishermen spend a great deal of time considering the weather, trying to work out what the weather is doing, suffering the weather and abusing the weather. We sniff the air, study the track and speed of the clouds. If the wind is in the north or the east, we frown. If the sun is blazing from a cloudless sky, we frown. If rain threatens, we frown; and if it arrives, we curse. We are very rarely happy about the weather, and very often unhappy. But I would not say that our unhappiness runs very deep, for it is most unusual for the weather to be so bad that it actually stops us fishing.

Widening the focus, and putting my fishing tackle to one side, I would venture a generalisation: that our weather suits us pretty well. This immediately begs the question: if that is so, why do we complain about it so much? It is related that Jonathan Swift, who complained more bitterly than most, went up to a stranger and asked him: 'Pray, do you remember any good weather?' 'Yes, sir,' came the answer, 'I can remember a great deal of good weather in my time.' 'That is more than I can say,' retorted Swift, 'I can never remember any weather that was not too hot or too cold; too wet or too dry; but, however God contrives it, at the end of the year 'tis all very well.'

It is not that we enjoy our weather, but that we feel safe with it. In many countries of the world, the weather is regarded – with good reason – as an indifferent or even hostile force, to be watched closely, appeased if possible and not to be trusted. Here, we instinctively feel that our weather is on our side. It has helped make these islands moist and fertile, enabling us to grow the crops and raise the livestock to feed us. In alliance with the seas that surround us, it has kept our enemies at bay. It encourages us to go about our business all year round, and to take our pleasure when we feel like it. It nurtures the national pastime of gardening and permits most outside activities, even though it regularly casts clouds over Wimbledon and Lord's. It does not smite us with typhoons and our tornadoes are modest affairs. It does not wither us with heat or paralyse us with snow and ice. We can afford to abuse it, confident it will not turn against us. We grouse about it as we do about old friends with endearing, if sometimes irritating, idiosyncracies.

Our weather is crucial to our apprehension of our country and our place in it. That sense of a common experience and understanding has made the weather an indispensable reference point for writers and painters. Everyone knows what Shakespeare is talking about:

> Shall I compare thee to a summer's day?
> Thou art more lovely and more temperate:
> Rough winds do shake the darling buds of May
> And summer's lease hath all too short a date.

In the same way, everyone knows and has been under a Constable sky. Constable said he had been born to paint his own England, and he knew that he had to get the weather right. So he learned, with great labour, to tell what Ruskin termed 'the truth of clouds', and in doing so he defined our image of the English countryside in the Arcadian past. Mountains of billowing cumulonimbus ascend, white, black and grey, split by rents of blue through which the shafts of sunlight pour down on the fields, the woods, the river, the rose-draped cottages, the cattle, the country folk about their business. Rain is rarely far away, but these are summer storms and we know that the sun will shine again soon. The moment is captured – look away and back, and you expect to see the mounds of vapour shifted, the sunlit copse in shade, the shadowed river sparkling. This is our England, our weather, familiar, ever-changing, 'constant in nothing but inconstancy'.

Storytellers depend on the weather to create a familiar place where their readers can feel at home. It conjures up atmosphere and setting, and often makes itself useful in developing plots. Rain and fog are depressing. Frost and snow are exhilarating, unless you are poor. Showers are handy for getting characters to shelter under trees or hasten indoors. Sustained downpours bring strangers into close proximity and give them something to talk about. Ice encourages skating, which in turn encourages sparkling eyes, tingling cheeks and flirtation. Extreme cold can be deployed to remove characters who have served their purpose, as can gales – witness the fate of Steerforth and Ham in *David Copperfield*. Sustained heat is particularly favoured for eroding conventional norms of behaviour and promoting lust, jealousy and nervous irritation as well as the shedding of in-hibitions often followed by clothes. In Jane Austen's *Emma*, it takes a day of uncomfortable summer heat at Mr Knightley's residence, Donwell Abbey, to reveal the seething brew of tensions concealed beneath the genteel surface of Highbury society; and it is the reappearance of the summer sun after days of dismal rain that coaxes flawed heroine and stuffy hero into each other's arms in the novel's climactic scene. In the supreme English weather novel, L. P. Hartley's *The Go-Between*, the boy Leo is enchanted and blinded by the power of summer, which simultaneously stokes up the dark and destructive passions around him, until the storm bursts and realisation, violence and tragedy are unleashed.

Once, of course, we counted the weather as being one of the favours bestowed on us by a God who regarded us with particular favour among the nations of the world. As recently as 1944, 'God's restraining hand' was widely credited for tilting the balance in the fortunes of war in our direction. In a book called *The War, The Weather and God*, George Vallance, an evangelist on behalf of the Plymouth Brethren, declared that 'the miracle of Dunkirk was BECAUSE OF THE WEATHER. Had not those waters been as still as a millpond it could never have happened. But the remarkable FACT is that the Nation had been at PRAYER the previous Sunday.'

Periodically, exceptional periods of wet, cold or drought prompted a suspicion that God's arrangements on our behalf might have gone temporarily awry. Towards the end of the sodden summer of 1860, the Church of England distributed a Prayer for Fair Weather to be read at divine service on 20 August. The Reverend Charles Kingsley, rector of the impoverished rural parish of Eversley in Hampshire and the author of, among much else, *The Water Babies*, refused and instead preached a sermon on the wrong-headedness of the prayer. It referred, he said, to the rain as a plague and a punishment. But, Kingsley objected, he had been given no proof of this. 'I have, rather, proof to the contrary,' he told his congregation. 'There is great reason to believe that these rains, over-heavy and hurtful as they seem, are really a boon and a blessing.' He said that to pray for fine weather was simply wrong. If the prayer was uttered with no expectation of it being answered, God was being mocked. And if there was such an expectation? 'I know little or nothing about the weather and God knows all,' Kingsley declared. 'Which is most likely to be right: God or I?'

That degree of confidence in providence has largely disappeared, and, at the same time, our common experience of our weather has become progressively more superficial. In Kingsley's day, it was still an immensely important factor in daily life. As Brian Cathcart pointed out in his book *Rain*, we find it almost impossible to imagine the extent to which, in bygone times, adverse weather inhibited communication, transport and economic life, and affected comfort and health. Innovations such as the umbrella and the mackintosh, the development of the railway system, the use of better building materials and advances in water-heating encouraged a detachment between Britons and the weather which gathered pace through the nineteenth century. In our own time we have grown used to being able to do what we need or wish to do irrespective of what the weather is up to. It has become incidental to life, rather than central. Of course, the experience of it varies. A hill farmer on the Welsh mountains or Cumbrian fells will expect to endure a degree of weather-inflicted discomfort inconceivable to molly-coddled, office-bound southern suburbanites. But even he will be comparatively warm and dry within his waterproofs, and will return from the storm-swept hillsides to hot water and central heating.

It is very rare for our weather to turn against us with serious intent. When this happens, we are always unprepared and undone. Railway lines buckle in the heat, an inch of snow reduces major roads to gridlock, floodwaters surge through town centres, coastal defence walls are breached, and newspaper leader writers demand to know why THEY — the government, government agencies, councils — can't get their act together. Inquiries are set up and researchers sent to places like Norway where they manage extremes more efficiently. Psychologically, we are startled and flummoxed, as if an old friend had suddenly taken a swing at us, and we become alarmed and angry. For a moment we sense hidden, frightening possibilities within the familiar mix of our elements. But this does not last. The snow melts, the heat moderates, the floods subside, the researchers come back from Norway to make recommendations which are ignored on the grounds of cost, the pattern reasserts itself, confidence is restored.

Foreigners are generally mystified by our response to our weather. They find it difficult to understand how anybody can be other than melancholic in a land where sunshine and warmth are so rationed, nor how a society can organise itself purposefully when the main external influence on it is so unpredictable and inconstant. They do not understand that our attitude has nothing to do with enjoyment, and everything to do with feeling secure. They search for the melancholy concealed beneath the stolidity, and theorise about the kind of people we are and the way in which our weather has acted upon us. The American Ralph Waldo Emerson — who liked the weather here because it reminded him of his native Massachussetts, but without the snow — found that 'the bias of the nation is a passion for utility', with a mind that 'turns every abstraction it can into a portable utensil', and a logic 'that brings salt to soup and oar to boat'.

We — being more conscious than visitors of the differences between us — are less inclined towards generalisations about the kind of people we are. We may suspect that our weather must have exercised its influence, but we are hard-pressed to identify the shared traits which might be attributed to it. What we do share is a kind of grudging affection for it, a belief that, for all its quirks, it somehow suits us; and, famously, the habit of talking about it.

Johnson's celebrated dictum — 'When two Englishmen meet, their first talk is of the weather' — is one of the unshakeable truisms about us. It is also an aspect of our self-image to which we are rather attached, in the questionable belief that it amounts to an endearing collective eccentricity. Johnson's next observation about the two typical John Bulls is less frequently quoted: 'They are in haste to tell each other what each must already know; that it is hot or cold, bright or cloudy, windy or calm.' It is true that most weather conversation is predictable, repetitive and plain dull. But Johnson was utterly wrong to assert that the weather itself is not worthy of notice. By turning his broad back to it, he was the loser.

The Sunday before writing these words, I played cricket on a lovely ground perched on a hill to the south of Newbury in Berkshire. The game was, as Sunday afternoon cricket is, a mixture of honest endeavour, modest accomplishment, incompetence and occasional flashes of skill, all unfolded at a leisurely pace. But overhead the drama of the skies was swift and compelling. One moment the sun shone warmly, bathing the turf and the belt of trees around the boundary in gold. The next, the blue was annexed by vast, billowing clouds burdened with grey. Sometimes the clouds were chased away before they could do any harm, but a couple of times sharp showers fell. The home side's innings prospered and our thoughts in the field turned to tea, and our own chance to bat. We trooped off to engage with egg mayonnaise and cheese and pickle sandwiches, cakes and buttered malt bread. Looking back, I saw the sky to the south-west darkening from side to side. By the time our innings began there was no blue anywhere and the gloom was menacing. Thunder muttered and a first drift of rain swept in over the trees as the players dashed to put the covers over the wicket. Within a few minutes the deluge had set in. The rain obscured much of the ground, beat on the roof of the clubhouse, churned along the gutters and down the pipes. Ponds sprang up across the outfield, while inside we drank beer, exchanged meteorological banalities and bemoaned our luck. By the time I left for home, the sun was dazzling and I had to shield my eyes against the glare off the standing water.

No one drowned or was struck by lightning. There was no damage to property or crops. Beyond the usual traffic jams, there was no inconvenience, no harm done other than the loss of half an inconsequential cricket match. It had been no more than a summer storm. The weather had merely gone through part of its repertoire, and given us surprise, excitement, theatrics and beauty to console us for the termination of our fun. Hazlitt described how he and Coleridge were taking refreshment at an inn when a thunderstorm burst outside, and how the poet 'went running out bare-headed to enjoy the commotion of the elements'. That is what Johnson missed.

There is an abundance of synonyms to describe the quintessence of our weather. Changeable, capricious, fickle, inconstant, mercurial, unpredictable – call it what you will, it comes down to the same, treasurable quality: that it banishes boredom and monotony, keeps us guessing and watching. 'Everyone talks about the weather,' Mark Twain is supposed to have quipped, 'but no one does anything about it.' But would we, if we could? I hope not.

Chapter 2

The Flame is Lit in Driby

THE LANE LEADS TO DRIBY AND NOWHERE ELSE. IT LEAVES THE MAIN road between Louth and Skegness on a ridge of the Lincolnshire Wolds, winds down through fields, then up, swings right and there you are. Only, so insignificant is Driby that you would hardly think yourself in a place worthy of a name at all; and if it weren't for the fact that the lane comes to an end, you would keep searching. There is a small farm on the right, and on the left a little mid-Victorian church now converted into a house, whose dark stone walls are tinged with green lichen. There is a pair of cottages, a square brick house, and at the end of the lane two more cottages, beyond which is the water treatment works, a cluster of ugly, square, flat-roofed buildings enclosed within barbed wire.

That is the sum of Driby today. But if you pause for a moment and study the contours of the land carefully, you may be able to detect an arrangement of grassy mounds and declivities hinting at an ancient, buried past. These are the remains of the earthworks and moat which once guarded the house at the heart of the manor of Driby, which was held before the Norman Conquest by Siward, who helped Hereward the Wake defend the Isle of Ely against William's men. After Siward came Gilbert de

Gaunt, who had Driby and much else conferred on him by a grateful conqueror; and after him assorted Simons and Roberts de Driby; and after them, through the female line, various Bernaks and Cromwells.

The last family of substance at Driby Manor were the Prescotts, who bought it in about 1580 and died out a generation or two later. The subsequent three and a half centuries seem to have passed without anything of note happening in Driby, bar the replacement of the old church of St Michael by the new in 1850. Not that the previous six centuries were packed with incident. But Driby does warrant two minor historical footnotes. One records an early outbreak of rural lawlessness, in 1369, when 'on the Feast of the Translation of St Hugh of Lincoln, Robert de Bernak was spoiled and beaten in Driby by false and malicious men, robbers and thieves, and Robert Pepir, his reave, and Henry his butler were wounded and slain'. The other chronicles the presentation in 1330 to St Michael's Church of its new rector, William Merle, a Fellow of Merton College, Oxford.

It was the second of these that had moved me to come to Driby. It would hardly be proper to follow the story of the British fascination with the weather without doing honour to the man who started it all.

As is the way with these shadowy medieval types, almost nothing is known of William Merle's life other than that he ministered to the souls of Driby, that he died in 1347, the year before the Black Death, and that for some unknown reason he was moved to maintain a daily record of the weather between January 1337 and January 1344. Even that little is not entirely sure, since the one subsequent reference to him – by the seventeenth-century Oxford antiquary Robert Plot – called him Walter and stated that he 'observed the weather here at Oxford

17

every day of the month, seven years altogether'. Furthermore, although the original manuscript of the weather diary describes him as '*per Magistrum Willelmum Merle socum domus de Merton*', his name does not appear on the extant lists of Merton Fellows for the period.

Never mind. The diary exists, a thin folio volume of vellum except for its seventeenth-century calf cover, the first to be devoted to the single, consumingly interesting subject of the weather in England. It is in Latin, in brown ink except for the first letter of each paragraph, which is decoratively inscribed in red. At the top of the manuscript another, later hand has provided a title – '*Temeperies* [a misspelling of "temperies"] *aeris oxoniae pro sentennio*' – which was translated in a late nineteenth-century edition as *Temperature of the Air at Oxford for Seven Years*. This is thoroughly misleading since it is a record of the weather rather than temperature, which Merle had no means of measuring; and was clearly made partly in Oxford but mainly in Lincolnshire.

Here is an extract, to give a flavour of the first British weather journal. It is from November 1342, 661 years to the month before I sat down to transcribe these words:

2nd heavy fall of snow. 3rd and 4th slight frost. 5th thaw. 6th W. wind with rain. 7th stronger W. wind than on the 6th. 8th and 9th slight frost, with hoar-frost. 10th cold without frost but after mid-day there was no cold until the 15th when there was a slight frost with hoar-frost. 20th, 22nd and 23rd light rain. 22nd strong S.W. wind. 21st wind but no so strong, and before 21st there was W. wind. 25th and 26th light rain. On the last day there was slight frost with ice and hoar-frost.

The outstanding failing of the weather journal as a literary form – its dullness – is amply illustrated by this sample. Only one of William Merle's entries has any intrinsic dramatic interest, and that is the one for 28 March 1343, when 'at mid-day there was an earthquake which was so great that in certain parts of Lyndesay [the district of Lincolnshire including Driby] the stones in the chimneys fell down after shaking in very great agitation and it lasted long enough for the *Salutatio Angelica* to be said distinctly'. This sensation aside, Merle's journal is a model of the commonplace. And how could it be otherwise? All he has are the elements familiar to us all: rain, snow, wind, sunshine, hail, dew, frost, fog, mist, cloud. Of itself, the weather in Lincolnshire on a particular day in 1340 is no more worthy of note than that in south Oxfordshire last Tuesday. The interest of Merle's journal is not in its contents, but its timing.

Naturally, climatologists intent on finding out what our weather has been up to over the past ages have a different perspective. The records of William Merle and his many successors – however insubstantial, incomplete, inaccurate, subjective and uninteresting – are fondly cherished. For historical detectives otherwise reliant on fragmentary allusions in assorted annals, chronicles and manorial account rolls, occasionally backed up by the enigmatic testimony of tree rings, pollen deposits and deep soil cores, a systematic record compiled by a man of education is climatological gold dust. They are happy to overlook the obvious statistical shortcomings in their eagerness to extrapolate the pattern. In that context, the most striking feature of the weather observed by William Merle is its familiarity. The winters were generally mild and damp, the one exception being twelve weeks of snow and frost between December 1338 and February 1339. The summer of 1338 was extremely hot, and there were considerable heat waves in the summers around then, although from 1341 onwards they were mainly cool and dismal. It adds up to the usual mixture: a bit of this, a bit of that, not too much of anything.

What interested me, as I stood in Driby one Friday morning in early April – fine, dry, temperature in mid-teens Celsius, high cloud, periods of pallid spring sunshine – was what went on in the weather observer's mind. What kind of man could take pleasure in a duty which to the majority of his fellows would appear punishing in its tedium and pointlessness? An understandably generous view was taken by the late Professor Gordon Manley, a giant among twentieth-century British climatologists, who, in the course of his epic investigation into the climates of the past, pored over a great many of the surviving weather journals. 'The prolonged maintenance of daily observations,' Manley wrote, 'demands an uncommon type of enthusiasm.' Ralph Thoresby, an antiquary and collector of curiosities, noted in his diary for September 1702 that he had considered embarking on a regime of weather observation at his home in Yorkshire 'but am discouraged by the charge and tediousness'.

I discussed the matter with the only living soul I could find in Driby. He was the owner of the farm, although he had given up farming himself, preferring to let his fields and concentrate on tending horses, some of which he was coaxing from one paddock to another when I accosted him. We agreed that one factor influencing the Reverend Mr Merle's decision to start his journal might have been the lack of much else to do in these quiet parts. 'Not a lot happens around here,' my acquaintance said as we stood side by side looking out across the gently undulating fields towards Sutterby, Bag Enderby, Somersby – where Tennyson was born – South Ormsby and various other villages ending in -by. 'Still, it's a nice enough place to go broke slowly,' he added cheerfully.

Two other meteorological works were attributed to William Merle by George Symons, the pre-eminent weather authority of late Victorian times, who oversaw the printing of a facsimile of the journal, with an English translation, in 1891. These were the *Tractatus de prognosticacione aeris* and the *Notula de futura temperie aeris prognosticanda*. I do not know what is in these works – except that they deal with the dark mysteries of forecasting – nor on what grounds Symons made the attributions. What is certain is that whatever science is in them will have derived from the same source as every other European text on the subject composed in the two thousand years after Aristotle.

The *Meteorologica* was one of the treatises in which Aristotle recorded his comprehensive account of the universe as seen from Greece in the middle of the fourth century BC. He sought to explain what was happening in the skies over his own head and those of his pupils and followers in the context of a cosmos with an unmoving earth at its centre. Since Aristotle's description of the weather over Greece was, with some minor variations, to dictate Europe's understanding of its weather until around the time Charles I lost his head, it's worth attempting a simple exposition of its fundamentals.

The Aristotelian cosmic system purported to identify the forces dictating the conditions of our world, our bodies and our minds. The boundary of our universe was marked by the moon, beyond which extended aether, or prime matter, through which the stars pursued their unchanging paths. There were four elements within our universe: the earth and its three surrounding, concentric circles of water, air and fire. Each element was invested with two of the fundamental qualities of hot and cold, which are

21

active; and dry and moist, which are passive. Thus the earth combined cold and dry, water cold and wet, air hot and wet, fire hot and dry. Among their several functions, the elements determined our dispositions and state of health. For each element there was a humour, and for each humour a temperament, thus:

ELEMENT	HUMOUR	TEMPERAMENT
Fire	Yellow bile	Choleric
Air	Blood	Sanguine
Water	Phlegm	Phlegmatic
Earth	Black bile	Melancholic

The body produced the humours in the course of digestion, with the heart – possibly with the help of the liver – heating them into vapours which rose to the brain to establish the temperamental disposition.

The key was that the forces within the universe came from the shifting and unstable relationships between the elements, and between the humours. When the elements were mingled, without any one dominating the others, the world was orderly and humankind could go about its business without fear of natural disaster. Similarly, when there was equilibrium between the humours (and therefore the temperaments) humans were healthy and reasonably cheerful. But this happy state of affairs could last only so long. Sooner or later one or other of the elements – followed by the humours, followed by the temperaments – gained the upper hand. The consequence was disease, gloom and bad weather.

As a thesis, it was complete. It explained and resolved every aspect of the visible world around us, and the invisible reality within us. It covered the making of the planet, the operation of rivers and springs, terrifying phenomena such as earthquakes and volcanic eruptions, the appearance and disappearance of the sun and the moon, the celestial manifestations of comets, shooting stars and the Milky Way. It made sense of an existence crammed with horrors, terrors, surprises and disasters of every kind; and as such, it continued to provide reassurance to our species for two thousand years and more.

The weather was, obviously, the single most important external influence on the human condition, and Aristotle had to impose some kind of intellectual order on it. *Meteorologica* means 'the study of higher things', the *-logica* being study, and the meteors being higher in a physical sense, in that they are imperfect mixtures of the four elements confined to the region below the moon, from which they dispatch the various familiar ingredients in an earthly direction. Even though we have moved on from the Greek and his falling meteors, the influence of his cosmology is still very evident, and not merely in the name by which the science of the weather is known. For instance, we still use 'the elements' as a synonym for weather, and talk of dew 'falling', when it does no such thing.

Aristotle's analysis of weather went only so far. His job was to elucidate the physical phenomena in a specific cosmological department, between the earth and the moon. He explained events, but he did not attempt to identify patterns, still less venture into weather forecasting. The task of shedding further light on the particulars was left to his pupil and friend Theophrastus. It was Theophrastus who – for example – pondered the mystery of thunder and determined that it came from the collision of the clouds. And it was Theophrastus who argued, with great good sense, that meteors could not possibly be directed by a divine hand, otherwise why would thunderbolts – generally regarded as the favoured instrument of divine punishment – frequently fall upon uninhabited areas, and strike indiscriminately against the virtuous and the evildoers.

By the time William Merle first peered at the skies over Driby and started scratching down his observations, the heavy hand of Aristotle's world view had been clamped on Western thinking for more than a millennium and a half. It was to be another three and a half centuries before its hold weakened significantly. The translation of the surviving works of the Greek philosophers into Latin during the thirteenth century had given classical thinking a mighty new lease of life. Two of Europe's greatest men of learning – the German sage and Christian divine Albertus Magnus and his pupil Thomas Aquinas – composed extensive commentaries on Aristotle's texts with the aim of synthesising Christian theology and classical Greek thinking and laying an intellectual foundation for the adoption of Christian doctrine throughout civilised Europe. But many historians have seen their influence on the spirit of inquiry essential to scientific advance as suffocating and negative. Thus Theophrastus's notion of the meteors going about their business free from any kind of superior control was intolerable to a doctrine founded on the premise that everything in the universe had been designed and was directed by a specifically Christian God. It followed that if some natural phenomenon was inexplicable within that context, it was meant to be so, and that to continue searching and questioning was to contravene God's intentions as interpreted by His earthly representatives.

This, most famously, was where Copernicus and Galileo came to grief. But the tyranny of Christian Aristotelianism inhibited the investigation of any natural phenomenon. Take the winds, which Aristotle stated came from a 'hot and dry exhalation' produced when the rays of the sun struck dry land. In his *History of the Winds* of 1622, Francis Bacon spoke vaguely of the 'ventilation of the earth'. An earlier authority, the virulently anti-Catholic divine William Fulke, maintained that some winds were moved around the earth, while others came from 'great holes, caves or dongeons . . . within the globe of the earth'. Both classes, according to Fulke, had been created by God to keep the air moving 'which, were it not continually styrred . . . would soon putrifie . . . and would be a deadly infection to all that hath breathe upon the worlde'.

Other aspects of the weather were interpreted more or less fancifully. A sixteenth-century French writer, Antoine Mizauld, declared that raindrops were round because their edges were rubbed off as they descended AND because their shape was intended to reflect that of the universe (in fairness to Mizauld, it took another five hundred years for the mystery of the raindrop's form – which is not round – to be solved). As late as the 1690s, a London bookseller and pamphleteer, John Dunton ('a willing and everlasting drudge to the quill', he called himself), asserted that thunder and lightning resulted from a 'coagulation' of Aristotle's 'moist exhalations' – produced by the action of the sun on water – igniting the so-called 'nitric ingredient'.

The truth was that no one had any idea how the weather worked, nor how to proceed with a reasoned inquiry into it. In such circumstances, every sort of fantastic speculation and nonsensical invention was legitimised. A well-known Elizabethan plagiarist and astrologer, Thomas Hill – who wrote one of the earliest books on gardening – said that pearls were created when oysters fed on dewdrops, and that poisonous creatures were less dangerous at night because the dew they drank neutralised their venom. Hill also advised that the best way to discourage lightning from striking the garden was to display the hide of a hippopotamus, a speckled toad and an owl with outstretched wings beside it; and that the skin of a hyena, a seal or a crocodile would deter hail.

There was a particular fascination with comets – defined by Aristotle as 'an ignited mass of exhalation at the uppermost limit of the atmosphere' – and other fiery apparitions. Some, according to Fulke, belonged to the upper air, and some to the lower, such as the 'fire drake', which 'flyeth along in the ayre and sometime turneth to and fro if it meat with a cold cloud to beat it back'. Another oddity of the lower air was the '*ignis fatuus*', otherwise known as the will-o'-the-wisp, a mysterious and unsettling phosphorescence sometimes encountered over marshy ground and in churchyards, and associated in folklore with spirits and fairies, specifically Puck and Robin Goodfellow. Thus did Falstaff mistake Bardolph's nose for 'an *ignis fatuus* or ball of wildfire'.

Unable to make much sense of weather patterns in Britain by sticking to principles laid down in Greece, the early authorities consoled themselves by concentrating on events, the more extraordinary the better. These, of course, were entirely explicable. God made them all: tempests, earthquakes, droughts, floods, hailstorms, lightning strikes, comets, gales, blizzards – each and every one a manifestation of divine displeasure at the wickedness of humankind. There was a keen public appetite for descriptions and interpretations of these marvels. A minor earth tremor, which was felt in many parts of England on 6 April 1580 and caused no deaths and very little damage, inspired no fewer than ten pamphlets – one of which, by Thomas Twyne, announced itself as 'a shorte and pithie discourse on that most strange and terrible work of the Lord in shaking the earthe'.

Accounts of showers of blood and other airborne wonders were very popular. Several were included in the *Britannia Baconica or Natural Rarities of England, Scotland and Wales*, which was compiled by an astrologically inclined clergyman, Joshua Childrey, and first published in 1660. One concerned a fall of warm blood onto Poole, which the author speculated might have been 'engendered of some vapour drawn up by the sun from that part of the sea where the cruel sea-fight was fought between the English and Dutch'. Showers of wheat were regularly remarked upon, and showers of frogs were not uncommon. In his *Natural History of Staffordshire* of 1686, Robert Plot reported a fall of 'frograin' on Lord Aston's bowling green at Tixall so prodigious that 'it had been found difficult not to tread on frogs in walking'. (In justice to Plot, a recent article in the journal *Weather* gave a sober and authoritative record of deluges of yellow honeybee excrement, skulls, skeletons and coffins – from a tornado-ravaged cemetery in New Orleans – sticklebacks, sand eels, flounders, herrings and hazel nuts, as well as numerous frog-falls, including one of pink amphibians on Stroud in October 1987.)

There was a particular fondness for stories about lightning strikes on account of their inherent dramatic qualities and the opportunity they gave for moralising about the justice of divine displeasure with human imperfection. Sometimes, however, the location and the character of the victims made it tricky to draw the moral. In *Admirable Curiosities, Rarities and Wonders* collected by another energetic scribbler, Nathanial Crouch, and published in 1685, there is a gruesome account of a thunderbolt directed at a church in the village of Withypool in Somerset 'during sermon-time' on 21 October 1632. The calamity announced itself with 'a very great darkness . . . so that they could not see to read', which was followed by a 'terrible and fearful thunder, like the noise of many great guns, accompanied with dreadful lightning'. The climax was terrible and amazing: 'There presently came such an extraordinary flame of lightning that filled the Church with fire, smoak and a loathsome smell like Brimstone; a ball of fire came in likewise at the window and passed through the Church which so affrighted the Congregation that most of them fell down on their knees . . . all giving themselves up for dead.' The minister, the Reverend George Lyde, was left untouched in his pulpit. But Mrs Lyde, records Crouch with ghoulish delight, was set on fire; while another woman 'had the flesh torn off her back almost to the very bones', and Master Hill had his head thrown against the wall with such force 'that he died that night'. Another member of the congregation had his head cloven and his brains 'thrown whole to the floor', and the hair on his head was 'stuck fast to a Pillar near him'. Whatever had been going on in Withypool to warrant such punishment Crouch either did not know or chose not to reveal.

For Crouch and other chroniclers, the failing of the British weather was that such sensations occurred so infrequently. Then, as now, our weather was mostly innocuous. One way of correcting this deficiency was to let the imagination loose on celestial manifestations. Crouch himself reported the appearance over the village of Maxfield in Cheshire one summer's day in 1662 of 'a great pillar of smoak in height like a steeple and judged twenty yards broad which making a most hideous noise went along six or seven miles'. More spectacular still was the staging of battles overhead. The *General Chronological History of the Air, Weather and Meteors etc*, published in 1745 by a Sheffield doctor, Thomas Short, included a number of these – including one in

1236 'especially at Rochabbey, Yorkshire . . . where companies of armed men were seen to ride out of the Earth on horseback with Spear, Shield, Sword and Banner . . . so lively was the sight to behold that Multitudes flocked from all places around . . . these apparitions were followed by a great Tempest of Rain which caused Monstrous Floods'.

As recently as March 1716 several people in Oxford, alerted by the sudden appearance in the sky of 'a huge body of light', watched as swords were drawn and battle was joined. Witnesses to the same event in Upton-upon-Severn even smelled the gunpowder and sulphur. Several commentators were quick to make a connection between the ethereal conflict and the execution a fortnight before of the Earl of Derwentwater, one of the conspirators in the Jacobite rebellion of the previous year. Even though the invention of instruments such as the barometer and the thermometer had, by then, made the weather accessible to the new empirical disciplines – although with mixed results, as we shall see – a strong affection for the unusual, the sublime and the inexplicable persisted. Papers with such titles as *Strange Frost Around Bristol*, *Surprising Effects of a Terrible Clap of Thunder*, *Observations of an Uncommon Gleam of Light* and *Hailstones of Unusual Size* continued to be regularly featured in the journal of the Royal Society, the *Philosophical Transactions*.

But at least the enforced union between Aristotelian science and Christian doctrine had long since collapsed under the strain of its inherent inadequacies and contradictions. As far as the weather was concerned, Aristotle's cosmology simply could not convincingly explain what came down on the heads of the inhabitants of these islands as they went about their daily business. And there was a more fundamental failing. What people really wanted – then as now – was not information about what the weather was already doing, but reliable intelligence about what was to come. Prudently, Aristotle himself had hardly ventured down the path of prognostication. His successors and disciples — such as Theophrastus and the Roman natural philosophers Seneca and Pliny the Elder — attempted to address this drawback. But a system based on the wholly unaccountable behaviour of meteors was of very little use to them in formulating rules for prediction. They were forced to turn to other sources.

Rising above the sweep of land between the Cheviots in north-east England and the Lammermuirs in south-east Scotland is a rugged and imposing hill with a suitably imposing name: Ruberslaw. There is a ditty about it and its weather:

> When Ruberslaw puts on his cowl
> And Dunion on his hood,
> Then a' the wives of Teviotside
> Ken there'll be a flood.

The day of my visit, Ruberslaw had on no cowl, nor Dunion anything resembling a hood. It was an afternoon in July, warm and breezy, the sun sometimes out and sometimes obscured behind bands of white and pale grey cloud. I left my car in the farmyard and trudged uphill through green meadows where the sheep — just shorn and startling in their whiteness — kept up their ceaseless nibbling. From below, the hill appeared long and flat-topped. But when I neared the top, I could see that it was split by a shallow dip, so that the grassy summit itself was guarded from beneath by a crescent of steep rock. A metal plaque set into the stone records a meeting here on Easter Day 2000 of parishioners from the villages of Bedrule, Denholm and Minto to commemorate the birth of Christ and 'to remember Christians through the ages who have worshipped God in this place'.

For it was on the heights of Ruberslaw and other remote and lonely eminences scattered throughout the Borders that those stern and unbending opponents of bishops and kings, the seventeenth century Scottish Covenanters, gathered for forbidden worship. Driven from their kirks, their ministers dispossessed and harried at every turn by Charles II's troops, they were forced to seek such places to escape their persecutors. One of those whose voices boomed from Ruberslaw's heights was Alexander Peden, 'a man of heavy hand and massive frame, of noble and impressive countenance', as a contemporary related, famed for his 'rich figurative discourse and deep oracular utterance'. On one occasion, so the story is told, Peden and his flock were trapped on Ruberslaw by pursuing dragoons. There was no escape, and Peden fell to his knees. 'Oh Lord,' he prayed, 'lap the skirts of thy cloak ower puir old Sandy.' With that, a mist sank on Ruberslaw so thick that a man could not see his hand in front of his face. When it lifted, not a Covenanter remained to be apprehended.

Sitting where Peden sent forth his oracular utterance, I found it hard to associate the scene before me with ancient hatreds and conflicts. The panorama was marvellous in its breadth and tranquil beauty: fields of half a dozen shades of green, farms folded into the creases in the hills, dark forest and cheerful copse, the Teviot a silver band winding its way in search of the Tweed, in the middle distance the rounded triple crest of Eildon, with the misty blue of Lammermuir beyond. There was no hint in the sky of rain, nothing to interrupt the silage cutter below me as it chewed its way through the pasture laying neat lines of cut grass on the buttery yellow stubble; nothing for the wives of Teviotside to fear.

Nevertheless, Ruberslaw's reputation is well-deserved. Standing as it does in the path of the prevailing southwesterly air stream, it gathers in the rain clouds as they charge over the border on their journey from the Irish Sea. A poet of these parts, John Leyden – who was a friend of Sir Walter Scott, and achieved distinction as a linguist, physician and administrator in India – wrote:

> When Ruberslaw conceives the mountain storm
> Dark Ruberslaw, that lifts his head sublime
> Rugged and hoary with the wrecks of time.

Keeping a weather eye out for its head sublime would have been a matter of common sense for those living and working in its lee, and remembering the lines about Ruberslaw's cowl and Dunion's hood a handy way to learn and pass on the message.

Every society in every land has accumulated its store of weather wisdom. There is no better explanation of its genesis than the one written by Richard Inwards to introduce his classic compilation *Weather Lore*, which was first published in its definitive form in 1893:

From the earliest times, hunters, shepherds, sailors and tillers of the earth have from sheer necessity been led to study the teachings of the winds, the waves, the clouds and a hundred other objects from which the signs of coming changes in the state of the air might be foretold. The weather-wise among these primitive people would be naturally the most prosperous, and others would soon acquire the coveted foresight by a closer observance of the same objects. The result has been the framing of a rough set of rules . . . about the weather and the freaks to which it is liable. Some of these observations have settled down in the form of proverbs; others have taken the shape of rhymes; while many are yet floating about, unclaimed and un-registered, but passed from mouth to mouth, as mere records of facts, varying in verbal form according to local idioms but owning a common origin and purport.

Necessity mothered invention, and the inventors were the great army of those whose lives and livelihoods were most directly affected by the weather. Some of the observations — such as the Ruberslaw doggerel — were purely local in their applica-tion. Others were much more general, and of these a few have proved remarkably durable. Perhaps the most familiar of all is

> Red sky at night / Shepherd's [or sailor's] delight
> Red sky in the morning / Shepherd's warning.

The science behind this is entirely sound. When the atmosphere is comparatively clear of clouds, it is still full of particles of dust which have the function of scattering the rays of the sun. But these particles are much less efficient in disposing of the red rays than the others which make up sunlight's spectrum. The result is that when the sky in the west is clear, the evening sunlight appears red and makes any residual cloud on which it shines burn red. Conversely, the red sky in the morning is an optical phenomenon which occurs when a rain-bearing bank of cloud leading an approaching warm front is lit from below as the sun comes up.

The connection between fine, settled weather and a red sky at night would have been noticed at the dawn of humankind's evolution. But it probably did not find its way into the written record until Theophrastus made the first attempt to draw up some rules for weather prediction in the fourth century BC. Much of the accumulated weather wisdom available to him was incorporated into a poem called the *Diosemiai*, written a generation or two after Theophrastus by the Greek poet Aratus, who was employed at the court of the King of Macedonia – including this:

> Or if Aurora tinge with glowing red
> The clouds that float around Phoebus' rising head,
> Farmer, rejoice! For soon refreshing rains
> Will fill the pools and quench the thirsty plains . . .
> If with clear face in his watery bed,
> Curtained with crimson clouds around his head,
> He sink, that night no rain or tempest fear;
> And tomorrow's sun will shine serene and clear.

By then the prophetic tendency of a red sky at night was firmly embedded in the popular and literary consciousness, where it has remained. In the sixteenth chapter of St Matthew's Gospel as rendered in the 1611 Authorised Version of the Bible (Richard Inwards pointed out that the incident was not included in the early texts) Christ responds to a demand from the Pharisees and Saducees for a sign from heaven by saying: 'When it is evening, ye say, it will be fair weather: for the sky is red. And in the morning, it will be foul weather today: for the sky is red and lowring.'

From the start, the quality of weather wisdom clearly depended on the closeness of the observer to Nature, from which the intuitive understanding of Nature's way was derived. Equally clearly, this relationship became threatened by cultural progress and city living. Two centuries after Aratus, much of his work was repackaged into a more attractive form by Virgil in the first book of the *Georgics*. Even then, Virgil was in the grip of nostalgic yearning for the simpler tastes and virtues of an earlier age, among which he numbered a true love of Nature and affinity with the land. Virgil celebrated his own respect for the dignity of husbandry and the wisdom that came with it. This included the ability – instinctive and acquired – to divine the portents provided by Nature of the weather to come:

> Wet weather seldom hurts the most unwise
> So plain the signs, such prophets are the skies
> (Virgil, translated by Dryden)

The underlying philosophy is that Nature as shaped by benevolent gods will tell us what we need to know, but only if we stay close enough to it. We only have to look at the birds:

> Huge flocks of rising rooks forsake their food,
> And, crying, seek the shelter of the wood . . .
> Then thrice the ravens rend the liquid air
> And creaking notes proclaim the settled fair.

Virgil's theme – the dislocation between us and Nature, resulting in the shutting of Nature's book to our understanding – has been a popular one ever since with commentators disenchanted with the march of progress. Joseph Taylor, the author of *The Complete Weather Guide*, published in 1814, lamented our impoverishment: 'In general, the senses of man who in their way of life deviate from the simplicity of Nature are coarse, dull and void of energy. But the animals, which retain their natural instinct, which have their organs better constituted, and their senses in more perfect state, perceive sooner and are more susceptible of the impressions produced in them by variations in the atmosphere.' The confidence of country folk through the ages in the ability of the beasts to divine coming changes in the weather may well have sound foundations, but it has nourished some debatable adages – such as that oxen will sleep on their left sides when fine weather is approaching, or that migrating geese will form a number in the sky which corresponds to the number of weeks of frost to be expected in the approaching winter.

Often the interpretation of the sign demands a minuteness of observation bordering on the impossible. How can one tell if cockles have more gravel sticking to them than usual, or if moles are putting up more earth, or if bees are travelling further from their hives, and spiders from their nests? These are classified as indications of approaching rain in a book published in 1785 called *An Essay on the Weather*, which was written by John Mills, a thoroughly reputable Fellow of the Royal Society and the author of the first comprehensive treatise on agriculture, *A New System for Practical Husbandry*. Sixty years earlier the rector of Slapton in Northamptonshire, the Reverend John Pointer, published his *A Rational Account of the Weather* in which he – as John Mills was to do – expressed his disappointment at the failure of the new-fangled meteorological instruments, particularly the barometer, to provide the certainties for which the age hankered.

Mr Pointer called on people to put their trust in Nature's signals. Among these he listed, as indicators of imminent rain, increases in the normal incidence of deer fighting, asses braying and shaking their ears, foxes barking, wolves howling and cats rubbing their heads with their forepaws. His reference to owls illustrates the care demanded of the observer: 'Owls hooting much is another sign of Fair Weather, tho' Owls hoot much in wet and dry weather, with this difference, in wet their hooting is more clamorous.' Mr Pointer did not restrict himself to animals and plants. He instances a lake at Penford in Staffordshire with prophetic tendencies: 'When rain approaches it becomes troubled, rising full of bubbles and in a little time thickening with a yellow scum which presently, as it rains, washes away. The worthy Mr Fowler, an inhabitant of the place, has freely confessed that he has often been admonished by it in time of harvest to bring in his corn.'

Weather lore was most liable to become unstuck when it was overstretched in the direction of pseudo-science and long-range forecasting. Virgil's lines about the moon can be excused as a poet's fancy:

> But four nights old (for that's the surest sign)
> With sharpen'd horns, if glorious then she shine
> Next day, nor only that, but all the month,
> Are void of tempest by land and sea.

But when processed by Francis Bacon into a reliable rule – 'when the moon in her fourth day appears pure and spotless, her horns unblunted and neither quite flat nor quite even but betwixt both, it promises fair weather for the greatest part of the month' – it became no more than another lunar fallacy.

The most popular eighteenth-century compendium of rural weather wisdom was a volume called *The Country Calendar, or the Shepherd of Banbury's Rules*. This had originally appeared in 1670 under the title *The Shepheard's Legacy*, the Shepherd in question being identified as John Claridge or Clearidge, whose flocks grazed at Hanwell, near Banbury in Oxfordshire. His rules – said to be the result of his 'Forty Years experience of the weather' — were resurrected under the new title in 1744, the work being generally attributed to John Campbell, an industrious, London-based jobbing author well known to Johnson and Boswell and well liked by them. Campbell transformed the original by appending to each of the rules verbose elucidations purporting to provide them with a sound footing in science, while dispensing with the Shepherd's advice on such practical matters as treating sheep rot. The guiding principle was that the weather observed recurring patterns. The Shepherd's confidence that he had identified those patterns had some curious applications. According to the commentary in the 1744 edition, 'the most useful of the whole collection of prognostications' was this: 'If the wind return to the south within a day or two without rain, and turn northward with rain, and return to the south, in one or two days as before, two or three times together after this sort, then it is likely to be in the south or south-west TWO OR THREE MONTHS TOGETHER, AS IT WAS IN THE NORTH BEFORE' (my capitals).

The twentieth-century British meteorologist George Kimble statistically analysed another of the Shepherd's Rules — that if the second half of February and the first ten days of March are mainly wet, the spring and summer are likely to be so too — and found it was wrong ten times more often than it was right. Making fun of the ancients and their soothsaying has long been a favourite sport of professional meteorologists, armed with their statistics, their instruments and their impregnable confidence in their own superior knowledge. Regularly, come 15 July, the producers of radio current affairs programmes in search of a 'light' item will set aside two or three minutes to discuss the various versions of the adage:

St Swithin's Day, if ye do rain
For forty days it will remain
St Swithin's Day, an' ye be fair
For forty days 'twill rain nae mair.

A historian of Anglo-Saxon times will be wheeled in to recount how, a century after the saint's death in 862, his remains were disinterred from the simple grave he had chosen for himself outside the walls of his church in Winchester, and reburied amid pomp and solemn ceremony within; and how the legend grew that he had called up the deluge as a protest against this transfer. The historian then gives way to the Met Office weather man who – amid much chuckling and condescension – explains that the saying is wholly unfounded and that he has the statistical information to prove it. But, as Philip Eden points out in his excellent *Daily Telegraph Book of the Weather*, this rather misses the point, which is that by mid-July, generally speaking, the character of our summer – fine, damp or an oscillation between the two – is established and persists until towards the end of August.

Many of the sayings about animal behaviour are clearly ridiculous. 'When dogs eat grass it will be rainy' and 'when the cat lies on its brain / then it is going to rain' come into this category. One of the old saws quoted approvingly in Robin Page's robust rejection of modern meteorology and its sophisms, *Weather Forecasting the Country Way*, is: 'When a cow tries to scratch its ear / a shower is very near. / When it clumps its side with its tail / look out for thunder, lightning and hail.' This is all very well, but does it mean one cow in a herd, or several, or a majority? How prevalent should the ear-scratching and tail-clumping be? Doubtless a true countryman such as Mr Page will have a true countryman's intuitive understanding. But the rest of us are likely to left scratching our heads, if not our ears.

The difficulty is to tell the sound sense from the nonsense. Robin Page's assertion that fish 'gambol about near the surface causing ripples and splashes' when rain is imminent is rubbish. But the behaviour of eels is another matter. In *Weather Lore*, Richard Inwards used some lines from John Marston's satire of 1599, *The Scourge of Villainy*:

> They are nought but eeles, that never will appeare
> Till that tempestuous winds or thunder teare
> Their slimy beds.

It is perfectly true that eels are able to detect the approach of the equinoctial storms that trigger their autumn migration down to the sea, possibly by means of sensory mechanisms capable of registering falling barometric pressure; and that in lakes they anticipate the time of departure by moving towards the mouth of the outflowing river. It is also true that, as the weather clears after rain, the insects on which swallows feed find it easier to dry their wings after hatching from water, and ascend into the higher air − hence the saying 'Swallows high / staying dry. / Swallows low / wet 'twill blow'. Another familiar sign of approaching rain is the closing of the petals of the scarlet pimpernel, which was observed four hundred years ago by the celebrated herbalist John Gerard and ascribed by him to the possession of prophetic powers. In fact the flower closes its petals when the moisture level of the air around reaches 80 per cent of saturation point − which is often the case when rain is about to fall.

Charles Darwin's grandfather, the physician, botanist,

educationalist and polymath Erasmus Darwin, wrote some lines (also attributed to the pioneer of smallpox inoculation, Edward Jenner) which gently mocked the plethora of popular rain portents:

> The soot falls down, the spaniels sleep,
> And spiders from their cobwebs peep.
> Last night the sun went pale to bed,
> The moon in haloes hid her head . . .
> Hark! How the chairs and tables crack.
> Old Betty's joints are on the wrack.
> At dusk the squalid toad was seen
> Hopping and crawling o'er the green.
> 'Twill surely rain — I see with sorrow —
> Our jaunt must be put off tomorrow.

The oral tradition which Darwin affectionately lampooned had become part of the cultural landscape long before the dawn of the scientific era in Britain, which can most conveniently be dated to the inaugural meeting of the Royal Society in 1660. For a time, the achievements of science and the new disciplines of inquiry threatened to make the oral tradition redundant. The fact that it survived, and still survives, is a measure of its inherent qualities. But it also reflected the considerable and chronic problems that science encountered when it took on the task of making sense of our weather.

Chapter 3

Founding Fathers

IT TURNED INTO THE MOST DELICIOUS AFTERNOON IMAGINABLE, A SORT of hesitant lifting of the curtain on what was to be the most glorious summer since 1976. The morning had been overcast and moist. But as I left the King's Arms, having disposed of my pint and toasted sandwich, the skies over Oxford brightened. The sun pulled apart the grey vapour and sent it courteously on its way. Just up the road from the pub, the golden stone of Wadham College glowed in the sunlight; as perhaps it did on the day in June 1650 when Christopher Wren – 'that miracle of a youth', as the diarist John Evelyn felicitously dubbed him – arrived to begin his ascent towards renown.

Like so much else in that heady time, scientific meteorology in Britain was invented by Christopher Wren and his closest colleague and one true friend, Robert Hooke. This was one of the great intellectual partnerships. In whatever field the two men tackled together – astronomy, mathematics, meteorology, chemistry, biology, microscopy, and most famously, architecture – they suited each other ideally. And it was here, in Oxford, that their union was forged. In fact, with a little imaginative licence, it is possible to pinpoint the exact location. If you enter the main gate of Wadham and stand beneath the tower at the centre of the western façade, you will be immediately below the celebrated astronomy room occupied by Wren's sponsor and protector, Doctor John Wilkins, then the Warden of Wadham. It is quite likely that Wren and Hooke first met here, and more than likely that their collaboration took shape here.

Wilkins was an unusual and interesting man, a resourceful survivor through turbulent times, an original experimenter in science and a tireless promoter of other people's clever ideas. At Wadham he gave full rein to Wren's phenomenal, precocious ingenuity. When Evelyn dined with the Warden in 1654, he marvelled at the full display 'of shadows, dials, perspectives . . . a way-infer, a thermometer, a monstrous magnet, conic and other sections, a balance in a demi-circle; most of them of his own or that prodigious young scholar, Mr Christopher Wren'. Wren was the brightest star drawn to orbit around Wilkins at Wadham. But there were others, most notably the intensely religious, sensitive and high-minded Irish nobleman Robert Boyle, by then established as Europe's leading theoretical chemist; and Boyle's assistant, Robert Hooke.

Hooke's personal peculiarities were abundantly documented by his contemporaries, so much so that his genius was sometimes overlooked. He was ugly – 'something crooked, pale-faced . . . his head lardge, his eie full and popping', according to John Aubrey; 'despicable . . . very crooked . . . with a meagre aspect', in the words of his biographer Richard Waller. He never married, but had a long sexual relationship with his niece Grace, which began when she was a girl. He kept his money in a chest beside his bed, refused to wear a wig, slept for no more than a very few hours each night, was mistrustful, jealous and very inclined to accuse others of stealing his work. One of these was Newton, whom he charged with appropriating the original concept of the nature of light, and who hated him with such virulence that virtually Newton's first act upon becoming President of the Royal Society was to order the removal of Hooke's portrait from the premises. Not many people, apart from Wren, had much cause to love Hooke. But no one, not even Wren, could match him for fertility of mind and expertise in the conduct of experimental work.

Hooke was born in the Isle of Wight, where his father – a devoted Royalist and High Anglican – was a curate in Freshwater. Following his father's death, possibly by suicide, the thirteen-year-old Hooke went to Westminster School in London, where he was cared for by the headmaster, Richard Busby. It was Busby who arranged a position for Hooke at Christ Church, Oxford, where he worked as a paid assistant for the anatomist Thomas Wallis and subsequently for Boyle.

The great question of the day for Boyle, Pascal and several other of the inquiring minds of Europe concerned air and its physical properties. Boyle had good reason to suspect that air was 'both heavy and ponderable, if we will not refuse belief to our senses'. But to proceed with the experimental work necessary to test his speculations, he needed to be able to work both with air, and in its absence – i.e. in a vacuum. In 1657 or 1658, Boyle had read about a German invention for removing the air from a closed vessel. The creator was a citizen of Magdeburg, Otto von Guericke, and Boyle lost no time in commissioning Hooke and a London instrument-maker, Ralph Greatorex, to make one for him to be installed in his laboratory next to University College. Hooke quickly became impatient with Greatorex's efforts and took on the task himself. He adapted von Guericke's original design extensively, and made an air pump which actually did – at least, when Hooke was operating it – what it was supposed to.

The air pump was pivotal in the long series of experiments that led to the formulation of Boyle's Law on the inverse proportion between the pressure and volume of a gas. It also had a starring role at the early meetings of the Royal Society, the association of the philosophers which had grown out of earlier collaborations in London and Oxford. Whenever distinguished visitors came to a meeting of the Society, the air pump was wheeled out to entertain and inform. Samuel Pepys, who had become a member of the Society in 1665 despite finding most of the technical aspects of science well beyond his powers of comprehension, described a meeting at which Boyle and Hooke performed the roles of conjuror and assistant: 'It is a most acceptable thing to hear their discourses and see their experiments, which was this day upon the nature of fire and how it goes out in a place where the air is not free, and sooner where the air is exhausted; which they show by an engine on purpose.'

The air pump was instrumental in bringing Robert Hooke to the Royal Society. In 1662, the members – embarrassed by a series of failures with the temperamental apparatus – persuaded Boyle to release Hooke so that he could become the first paid Curator of Experiments. By then Hooke's incredibly agile and versatile intelligence had already exploited the potential in his pump in quite another direction – towards the mysteries of the weather, and a tube filled with quicksilver.

I wandered around the garden at Wadham, admiring the cut of the grass, the stately cedars and horse chestnuts and slender ash trees, the banks of colour in the borders against the pale, seasoned stoned walls; and picturing the members of Warden Wilkins's glittering circle as they paced energetically beneath the foliage, batting back and forth curious notions concerning the Copernican hythothesis, the circulation of blood, the behaviour of comets and stars and sunspots, the phases of Mercury, the recent improvements in telescopes and micro-scopes and all manner of stimulating aspects of natural philosophy; pausing every now and then to admire the celebrated transparent beehive designed and built by Wren, or the statue contrived by Wilkins so that it gave voice through a concealed tube. On the way out I asked the porter if I might see the rooms in the gate tower where the air had once been filled by their abstruse speculations. He looked at me as if I had proposed committing an indecent act, and informed me sternly that the rooms were private and certainly not available for inspection by casual passers-by. It occurred to me as I looked back from Parks Road at the oriel through which the after-noon and evening sun would have streamed into Wilkins's astronomy room, that I might have had a warmer welcome had I turned up 350 years earlier.

I walked past the Bodleian Library and the Radcliffe Camera to the High, with the idea of paying my respects to Boyle and Hooke. Although nothing remains of Boyle's lodgings and lab-oratory, there is a plaque set into the outer wall of University College, commemorating the fact that he 'here discovered Boyle's Law and here made experiments with an air-pump designed by his assistant, Robert Hooke, inventor, scientist and architect, who here made a MICROSCOPE and thereby first identified the LIVING CELL'.

The porter at University College was more accommodating than his Wadham counterpart, and directed me along a musty, stone-flagged corridor to the place where Boyle's rooms had been. The space was occupied by an outlandish monument to Shelley, who was actually sent down from the college for distributing an atheistic pamphlet. It consists of a sculpture executed by the esteemed Victorian artist E. Onslow Ford, in which a white effigy of the poet – 'laid out naked and drowned like a turbot on a slab', as one observer put it – lay above a bare-breasted bronze Muse of Poetry; the whole displayed beneath a flaking blue dome studded with stars, and enclosed by walls of deep chocolate brown. Rather overwhelmed by this horrible sight, I set off for the station and read about barometers on my journey home.

The invention of the barometer is usually credited to the Italian Evangelista Torricelli; although Nicholas Goodison, in his book on English barometers, describes this attribution as 'a naïve simplification'. Certainly the story is a complicated one, the fullest version being set out in *The History of the Barometer* written by an indefatigable Canadian meteorologist and historian W. H. Knowles Middleton, and published in 1964.

Torricelli was born in 1608 in Faenza, northern Italy. As a young man he was sent to study in Rome, where he came under the influence of the greatest scientist of the age, Galileo. The nature of air was one of the many riddles pondered by Galileo, who seems to have been dubious about the notion of it having a weight, but inclined to recognise the possibility of a vacuum. This in itself was highly contentious, not to say heretical, since the Catholic Church asserted that God would not permit such a version of nothingness, and so nor would they. In the late 1630s Galileo, by now blind, was living near Florence, where – despite the years of harassment and persecution by the Inquisition – he persisted in his refusal to withdraw his public support for the Copernican account of the universe, which held that the sun and not the earth was its centre and chief force. He was joined there in 1641 by Torricelli, who remained in Florence after Galileo's death the following year, his reputation being sufficiently high for the enlightened Duke of Tuscany, Ferdinand II, to appoint him court philosopher and mathematician.

The idea that air could have a weight and thereby exercise a downward pressure on the surface of the earth was a difficult one for the early seventeenth-century thinkers to come to terms with. It required something akin to a leap of the imagination to picture a column of invisible gas reaching up into the atmosphere and pressing down on every head. Unlike his mentor, Torricelli made that leap and was able to conceive of a way to prove it. In 1644 he supervised a famous series of experiments, in which a tube filled with quicksilver was inverted in a dish containing a quantity of the same liquid metal. Torricelli explained in a letter to a friend why the mercury in the tube was held at a height of about 30 inches: 'I assert that it is external; and that the force comes from outside. On the surface of the liquid in the basin presses a weight of fifty miles of air.' He also talked – but apparently did no more than that – of making an instrument 'which might show the changes of the air, now heavier and coarser, now lighter and more subtle'. '*Noi viviamo sommersi nel fondo d'un pelago d'aria elementare,*' he concluded: 'We are living at the bottom of a sea of air.'

Torricelli died in 1647, and his experiments were not published, quite possibly because of fear of Church hostility. But they were talked about, most notably by a mathematically inclined French prelate, Father Marin Mersenne, who was a friend of all the notable French scientists of the day, including Descartes, Fermet and Pascal, and whose voluminous correspondence played an important part in disseminating new ideas and discoveries around Europe. Mersenne apparently witnessed the

Torricelli experiments; and while he himself did not believe that the mercury was held up by the weight of air, he was swift to communicate the essentials of the procedure to inquiring minds on both sides of the Channel. Many years later John Wallis – a respected mathematician and cryptographer – claimed that he and 'diverse worthy persons, inquisitive into natural philosophy' had considered 'the Torricellian experiment in quicksilver' in London as early as 1645. The 'diverse worthy persons' included Wilkins, the noted physicians Jonathan Goddard and George Ent, the astronomer Samuel Foster, and Theodore Haak, a German who served as secretary to the Elector Palatine, Prince Charles Louis. In 1648 Haak wrote a letter to Mersenne in which he reported on various experiments with tubes of mercury to test air pressure at different heights.

A few years after that, Otto von Guericke was making use of his air pump to create the vacuum at the top of the Torricellian tube necessary for the mercury to hold its true level. Von Guericke is also reported to have constructed a variant which used water instead of mercury. Water, because of its comparative lightness, required a tube 30 feet long which was attached to the side of von Guericke's house in Magdeburg, with a little man floating on a cork at the top whose upward and downward movements served to amuse passers-by.

A column of mercury in a barometer varies in height according to changes in air pressure, and is calibrated to measure those changes. When pressure increases, the height of the mercury rises; when it decreases, the mercury drops. High-pressure areas (or 'highs') are formed in the upper atmosphere by converging winds which bring air together, increasing its mass and weight, and spiral clockwise around the system. Under the impetus of its own weight, air sinks towards earth, causing any water droplets suspended within it to evaporate, hence the association between high pressure and fine weather. Low-pressure systems, by contrast, tend to develop much nearer the earth's surface. The winds spiral anticlockwise, breaking up the air mass and causing pressure to fall. Rising air in low-pressure systems carries water vapour upwards, which condenses into droplets to form clouds. These, when large enough, will produce rain or snow, which is why falling pressure often signals wet and windy weather.

There is some doubt as to who first noticed the correlation between changes in the weather and the movements of quick-silver. According to Knowles Middleton, the honour goes to the same Grand Duke Ferdinand of Tuscany who employed Evangelista Torricelli. The Duke – whose interest in the weather caused him to set up a network for recording observations extending from Florence to Milan, Bologna, Parma and Pisa – was credited by a biographer with the 'new and curious' obser-vation that the mercury fell in damp weather. Certainly Hooke, Boyle and Wren were aware of the phenomenon in the early 1660s. But it was Hooke, armed with his improved air pump and uniquely adept in securing the required vacuum in the Torricellian tube, who pressed ahead with what he called his 'baroscopical index'.

In September 1664 Hooke moved to rooms set aside for him in Gresham College in Bishopsgate Street, London, where the Royal Society had established its headquarters. He wrote to Boyle:

I have also since my settling at Gresham College constantly observed the baroscopical index, and have found it MOST CERTAINLY TO PREDICT CLOUDY AND RAINY

WEATHER WHEN IT FALLS, AND DRY AND CLEAR WEATHER WHEN IT RISETH VERY HIGH [my capitals], which if it continue to do, I hope will help us one step towards the raising of a theoretical pillar, or pyramid, from the top of which, when raised and ascended, we may be able to see the mutations of the weather at some distance before they approach us, and thereby being able to predict and forewarn, many dangers may be prevented and the good of mankind very much promoted.

Quite what Hooke meant by his theoretical pillar or pyramid is obscure. It may be that he envisaged an actual building, sufficiently lofty for advancing weather to be followed by telescope; an early version of that enduring institution, the Met Office. As so often, Wren had provided the crucial stimulus for one of Hooke's ideas to take wing. As early as January 1662 Wren displayed to the Royal Society a prototype for an automatic rain gauge 'which emptied itself when filled to a certain height'. By the following year Wren's concept had expanded into what was termed a weather clock – a device for recording rainfall, wind, temperature, hours of sunshine and the weight of air. Hooke was instructed by the Society to add making the weather clock to his commitments, which at that time included preparing for publication his classic account of the revelations of the microscope, *Micrographia*, observing the motions of comets and the planet Jupiter, investigating the possibility of human flight, keeping a dissected dog alive by blowing air into its lungs through a tube attached to a pair of bellows, and a good deal else besides. Not surprisingly, it was to be fifteen years before the weather clock was ready. During that period Hooke worked intermittently on the various components, as and when his other duties allowed, but always concentrating on the possibilities of the baroscopical index.

In 1665 Robert Boyle published a dense and learned paper entitled *New Experiments and Observations Touching Cold*, which Hooke, needless to say, actually saw through the presses. In it, the Torricellian tube, complete with its column and basin of mercury, its vacuum and its wax-sealed top end, was, for the first time in print, referred to as the barometer. The birth of that soothing and enduring ritual, the tapping of the glass, was close at hand.

On the last Monday in October 2003 I travelled to Hampton Court Palace to inspect a selection of barometers which must have received a fair amount of tapping in their time. Blazing summer had given way to blazing autumn. As I came out of the railway station I was blinded by the sunshine, and I had to shield my eyes as I searched for a bus to take me over what was left of the river after months of drought. From the upper deck I could see into the park. The ponds were shrunken and the grass had dried to pale hessian. The oaks and sycamores lining the road to the Palace looked crisped and queasy. There was not a breath of breeze to stir the bronze foliage. Along the eastern flank of the blue sky innocuous white clouds were piled up, as if awaiting instructions. It was the kind of day that would have been much appreciated, on account of his chronic asthma, by that small, thin-faced, beaky-nosed Calvinistic king, William III. But unfortunately for William, the years between his grudging accession to the throne in 1689 and his death in 1702 were remarkable for some of the most dismally cold and wet weather these islands have ever endured.

Soon after their accession, William and Mary decided to make

Hampton Court Palace their main London residence, partly because it was more private than Whitehall, but mainly because the air upriver was much more wholesome than the stink which generally prevailed around the seat of government. When not engaged in military campaigns or dalliance with his various mistresses, William liked – inasmuch as this famously 'unamusable' man liked anything – to be at Hampton Court, where he could indulge his passion for hunting and where his doctors could attend to his delicate health.

To assist in deciding which activities might be recommended for particular days, several barometers were distributed around the palace – one in the King's bedroom, which was contained within the state apartments designed for him by Wren with views of the avenues and gravelled walks and clipped evergreens of the formal garden, with the park beyond. The instrument was made by Daniel Quare, one of the greatest craftsmen of the age, and as adept with barometers as he was with clocks and watches. It is of the pillar type, designed to stand on its own rather than be hung on a wall, with hinged brass feet below its slender ivory body, which supports an engraved gilt brass hood containing a silvered register with weather indications engraved in English and French. The work is of exquisite quality, although I was initially unable to appreciate this from the distant position which visitors are compelled to take. After I had spent some time craning over the rope to squint at Quare's handiwork, the attendant, a pleasant French woman in cod Tudor costume, took pity on me. She sent for her supervisor, who appeared dressed like one of Cardinal Wolsey's secretaries, and lifted the rope so that I could examine the barometer more closely.

Together the supervisor and I then marched to the King's Private Drawing Room to look at the other Quare barometer at

Hampton Court. This is one of the earliest English angle barometers, which worked in the same way as the standard pillar type, with the tube containing the mercury rising from a concealed cistern. The clever adaptation is said to have been the idea of Charles II's 'Master Mechanic', Sir Samuel Morland, the inventor of the speaking trumpet and several mathematical calculators, as well as a pioneer in the use of steam power. Just below the lowest point on the mercury scale the tube is taken off at a dogleg to the right. The effect is a very considerable magnification of the vertical movement of the mercury between the critical heights of 28.5 and 30.5 inches enabling very small variations to be easily observed. In the case of Quare's angle barometer made for William III, the mercury is able to move 20 inches between these two points, providing a tenfold magnification. Aesthetically, however, the effect of the dogleg is curious rather than pleasing, despite the fineness of the ornamentation.

At this point in my barometric excursion, I had hoped to inspect one of the very few surviving instruments made by the 'father of English watch-making', Thomas Tompion. This is an example of the wheel barometer invented by Hooke, with whom Tompion worked closely. Instead of having a cistern of mercury with a straight tube rising from it, Hooke's design had an enclosed bulb – or 'bolt-head', as he called it – at the top, with a tube descending from it and then bent upwards into a short limb, open to the air. The level in this open limb fell as pressure rose, the movements being registered via a float and an elaborate system of pulley wheel and counterweight on a dial, or wheel. The advantage of Hooke's method was that it could incorporate a very much magnified scale, showing movements of 0.1 of an inch. But its failings – which prevented it from being widely adopted – were that the movement of the mercury was invisible to the naked eye, and the performance of the measuring mechanism was significantly affected by changes in temperature.

The version presented by Tompion to the King is − apparently − exceptionally flamboyant, cased in oak, pine, walnut and mulberry, with ormolu mounds, and a resplendent dial like a clock face, on which the states of the weather − Stormy, Much Raine, Raine, Falling Raine, Changeable, Rising Faire, Faire, Clear and Settled Faire − are each highlighted in an engraved circle. However my friend the major-domo informed me that the Queen had recently sent for it to be hung at Windsor Castle. So we proceeded to the Queen's Gallery, where two barometers attributed to Tompion hang either side of the fireplace. They are so different, and the one on the left − even to my untutored eye − so palpably inferior that I raised a metaphorical eyebrow; and my friend admitted, rather shamefacedly, that doubts about the attribution had been expressed before.

Nicholas Goodison does not even mention it in *English Barometers*. But the one on the right − which he believes may have been delivered shortly after William's death − receives his warmest commendation. The case is of oak veneered with burr walnut, and the mounts are of ormolu. The barometer itself is of the syphon type favoured by Hooke, with the short limb displayed; or, rather, that would be the case had not the tube been replaced at a much later date by one of entirely the wrong kind. The result, in Goodison's stern words, is that 'the barometer cannot at the time of writing function intelligibly'. Nonetheless, it is still a gorgeous artefact.

I looked out of the window on to the garden. The only relief from the sun was in the shade beneath yews clipped to resemble toadstools. Between and beyond them the grass paths looked dead. The indicator on Daniel Quare's angle barometer was pointing at Falling, but the sky gave no reason to hope that it would ever rain again. In fact, on the night of the next day, it started raining and when I got up early the following morning it was still raining, the water hissing gently against the corrugated iron roof of my shed and gurgling in the gutters, sounds I had almost forgotten.

On 7 October 1663 Robert Hooke read to the Royal Society a paper entitled *Method for Making a History of the Weather*. It reveals how thoroughly he had already considered meteorology as an integrated scientific discipline, and the contribution the new instruments could make to it. Hooke told the members it was 'requisite to observe' the strength and direction of the wind, the temperature (by means of a sealed thermometer), humidity (using a hygroscope, in which variations in the moisture content of the air were registered by the ripe beard of a wild oat) and air pressure — 'best of all with an instrument with quicksilver, contrived so . . . it may sensibly exhibit the minute variations of that action'. In addition, Hooke recommended that observations should be recorded of the clouds, the sun and the moon and their haloes and rings; the effects of the weather on creatures and plants; the occurrence of thunder and lightning and extraordinary tides; the rising and drying of springs; and the appearance of 'comets or unusual apparitions, new stars, *igni fatui* or shining exhalations or the like'. Finally Hooke suggested a standard 'scheme' for arranging the observations on a monthly basis, and a glossary of standardised terms and scales of measurement.

On and off through the succeeding years Hooke worked on Wren's weather clock, which, as the concept expanded, he came to refer to as the 'weather-wiser'. When finally completed in 1678, Wren's original idea had been augmented into a comprehensive automated weather recorder of very great complexity and fantastic ingenuity. A large pendulum clock, capable of running for a week between windings, slowly unrolled a cylinder of paper on which a hammer linked to a barometer, a thermometer, a wind vane, a hygroscope and a self-emptying rain gauge delivered a series of punches every fifteen minutes. The members of the Society were permitted to inspect the apparatus for the first time on 29 May 1679, an earlier demonstration having been abruptly cancelled by the ever-suspicious Hooke because of the presence of a non-member. The record states that all the measurements were set down 'so as to be very legible and certain'. The weather-wiser evidently did function, after a fashion. But the operation and maintenance of it were taxing and its performance was erratic – one basic flaw being that it could not be left out in the rain because the roll of paper became sodden and the instruments began to rust. Hooke subsequently modified it in an effort to simplify it, but there is no record of it ever being used to produce a sustained series of data. It was ahead of its time, long ahead. It was not until the twentieth century that its most original feature – the method of punched data collection – achieved widespread use.

Of the several components of Hooke's weather-wiser, it was the barometer which secured the strongest hold on the public imagination. The other instruments – even the ingenious self-emptying rain bucket – were not of themselves elegant or interesting, and demanded long periods of dedicated scrutiny to furnish information of any value. But the barometer was different. The variations in the height of that gleaming, intriguing column of mercury could be instantly appreciated: a close look and a quick tap at the glass sufficed, assuming the indicator had been set at the previous day's level. The fact that it worked just as well inside as in the open air made it amenable to every kind of extravagant and outlandish ornamentation, and meant that it could be viewed in comfort whatever the conditions outside. Most alluring of all, it seemed to offer a short cut to an understanding of the otherwise baffling mysteries of our weather; and — even better — the promise of advance warning of change. The combination was irresistible.

However, for a lengthy period, the study of the Torricellian tube was confined to the members of the Royal Society and a handful of other virtuosi, for the simple reason that there was hardly anyone who was able to make them. It was not until the late 1670s that the commercial possibilities began to be exploited. The credit for this was given by the historian Roger North to his elder brother Francis, who was Charles II's Lord Chancellor before Jeffreys of infamous reputation. As well as being an exceptionally highly paid lawyer and judge — at one time he estimated his income at £7000 a year, a prodigious sum in those days — Francis North was a man of great culture, with a keen interest in the new sciences. According to his brother:

> His Lordship was much affected by the discoveries which fell in consequence of the Torricellian experiments; whereby a new world of air, compressing everything it touches, is reveal'd. He could not but observe a manifest connection between the alteration of the mercury station and the course of the winds and weather: but could not fix in his mind any certain rules of indication, but rather the contrary, viz. that events failed as often as corresponded with the ordinary expectation. But yet he would not give it over for

desperate, and hoped that a more general observation might generate a prognostic of the weather from it than was yet known. And that must be expected from a more diffuse, if not a universal use of it, which could not then be thought of; because the instruments were rare and confined to the cabinets of the virtuosi.

In the first instance North sent for a well-known London instrument-maker, Henry Jones, and – having 'shewn him the fabrick' – urged him to make and sell barometers. But Jones failed in some way to satisfy, so North summoned another craftsman, Henry Wynne, who 'pursued the manufactory to great perfection and his own no small advantage' at his shop in Chancery Lane. Over the next few years several clock-makers expanded into barometers, and they are said to have been available at Tompion's workshop in Water Lane by 1677.

In 1688 John Smith, a member of the Clock-makers' Company and an early authority on horology, produced a short guide entitled *A Compleat Discourse of the Nature, Use, and Right Managing of that Wonderful Instrument, the Baroscope or Quicksilver Weather-glass*, which was intended to promote sales of barometers, particularly those made by Smith himself. Smith favoured the straight-tube, cistern type, on the grounds that the small movements of mercury displayed as a result of the greater magnification of Morland's angle barometer and Hooke's wheel barometer 'are but seldom followed by any considerable variation in the state of weather; but those motions of the mercury as are indeed tokens of any great change to wet or dry, these are sufficiently manifest in the common baroscope'. Smith's scale displaying the correlation between the height of the mercury and states of weather was much the same as that proposed by Hooke:

28 inches	Great Storms
28.5	Much Rain
29	Rain
29.5	Uncertain
30	Fair
30.5	Settled Fair
31	Very dry

The visual appeal of this scale was, and remains, potent, and Smith's calibration – with minor variations – is still commonly used today. At the same time, however, the scale contributed significantly to the dissatisfaction with the barometer that developed during the eighteenth century. Smith himself was aware that what mattered was the *movement* of the mercury, not the position on the scale. He pointed out that if it fell half an inch from Settled Fair 'it may rain notwithstanding the quicksilver does still stand at Fair'. But Smith's words of caution were not heeded, and it was not until much later – well into the nineteenth century – that meteorologists came generally to realise that the prime function and value of the Torricellian tube was to indicate change, rather than to make a definitive statement about what the weather would be like.

The scientific revolution that gathered pace across Europe in the course of the seventeenth century was driven on by a supreme confidence in the power of the human intellect. The 'ingenious pursuers' celebrated by Professor Lisa Jardine flung off the shackles fastened by the ideologues who had controlled thinking in the names of God and Aristotle. They were not prepared to accept that any aspect of our universe was out of bounds to investigation. The notion that some mysteries should be left alone because that was what God intended was almost sacrilegious to them. They believed that, through observation and experimentation, all citadels could be breached; and that every working of our world and the air and the skies above, and the moon and the sun and the other planets and stars was determined by laws, the laws of Nature, which made all discoverable. And, one by one, the citadels did fall and give up their treasure. Galileo tracked the planets. Harvey followed the circulation of the blood. Boyle set down a law to measure air pressure. Newton calculated the gravitational pull of the earth. Flamsteed fixed the positions of the northern stars. Wren discovered how to measure the progress of an eclipse, and how to build the greatest dome in the world. Hooke grew moss on a dead man's skull, observed and drew a louse holding a human hair, analysed the beards of goats, the muscles of lobsters and the stinging parts of nettles, and solved deeper mysteries besides.

But meteorology proved to be an obstinately hard nut to crack. Hooke himself was well aware that the relationship between air pressure and the state of the weather was a good deal more complicated than a glance at the barometer might suggest. In December 1664 he reported to Boyle that his baroscopical index 'has risen a little these four or five days and has continued to do so, notwithstanding the variety of winds and the multitudes of rains that have lately fallen'. He, Boyle, Wren and the others could not have realised that – without being able to observe accurately what was happening in the atmosphere – even to hypothesise a coherent account of the weather was beyond their intellectual powers. In the event, they were necessarily restricted to energetic and ingenious speculation which produced the occasional disjointed insight amid much that was plain wrong. When Hooke tried to explain high barometric pressure, he could not escape Aristotelian terminology, and his best effort was to suggest that 'exhalations' were added to the wind by winds blowing from the east which mixed readily 'by reason of congruity'.

The faith of the ingenious pursuers that nothing in our universe was beyond their powers of comprehension was their strength. But it could also be a form of blindness. They placed their faith in observation and experimentation; and if that failed, their response was to declare that what was needed was more of both. In meteorology's case, Hooke – who did more sustained work on the subject than anyone else – knew all too well that the store of relevant knowledge was utterly inadequate. His *Method for Making a History of the Weather* was intended to address this deficiency. Having listed the various phenomena to be recorded, he wrote: 'These should all, or most of them, be diligently observed and registered by someone that is alwayes conversant in or neer the same place. Now that these, and some other hereafter to be mentioned, may be registered so as to be most convenient for the making of comparisons, requisite for the raising of *Axioms*, whereby the cause of laws of weather may be found out.'

Hooke's hopes were echoed forty years later by the philosopher John Locke, who was an assiduous watcher, and recorder of the weather. In a letter offering his weather journal to the Royal Society, Locke wrote:

I have often thought that if such a register as this one, that were better contrived with the help of some instruments that for exactness might be added, were kept in every county of England and so constantly published, many things relating to the air, winds, health, fruitfulness etc might by a sagacious man be collected from them, and several rules and observations concerning extent of winds and rain etc be in time established to the great advantage of man kind.

Unfortunately, neither Locke's journal nor the diary maintained from 1672 by Hooke came close to fulfilling these conditions. Both men were far too occupied with other much more stimulating projects to devote to the weather the enormous amount of time and effort evidently required for its laws to be revealed. If progress were to be made, men suitably circumstanced, equipped with the necessary single-mindedness and dedication, had to be recruited to the cause.

Chapter 4

With Time on Their Hands

THE VILLAGE OF LYNDON IN THE COUNTY OF RUTLAND IS AS YOU IMAGINE all of rural England used to be. It is approached along an avenue of oaks and ash trees and limes. There is a cluster of cottages and houses, a few of them red-brick but most of soft, weathered pale stone like crumbly cheese; some tiled, plenty thatched. The church, with its sturdy, battlemented tower, is of the same stone, and stands serenely among yews, sycamores, limes and horse chestnuts. The village's single road curves around one end of the churchyard. At the other end there is a stone arch and a gate, which leads to Lyndon Hall.

The Hall is as it should be, in proper proportion to its situation. It is sizeable but not at all grand, handsome but not at all ornate or extravagant, of the village but keeping a proper distance from it. With its steep hipped roof, high chimneys and moderately imposing façade in that mellow stone, it is a statement on behalf of the family which has occupied it since it was built. It says, quietly and firmly: yes, this is the big house but not that big, as you can see; and, yes, we own everything around here, but we don't throw our weight around; and, yes, we have done pretty well for ourselves, but we belong here and here we intend to stay, and if you have anything to say to us, you are welcome to walk up and make yourself known, and we will be happy to give you a hearing.

Two brothers Barker — the elder Abel, the younger Thomas — bought the Lyndon estate in 1662. They came from Hambleton, a little way to the north; and since they paid £10,000 for it, they were obviously men of considerable substance. It was Abel, later Sir Abel, who commissioned the building of Lyndon Hall. On his death, his property passed to his son, Thomas. But Thomas had no children, so when he died the whole estate reverted to the other branch of the family, now headed by a cousin, Samuel Barker. This Barker, a considerable scholar in Hebrew, was married to the daughter of a very curious clergyman, William Whiston.

If Whiston is remembered at all today, it is as one of those who laboured long and fruitlessly to claim the reward offered for a reliable method to calculate longitude. But in his time he was celebrated, even notorious, both for his achievements in mathematics and for his highly individual theology. Having heard some of Newton's lectures at Cambridge, and studied the *Principia*, in 1696 Whiston published his *New Theory of the Earth*, in which he explained the Creation, the Flood and all subsequent natural occurrences with reference to the activities of comets. In 1703 he succeeded Newton as Lucasian Professor of Mathematics at Cambridge, but was removed from the post some years later after publicly questioning the divinity of Christ. Whiston was famously difficult to silence, once rebuking some friends along the lines that they might as well ask the sun to leave the firmament as urge him to keep quiet about the nature of the Trinity. In his later years he devoted himself to the problems of longitude and the composition of biblical commentaries, announcing in 1746 that Christ's reign on earth would begin in twenty years, after which – as he put it – there would be 'no more gaming tables in Tunbridge Wells or infidels in Christendom'.

Whiston died at Lyndon Hall in 1752 and was buried in the churchyard beneath a headstone that referred to his 'excessive knowledge in various parts of literature' as well as 'his sufferings for conscience sake'. In the same place, along with a good many other Barkers, rests Whiston's grandson, Thomas Barker, the man who answered the call, and put Lyndon on the weather map.

The summons from Hooke and Locke for gentlemen of leisure, education, means and scientific enthusiasm to dedicate themselves to the rigours of systematic weather observation received a patchy response. One of those who enlisted for a time was Sir Philip Skippon, a member of an old Norfolk family whose father – also Philip – had been one of Cromwell's most trusted generals. Sir Philip kept an extensive general diary in the period 1667–77, into which he incorporated a detailed weather record running from January 1673 to November 1674 consisting of daily observations of the wind, temperature and barometric pressure, as well as brief descriptions of the weather. It is of interest if you wish to know, for instance, what March 1673 was like (stormy and cold with 'much snow' on the 13th, 14th and 15th until the 23rd, when 'pleasant spring weather' set in, interrupted on the 29th by a 'great storme of haile as big as large pistol bullets and great thunder claps'). But overall, Sir Philip does not emerge as a rival to Pepys as a chronicler of his times. Nor is his diary of much use as a source of data. He used an unusual and obscure temperature scale, and close study of his barometer readings by Professor Manley revealed that the instrument did not work properly, almost certainly because the vacuum at the top of his tube of mercury was imperfect. No explanation is offered for the abandonment of the daily record, although the fact that Sir Philip continued with his general diary for another two years suggests that he may merely have become bored with it.

A rather more assiduous and reliable recorder was the Reverend William Derham, who was rector of the village of Upminster in Essex for many years, and later Canon of Windsor. Derham was a sane and admirable specimen of the breed of amateur scientist. He contributed many papers to the Royal Society on subjects as varied as the behaviour of wasps and the deathwatch beetle and the legends of the will-o'-the-wisp, as well as annual bulletins on the weather in Upminster. The first of these was published in 1697, and two years later Derham acquired a 3-foot-long thermometer which he had the wit, unusual at that time, to hang outside, in the shade. For the next eight years he recorded the temperature three times a day at fixed hours, as well as noting wind direction, measuring rainfall and logging barometric pressure. Derham collaborated closely with Richard Towneley, the head of an ancient and wealthy Catholic family in Lancashire. Towneley was a classic virtuoso, a talented experimenter in several branches of science who was credited by Robert Boyle with the original hypothesis that became Boyle's Law. The weather of Lancashire was close to Towneley's heart, and for several years the records he made at Towneley Hall, near Burnley, were published with William Derham's in the Royal Society's *Philosophical Transactions*.

According to Professor Manley, who knew more about these matters than any man who ever lived, William Derham's records were sufficiently accurate and consistent to form 'a reasonable estimate of the air temperature by today's standards'. Manley made extensive use of them in his epic labour of calculating and compiling a continuous record of mean temperatures over central England running from 1659 to the 1950s. He had a keen interest in dusty old weather diaries, and an affinity with those who kept them amounting almost to affection. Whenever one was recovered from an attic or cellar where it had been gathering cobwebs, and sent to the Royal Meteorological Society, Manley would be summoned and a notice would subsequently appear in either the Society's journal or the journal *Weather*, reporting on its 'interesting' and sometimes 'remarkably interesting' character.

Neither of these epithets could possibly have been applied to an extended journal composed in 1703 by a country gentleman with an abundance of time on his hands, which, for some reason, escaped Manley's attention. The author neglected to put his name on it, but he has been tentatively identified by the American meteorological historian Jan Golinski as one Thomas Appletree; of whom nothing is known beyond that he was born in 1680 and died in 1728, that he went to Oxford and studied for the bar but never practised, that he lived a life of some ease on his property in Worcestershire, and that he suffered from acute verbal flatulence.

The Appletree journal was vetted by a colleague of Gordon Manley's, C. E. Britton. Having transcribed its more than two hundred pages of minute writing, an exhausted and disgruntled Britton scrawled at the top of the typescript version now in the Met Office archive: 'For turgidity of style *ad nauseam* this work must be surpassed by no other writings in any branch of writing whatever.' Although Jan Golinski makes considerable claims on behalf of Thomas Appletree's 'highly detailed and richly expressive' descriptions, Britton's verdict is a good deal nearer the mark. This – the entry for 25 August 1703 – is a representative sample of Appletree's prose style:

Most sweet and agreeable, vast, wide, diffusive [?? indecipher-
able] . . . an incredible Penetration and reach of ye eie into
ye huge abyss of Ether; I stood gazing, lost and transported
with admiration and wonder; v. delectable free smooth
complacency of ye mighty grand August and magnificent
amphitheatre of Nature; ye spacious hemispheres, ye canopy
of ye sky supported by distant hills; arch of heaven with
mountains for its pillars, ye stately architrave of clouds and
Azure interlaced in a most ravishing, regular and yet
unbounded variety: Horizon receded backwards and
discovered an unspeakable superb majestic scene.

Some of the entries run to more than twenty pages for a
single day, and it is hardly surprising that a few days after the
verbal downpour quoted above, the young man should be
complaining that 'our language is exceeding scanty and barren
of words to express ye various notions I have of Weather . . . I
tire myself with primping for apt terms and similes . . . I cannot
invent a language commensurate to vast and infinite properties
discoverable in Meteorology.' Nor is it any wonder that by
Christmas he was clearly sick of the burden he had devised for
himself, referring longingly to 'the pristine innocent Gulf of
Oblivion' which would 'wean me from this Tiresom and
Tyrannic custom of keeping and so laboriously penning this
Book of Life'. At the end of the year he gave it up, and, apart
from an unpublished paper entitled *Essay Philosophical of the Cause
of Unequal Growth in Vegetables*, the voice of Thomas Appletree was
heard no more.

Jan Golinski may well be right in arguing that such enterprises
as Appletree's should be judged as individual contributions to
a general effort to 'civilize nature' rather than as sources of
data. Certainly the Appletree journal is useless to the historical

climatologist, as it contains no readings of temperature, baro-metric pressure or anything else. And the fact that the author himself became so bored with it suggests that as a mechanism for bringing the forces of Nature under control, it may have had its limitations.

Although both were fortunate members of the landed gentry, Thomas Barker of Lyndon was the antithesis of Thomas Appletree of Worcestershire in every other way. Where Appletree was windy, sententious, incapable of methodical observation and fatally given to overblown effusions about the effect of the weather on his soul, Barker was self-effacing, meticulous in his studies and record-keeping, a man of exceptional diligence and steadfastness. As a result, while Appletree never emerged from his well-merited obscurity, Barker achieved work of permanent scientific value and became acknowledged as the leading weather authority of his day.

I spent some time in the churchyard at Lyndon searching for Thomas Barker's gravestone, pausing every now and then to listen to the insistent racket of birdsong bursting from the trees and to frown at the bilious green copper roof stuck on the church's nave and aisle. But the same Rutland weather that has softened and mellowed the stone of the church, the Hall and the other old buildings has done its work on the plaques recording the various Barkers, so that it is no longer possible to decipher which belongs to which. On the grass beside the lane is a notice inviting passers-by to picnic on the Church Lawn. I had no picnic, but I sat there anyway, in the shade of two soaring wellingtonias, and speculated idly on what it could have been about the weather here 270 years before that moved a young lad to devote his time to writing it down.

The first entry in Thomas Barker's weather journal records a 'remarkable hot day' in June 1733. Three years later he embarked upon the systematic daily log that he was to maintain, with one or two brief interruptions, for more than sixty years. It's a reasonable bet that the boy was encouraged in his meteorological endeavours by his learned grandfather, Whiston, and his learned father, Samuel Barker. But whether his great project had anything to do with periodic appeals from the Royal Society, or whether it sprang to life independently, is not known. Elsewhere in England, like-minded enthusiasts were doing their bit. In London, James Jurin, a well-known physician and pioneer of inoculation against smallpox who served as the Royal Society's secretary for some years, maintained a weather record in Latin until a few days before his death in 1750. Several other medical men, interested as Jurin was in the links between weather and health, also kept journals – among them the country's leading expert on fevers, John Huxham of Plymouth, and Clifford Wintringham of York, who gamely refused to give his up despite what he referred to as 'the continual tediousness of making these observations over several years'.

If Thomas Barker ever felt oppressed in the same way, he kept it to himself. The Barker journals have two distinct, complementary strands. One is the record of readings taken, usually twice a day, from a barometer and thermometer hung inside Lyndon Hall, and – from 1763 onwards – from a second thermometer placed in the shade outdoors, as well as measurements from a rain gauge, observations of cloud formation and wind direction and strength, plus brief comments. The second consists of a continuous narrative description covering the years 1733–95, woven together from his data and comments, and entitled *A General Account of the Weather*. Although the focus of this narrative is meteorological, there is a good deal about the farming of his estate, covering the sowing of crops, grass-cutting, hay-making, the wellbeing or otherwise of livestock, and the progress of the harvest. Unlike Thomas Appletree, Barker is mercifully sparing in his moralising, one exception being a comment written at the end of 1748: 'The latter end of last summer the murrein again visited this country and spread like wild-fire carrying destruction with it . . . I believe several thousands of beasts must have perished by it in this small county . . . God grant that the people of the land may turn away the wrath of God by true repentance, and that we may sin no more, less a worse thing come unto us.'

Barker's records reveal that, although winters were frequently much more severe than they are now, and the summers generally not so warm, the dominant theme of our climate — its inconstancy — was as noticeable then as now. Occasionally conditions were so extreme as to stimulate Barker to a more extended account. The atrociously cold winter of 1739–40 was one example. The freeze set in on Christmas Day, and on the night of 28 December a marrow-chilling east wind arose. Reviewing the winter, Barker wrote:

About three inches of snow fell in the first three days of January. After the snow it froze most days and every night until February 16th . . . February 2nd when the Ice was the thickest, I found it 11.5 inches thick in a pond. Trees were split by the frost and plants shrivelled . . . The small birds which were plentiful before the frost were almost all destroyed by it and were three or four years before they recovered their usual numbers . . . This frost exceeded almost all others of which we have account . . . the strong freezing wind on Dec 28, 29 and 30 was so inexpressibly sharp

that few who could help it cared to face it, and some Post
boys who were forc'd to go into it were kill'd by it.

Almost half a century later, over the winter of 1788–9,
northern Europe was subjected to two months of savage cold
and blizzards. The learned men of the Académie Royale des
Sciences in Paris wanted to know how England had fared. The
formidable President of the Royal Society, Sir Joseph Banks, was
approached, and he turned to Thomas Barker, who reported
that the cold had been such 'as to burst bottles within doors
and to freeze water immediately in the act of pouring it into a
cold basin', but that, as a whole, 1740 had been more severe.

It is evident that Barker was by then regarded by the scientific establishment as the leading weather expert in the land.
From 1771 a digest of his observations was published each year
in the *Philosophical Transactions*, together with a commentary. The
last, dealing with conditions in 1798, was as meticulous as ever.
The highest barometer reading was 30.19, on a day in February,
and the lowest 28.21, in November. The top temperatures was
84 degrees – by now the Fahrenheit scale had been generally
adopted – and the lowest 5.5 degrees, almost 27 degrees of frost,
in late December. The last sentence from Thomas Barker was
entirely typical:

The autumn was fine, with few frosty mornings; yet one or
two severe nights in October, before the greenhouse plants
were housed, killed many of them, especially the Geraniums;
but it was afterwards warm and wet again, and continued
pretty fine for the season till the middle of the season, when,
after some misty weather, followed by very severe frost in
the last week, it was exceedingly cold, and the thermometer
was down one day at five-and-a-half, which I never saw it

but once before; and the frost continued, though not so severe, till the middle of January 1799

With that, the voice that had informed anyone who was interested about the weather in Rutland for more than six decades fell silent. Barker was by then nearly eighty, and he may well have felt that he was no longer up to the demands of inspecting his instruments and recording their readings twice a day; and that if he could not maintain his regime properly, it was better that he gave it up altogether than lower his standards.

From himself we learn almost nothing of his personality, other than what can be deduced from his work: that he was insatiably curious, and painstaking, determined and diligent almost beyond belief. But there are one or two glimpses of Barker from other sources. By a happy accident, the brother of the woman he married shared many of his interests; the two men became as firm friends as the considerable distance between their homes would allow. The friend also had a talent which the Rutland squire would not have dreamed of claiming: he was a born writer. His name was Gilbert White.

I was in Selborne on a morning in mid-June in our summer of summers, 2003. It was hot, but the air was fresh and carried the scents of the wild flowers and the woods. If you do not know Selborne, as I did not, the dramatic quality of the landscape comes as a surprise, even if it does not quite live up to the verses with which the village's lovable son introduced his immortal book:

> See, Selborne spreads her boldest beauties round
> The varied valley and the mountain ground
> Wildly majestic!

Behind Gilbert White's house, The Wakes, the great beech wood known as The Hanger rises abruptly like a green cliff. Along the ridge above runs the down, or sheep-walk, as White knew it. If you stand there and look east, the land plunges from your feet, then levels out and extends far away towards the downs of Sussex and Surrey, still today much as White saw it then, 'a very engaging view, being an assemblage of hill, dale, woodlands, heath and water'.

I took the path that zigzagged up the southerly flank of The Hanger, which had been cut by White and his brother John exactly 250 years before. A soft, warm breeze stirred the tops of the beeches, whose slenderness and height were somehow exaggerated by the steepness of the slope. There were walkers ahead of me and behind, with staffs and rucksacks and heavy boots, suggesting an arduous slog through hard terrain ahead. I sat where White placed his own seat – 'a rural, shelter'd, un-observed retreat' – and looked down. Nearby a couple paused to give water to a white dog called Digby. I took the path along the top of the wood, then another down through the trees. The air beneath the canopy of leaves was moist and still, heavy with the smell of humus and beechnuts. Above the straight, pale trunks of the trees, the foliage burned golden where the sun's rays fell. I came down the meadow known as Dell Field, where thick grass bright with buttercups and cowslips rustled with the wind. A chain saw growled somewhere, loud enough to make me wish that it would give way to the axe thud of White's day.

Back in the village, I sat by the oak tree which stands on the patch of open ground next to the churchyard 'vulgarly called The Plestor', and read the passage from *The Natural History of Selborne* in which White recorded the fate of the noble tree which shaded the spot long ago:

. . . a vast oak, with a short, squat body and huge horizontal arms extending almost to the extremity of the area. This venerable tree, surrounded with stone steps and seats above them, was the delight of old and young, and a place of much resort on Summer evenings; where the former sat in grave debate while the latter frolicked and danced before them. Long might it have stood, had not the amazing tempest in 1703 overturned it at once to the infinite regret of the inhabitants and the Vicar, who bestowed several pounds in setting it in its place again; but all his care could not avail; the tree sprouted for a time, then withered and died.

When the great oak was toppled, another witness to Selborne's history, a yew, had already been standing for several centuries in the churchyard. It continued to do so throughout White's time and long afterwards, until 25 January 1990, when another great storm pushed it over. Again the people and vicar of Selborne put it back upright. But, like the oak, its spirit departed. The skeleton has been left, its immense, shattered trunk embraced by sweet honeysuckle.

I walked around to the north side of the church in search of White's grave. It takes some finding, not because of neglect, but because of its extraordinary modesty. The stone just peeps above the scythed grass, and because of the angle at which it leans it is necessary to kneel and squint at it before the inscription can be deciphered. It reads: 'G. W. 26th June 1793'. That is all, but it is enough to give a flavour of this most unusual and appealing man.

Gilbert White was born in 1720, in Selborne, where his grandfather was vicar. He was sent to the grammar school in Basingstoke and thence to Oriel College, Oxford, where he became a Fellow. White served as curate to his uncle Charles at Swarraton in Hampshire, and subsequently held the curacy at Faringdon in the same county, which was close enough for him to live in Selborne. In 1784 he finally became curate of Selborne itself. Although White travelled extensively in southern England, visiting members of his large family, and the friends he had made at Oxford and through his enthusiasm for natural history, his whole life was shaped by his determination to live and die in the village where he'd been born. With that came his life's work, which was to minister to the souls of that place and to make a record of them and it.

In 1751 White began to keep a Gardener's Kalendar to record his observations on the life in and around Selborne. He maintained it until 1767 when it was supplanted by a more elaborate journal printed by his brother Benjamin to a design of a well-known figure in London's scientific circles, Daines Barrington. Barrington was one of those fortunates liberated by inherited wealth and good connections from the burden of having to earn a living, and thus able to follow their whims. For some years he served as a judge – 'not intentionally a bad judge', Jeremy Bentham wrote, 'though he was often a bad one' – before retiring from the bench to pursue his wide range of enthusiasms. Meteorology was among them, but it had to compete for his time and limited capacity for inquiry with many others, including ancient statutes, King Alfred, polar exploration, the universality or otherwise of the Deluge and the origins of card-playing. Barrington's researches into the Cornish language and his attempts to locate the last remaining speaker of the language, roused the ridicule of the popular satirical poet Peter Pindar who wrote:

> Hail, Mousehole! Birth-place of old Poll Pentreath,
> The last who jabbered Cornish, so says Daines,
> Who, bat-like, haunted ruins, lane and heath
> With Will-o'-Wisp to brighten up his brains.

Barrington himself was well aware of his own shortcomings – 'I have, perhaps, published too many things,' he commented ruefully. But he deserves the nation's gratitude for being Gilbert White's devoted friend, and for encouraging White to write to him and to another naturalist, Thomas Pennant, the series of letters which eventually comprised *The Natural History*.

The book which immortalised the self-effacing curate of Selborne was published in 1787. Its excellence was recognised at once, although no one could have predicted that it would secure and hold a place high in the ranks of the classics of English prose. It does so because there is no book like it. For one thing, it paints an incomparably vivid and truthful picture of a place and the life in and around it. But that is the easy aspect of White's genius to classify. The other is more elusive, but the elements include charm, sweetness and innocence, as well as modesty, honesty, humour and wisdom. These were also, according to those who knew him, the qualities of the man himself. To them may be added another: a complete absence of self-importance or self-consciousness. No doubt these – as much as the shared passion for science and natural history – served to attract the man who became his brother-in-law, Thomas Barker of Lyndon.

Two early entries in Barker's journal – one referring to a flight of geese on the last day of March 1736, the other to the hearing of a cuckoo a week later – are initialled G.W., and it seems likely that Barker was accompanied by the fifteen-year-old White who was then staying with his aunt and her clerical husband at Whitewell rectory, two miles from Lyndon Hall. As a young man White made several more visits, as did his younger sister, Anne. Barker himself visited Selborne in 1749 and again the following year, by which time his engagement to Anne had been announced. White's old friend John Mulso wrote to congratulate him: 'I heartily wish your sister much happiness in her new state: with her cheerful and easy Temper she will be ye best wife in the world to Mr Barker and may manage to her own Content and his Advantage that extreme Abstractedness and Speculativeness to which I hear he is naturally prone.'

Over the years White and Barker corresponded regularly on matters abstract, speculative and factual. White refers in *The Natural History of Selborne* to Barker's rainfall readings, while Barker occasionally included data gathered from White and his brothers John and Thomas in his dispatches to the Royal Society. Gilbert White appears to have paid his last visit to Rutland as early as 1759, but the Barkers and their children continued to make sporadic forays to Selborne, the last in the late summer of 1783. Barker, then aged sixty-one, left Lyndon on horseback on the Monday morning, arriving at Selborne on Wednesday evening, having covered 118 miles. White wrote to his niece, Mary, to say that Barker '. . . still has a streight belly, and is the same agile being that he used to be: he rises at six and cannot sit still; but starts up the moment he has dined and runs away to Hawkley Hanger or St John's Hill . . . This morning Mr B ran round Baker's Hill in one minute and a quarter; and Sam [his son and White's favourite nephew] in somewhat less than a minute.'

That summer, 1783, was memorable in other ways. In June, the volcano of Laki, in south-east Iceland, had erupted, blasting a colossal load of dust and debris into the upper atmosphere. This formed a shroud over the skies of Europe which caused extreme weather conditions for many months. Thomas Barker's account of its effects in Rutland was characteristically sober:

During this showery time [mid-June] began what was very remarkable all the rest of the summer, an uncommon haziness; the air was all thick both below the clouds and above them, the hills looked blue and at a distance could not be seen; the sun shone very red through the haze and sometimes could not be seen when near setting; there was more or less of this haze almost constantly for a month . . . and neither rain nor fair, wind nor calm, East or West Winds took it away; and it was the same all over Europe and even to the top of the Alps. This haze was very like Virgil's description of the summer after J. Caesar's death, which was probably the same case — *sum capit obscura nitridium ferrugine texit* — for rusty iron is a very good description of the colour the sun shone.

In total contrast, Gilbert White's response was that of an artist and all the more effective for his unconsciousness of his artistry. The passage in *The Natural History* begins: 'The summer of the year 1783 was an amazing and portentous one, and full of horrible phaenomena.' From that opening, White proceeds to note conditions very similar to those described in his brother-in-law's plodding prose. But his account is full of vivid touches: the sun looking as black as a clouded moon, and shedding a 'rust-coloured ferruginous light'; the heat so intense 'that butcher's meat could hardly be eaten on the day it was killed'; the swarms of flies driving 'the horses half-frantic and making driving irksome'; the country people who 'began to look with superstitious awe at the red, louring aspect of the sun'. And instead of a vague reference to 'the same all over Europe', White picks out the instances of Calabria and Sicily being 'torn and convulsed with earthquakes, and about that juncture a volcano sprung out of the sea off the coast of Norway'.

White took his meteorological duties seriously. He recorded barometric pressure and temperature both at his own house in

Selborne and at that of a friend in the village of Newton Vallence, a mile or two away. In 1778 his brother Thomas gave him a 'rain-measure' and from then he systematically recorded the rainfall, comparing his results with those of brother-in-law Barker in Rutland and Doctor Huxham in Plymouth. But his practice was to weave his weather observations into the larger tapestry of rural life presented in his journal. Thus we hear that on the last day of 1783 ice is freezing under people's beds, water bottles are bursting and the snipe have been driven off the moors and up the streams towards the spring heads to find running water. On 24 January 1784 White hears that the temperature at Totnes was as low as 6 degrees Fahrenheit. A few days later the hares nibble the buds off his espalier pear trees. The next day a curlew is shot near The Priory. Shortly after that a neighbour shoots at a pair of hares from his window, killing one and wounding the other, and giving White reason to hope that 'our gardens will not be so much molested'. On 4 February: 'Hard frosts. Paths thaw. Fleecy clouds. Sky muddles. Halo.' A week later the hares are back in his garden.

For the letters to Barrington and Pennant, White worked up his journal entries into more rounded and coherent narratives, while somehow retaining the air of spontaneity which makes them so vivid. The last six letters in the book all deal with the weather. Three are devoted to various remarkable frosts, two to hot summers and the last to thunderstorms, 'with which' – White noted – 'we are very seldom annoyed'.

Although White was a well-educated man and extremely knowledgeable about natural history, he subscribed unquestioningly to the meteorological fallacies of the day. For instance, he explained that the appearance of 'honeydew' – a sticky secretion left on plants by aphids – occurred when 'in hot weather the effluvia of flowers in fields and meadows and gardens are drawn up in the day by a brisk evaporation and then in the night falls down again with the dews in which they are entangled'. He accepted that an increase in the vociferousness of 'roost-cocks' and crows in severe winter weather was a 'prognostic' of a thaw, as was a sudden inclination on the part of moles to 'heave and work'. 'From the latter circumstance,' White wrote, 'we may conclude that thaws often originate underground from warm vapours which arise; how else should subterraneous animals receive such early intimations of their approach?'

Gilbert White's willingness to accept untested and often fanciful speculations to explain the observations he so carefully recorded is a measure of the state of meteorology at this time. The work of Newton and his colleagues and followers had demonstrated to the satisfaction of enlightened Britain that the material universe was organised by identifiable, comprehensible principles. Pope's famous lines − 'Nature and Nature's laws lay hid in night / God said, let Newton be, and all was light' − summed up the confidence of the age. It was as if a set procedure had been agreed for the solving of problems. Observations and experiments were undertaken. Hypotheses were advanced, tested and either proved or found wanting. Further evidence was sought, and refinements in the experiments were made. Eventually knowledge was obtained, and more of the absurd superstitions of the past were banished.

But the empirical method which brought the motions of the planets to order and unlocked the secrets of physiology, physics, biology and mathematics − to name but a few − proved sadly inadequate when it came to working out what the weather was up to, and even more useless for establishing what it might have in store. This was not for want of effort. Throughout civilised Europe great quantities of data were being accumulated, from which the laws of the weather – for such there must surely be – might be deduced. In 1778 the Société Royale de Médecine in Paris began establishing a network of weather stations across France, whose volunteers were required to record readings and observations three times a day. By the mid-1780s more than eighty correspondents had enlisted, from as far away as Russia, America and Asia. The illustrious French scientist Antoine Laurent Lavoisier asserted that with the requisite data 'it is virtually always possible to forecast a day or two in advance how the weather is likely to be'. Unfortunately for Lavoisier's confidence, the Société Royale was abolished after the Revolution and Lavoisier himself was guillotined.

At roughly the same time, one of Europe's most enlightened rulers, Karl Theodor of the Rhineland Palatinate, founded the Societas Meteorologica Palatina, and appointed his chaplain, Johann Hemmer, as its director. Hemmer recruited a team of observers across Europe and equipped each of them with a set of uniformly calibrated instruments, with instructions to send their thrice-daily readings for collation and interpretation at the Society's headquarters in Mannheim. This exercise produced a vast quantity of information about the weather as experienced from Siberia in the east to America in the west and Greenland in the north. But it did almost nothing to advance the primary objective, which was reliable prediction. The reason was simple: no means of communication then existed which could outpace weather systems – or even come close to keeping up with them.

The great disappointment for the weather observers of the eighteenth century was the instrument which had promised so much, the barometer. Barometers had become immensely popular within a few years of coming on to the market, partly because of their novelty and pleasing appearance, and partly because of the promise that they would divine the weather before it arrived. The barometer's cause was not helped by the absurd claims made for its prophetic powers. In the 1690s a cod scientist called Gustavus Parker boasted that his mastery of the Torricellian tube enabled him to make accurate forecasts for up to six weeks ahead. This provoked a crushing response from the well-known instrument-maker and self-styled Torricellian operator John Patrick, who thundered: ''Tis evident from consulting the journal that he [Parker] missed the wind and the weather more days than he has hit right, from which I infer that it is not a solid basis he builds upon, but purely imaginary.'

In 1730, Edward Saul, a Fellow of Magdalen College, Oxford, and Rector of Harlaxton in Lincolnshire, produced a pompous little book called *A Historical and Philosophical Account of the Barometer or Weather-glass* whose title page promised a 'MODEST ATTEMPT from thence made towards a rational ACCOUNT and probable judgement of THE WEATHER'. 'The weather-glass,' Saul wrote, 'being of late grown into common use and in most houses of figure and distinction being hung up as a philosophical or ornamental branch of furniture; and supplying often matter for discourse upon the various and sudden changes of it; it may not perhaps be unacceptable to many persons who daily see the effect and are not rightly apprized of the cause to explain the Nature and Reason of it.' Although Saul's advice on how to read the mercury was unexceptionable, his elucidation of the 'Nature and Reason' was the usual mixture of guesswork and denigration of rival theories. He asserted that the mercury stood high in calm weather because 'the pressure is direct, uniform and steady', and low in wet weather because 'by the interposure or fluctuation of clouds and vapour, it is broken and interrupted and thereby diverted and diminished'. Among various imposing statistics furnished by Doctor Saul was his estimate of the weight of the air 'impendent over England', which he put at 1,576,735,875,000 tons.

Unfortunately for Doctor Saul and the other pseudo-scientists, the barometer's unreliability became a favoured target for ridicule. Doctor Johnson mocked the vogue for the instrument in characteristically rough fashion in an issue of *The Idler* in 1758: 'The rainy weather, which has continued the last month, is said to have given great disturbance to the inspectors of barometers. The oraculous glasses have deceived their votaries; shower has succeeded shower, though they predicted sunshine and dry skies; and by fatal confidence in these fallacious promises, many coats have lost their gloss and many curls have been moistened to flaccidity.'

The barometer's failings stimulated a new interest in rural weather wisdom. In *The Shepherd of Banbury's Rules*, the instrument is abused for its inability 'in prognosticating a change in the weather at distance, and it is from the experience of this that they are so little esteemed, so lightly regarded, by the common people'. Doctor Thomas Short regarded what he called The Book of Nature as much superior to any meteorological instruments, stating as a fact that the wisdom of rural sages was divinely appointed. John Mills, in *An Essay on the Weather*, criticised the philosophers who had 'despised or neglected the remarks of illiterate country people', and expressed what seems to have been a general feeling of dissatisfaction at the lack of progress in solving the meteorological mysteries: 'It might have been expected that, considering the great improvements which have been made in natural philosophy, an accurate account of the weather would now have been attained; yet the earliest authors who have treated of husbandry seem to have established more certain prognostics of the weather peculiar to their climates than any have done in ours.'

Mills retained some faith in the barometer, and attempted to synthesise the best of the scientific and the intuitive. An anonymous pamphlet entitled *The Meteorologist's Assistant*, which appeared in 1793, poured scorn on the 'sanguine but misguided advocates' of the barometer for 'extolling it as a certain fore-teller of the weather', and chided its critics for 'asserting it is not at all to be depended on'. 'The truth,' the level-headed pamphleteer stated, 'will be found, as it generally is, between the two extremes.'

Meteorology's intractability counted against it. First-rate minds tended to avoid the extended and laborious data gath-ering it necessitated, and as a result it failed to acquire the status of a primary branch of science. It remained a shadowy, ill-defined place, open to invasion by all kinds of self-declared experts, where, in the absence of any testing procedure, speculations could be launched and kept airborne almost indefinitely. Thus Doctor Saul, in advancing his own fallacious explanation of air pressure, derided John Wallis's notion that the air became lighter as it shed the rain it was carrying. In *A Rational Account of the Weather* the Reverend John Pointer damned the barometer, while commending the suggestion of the 'Reverend and Ingenious Mr Robinson' – Thomas Robinson, rector of Ousby in north Cumberland for fifty years, a devotee of football and author of *An Anatomy of the Earth* – that winds were created 'in the greatest probability . . . from vast swarms of nitreous parti-cles arising from the bottom of the sea'. John Mills made a decent stab at explaining raindrops as being formed 'when the watery particles composing a cloud approach so near to each other that they unite into drops, which, becoming specifically heavier than the air, they fall down'. But his definitions of dew as 'most frequently the sweat of plants', and fog as 'exhalations either rising slowly from earth or returning slowly to it' are Aristotelian old hat.

While assorted self-appointed authorities persisted in their fruitless efforts to make sense of the weather, others continued with the mundane task of compiling data, though none was as assiduous as Thomas Barker. I have examined several of these journals, and they do not make for stimulating reading. Needless to say, most were kept by men. One exception – praised by Gordon Manley as 'an unusual revelation of a remarkably interesting character' – was the work of the exotically named Constantia Orlebar, whose family had been landowners in Northamptonshire since the twelfth century. Miss Orlebar lived with her two spinster sisters at Ecton, about five miles from Northampton, and she kept a record of its weather, without any instrument readings, for twenty-two years until shortly before her death in 1808. One entry, for 30 September 1794, suffices to give the flavour: 'Early very hasty rain, changed to be fine – cloudy sunset – wind arose and was a turbulent wet night.'

Despite the labours of Thomas Barker, and the contributions of Gilbert White and lesser lights, nothing even resembling the national weather database called for by the Royal Society came close to being assembled. The 'uncommon type of enthusiasm' referred to by Gordon Manley as being necessary to sustain dedication over a protracted period was uncommon indeed. It was not until Manley himself assembled his mean temperature series from 1659 onwards that a semblance of order was imposed on these dusty old records, and coherent sense drawn from them.

Although connoisseurs of weather facts may regret that the example set by Barker in Lyndon, Derham in Upminster, Towneley near Burnley, White in deepest Hampshire and a few others was not more widely followed, the rest of us are likely to take a relaxed view of this statistical paucity. Anyway, there is a consolation. Data may be in short supply, but there is a wealth of testimony about what living with our weather was like.

Chapter 5

Hay and Ice

THE OLD CHAP FORKING MANURE ON TO HIS VEGETABLE PATCH WAS happy to give his back a rest and tell me what had happened to the village in the forest since he was a lad. 'Used to know everyone here,' he said, waving a mucky hand. 'Every single person. And their business. Now, mebbe a dozen out of a hundred and fifty or so. And them just the old ones, like me. See, in them days everyone worked for the Forestry. Was them that built the 'ouses. Then Mrs Thatcher said they could buy 'em, so they paid nine thousand for 'em then sold 'em for sixty thousand. Shoved off to Thetford, places like that. Load of outsiders moved in, didn't they?' He shook his head at the folly of it.

I complimented him on his soil, which was in dark, fertile contrast to the yellow sand on which the village stood and which lay beneath the mantle of frowning pine trees stretching away on every side. 'Well, see,' he replied, clearly pleased, 'this is where the potting shed for the 'all was, with the vegetable garden next door, so's there was always plenty of muck put down 'ere. My father was a warrener for the Estate, see.' I wasn't sure what a warrener was. 'Well, he was in charge of the rabbits, wasn't he? And other game, deers, pheasants and such. But mainly the rabbits. That's all I remember eating. Rabbits.'

There was a time not so long ago, when rabbits still played a vital part in sustaining life in this harsh corner of East Anglia. The tenants of the little farms used ferrets, lurchers and nets to capture them in their tens of thousands around the warrens which pockmark the open ground between the trees, and depended on selling the pelts and meat to pay their rents. There was even a factory at Brandon, a few miles away, where the pelts were made into hats and fur coats, although the main employment in Brandon was the ancient craft of flint-knapping, which has left its mark in every settlement in these parts. Brandon flint-knappers supplied the gun flints for Wellington's army, and as recently as the 1930s the Emperor Haile Selassie sent officials there to get flints for the rifles of the Abyssinian army. The aptitude with flint in the Breckland – as the district is known – goes back thousands of years, for prehistoric man learned to use it to make his weapons and knives and axes. Now, of course, the knappers and pelt-stitchers are no more. The rabbits, however – left pretty much in peace these days – are thriving.

I asked my informant about the fate of the 'all, for which his father had worked. 'Pulled it down, didn't they? In the Twenties, I think.' The last squire, Colonel Edward Mackenzie, had sold up some time before, leaving Downham Hall – described in Kelly's Directory of 1883 as 'a noble mansion built of white Suffolk brick situated in a well-timbered park' – to sink into decay. It and everything else for miles around was acquired by the Forestry Commission; and by the time the 'all was demolished, the Commission was already engaged on its mission to cover the sandy wastes with the blanket of trees that is Thetford Forest. The Commission made the village of Santon Downham the administrative centre for the forest, and built houses in pine, brick and a little flint for the foresters around the clearing a little way to the north of where Downham Hall had stood. In the 1950s everyone, including my friend, worked for the Commission. Now almost no one does, although there is still an office down near the river.

I thanked the old boy and he turned back to his brassicas. I walked down the lane and crossed a brick bridge over the Little Ouse, thereby leaving Suffolk for Norfolk. It was a soft, sparkling spring day, the air filled with birdsong. I sat down on a hummock by the stream. The clear water ran with surprising liveliness over beds of weed whose rich emerald was set off by the yellow of the sand beneath. The banks, too, were lined with gold. In one way or another sand has shaped this place's destiny through the ages, as well as burying its past. It was the reason I had come here.

Back in Suffolk I approached the Church of St Mary – the Church in the Forest – through the trees enclosing the church-yard. It is a lovely, mellow, peaceful, welcoming building, with a fifteenth-century tower at the western end and a Norman font at the eastern, and many curious features in between – most notably a carved stone panel over the south doorway depicting a creature resembling a llama with a ruff around its neck in the act of swallowing some symbolic plant which sprouts again from below its tail. Pevsner says it's a lion with a fleur-de-lis; while another writer suggests it could be the Paschal lamb, although it looks even less like a sheep than the king of the felines. A former rector of Santon Downham, Canon John Fitch, speculates in his booklet about the church and its history that it might be a wolf – standing for evil – shown swallowing the Tree or Vine of Life, which grows indestructibly from the animal's backside.

One of Canon Fitch's predecessors, Richard Kendal, was turned out of the living in 1644 for 'refusing to contribute to the Rebellion, swearing, haunting inns, being distempered with liquor, keeping malignant company and for saying in a sermon six or seven years before that Puritans were hypocrites'. By then, or not long afterwards, the Downham estate had come into the possession of Thomas Wright, a member of an old Norfolk family. It was Mr Wright who secured for Santon Downham its place in the slim history of British natural disasters: as the village that was buried in sand.

In a dispatch to the Royal Society, the squire told how, over a period of many years, the 'impetuous south-west winds' had loosened the surface of 'some great sand-hills' by a warren at Lakenheath, five miles to the south-west. Since 'the first eruption thereof (which does not much exceed the memories of some persons still living)', the sands had rolled across the barren land, picking up mass as they went. ''Tis between 30 and 40 years,' Mr Wright related, 'since it first reached the bounds of this Town; where it continued 10 or 12 years in the outskirts without doing any considerable mischief.' But at length the gales set the sand moving again 'above a mile in two months time, and over-ran 200 acres of very good corn'. Now it was into the village itself 'where it hath buried and destroy'd divers Tenements and other Houses', and threatened Mr Wright's own home. It filled the yard and the avenue to his front door and crept up to 'the Eves of most of my out houses'. He managed to defend the main building by putting down furze hedges, one on top of another as the level of the sand rose, until the banks were 60 feet high. He then stabilised the surface 'by laying some hundreds of loads of Muck and good earth upon it', and cut a passage through to his door, removing 1500 loads of sand in the process.

Mr Wright saved his home. But others were not so fortunate,

or resolute. Many houses at the eastern end of the village simply disappeared and 'our Pastures and Meadows (which were considerable both for quality and quantity) over-run and destroyed'. The progress of the sands was finally halted by the natural barrier of the river, three miles of which was so filled as to make it impassable to boat traffic. Without it, said Mr Wright, 'doubtless a good part of that county [Norfolk] had ere been left a desolate Trophy of this Conquering Enemy'.

In 1677 the diarist John Evelyn spent three weeks at Euston, about ten miles south-east of Santon Downham. His host was Henry Bennet, who had been enriched and created Earl of Arlington by Charles II for having acted as his exceptionally devious negotiator in a series of European treaties, as well as assisting in the equally important matter of managing the King's mistresses. Bennet was widely disliked and distrusted, on account of his scheming, his clandestine Catholicism and his self-important demeanour; once the King tired of him, he was rapidly relieved of his public offices, whereupon he retired to Euston to spend a great deal of money making his country seat into a suitable reflection of his own estimation of himself.

Evelyn described it as 'a very noble pile consisting of four pavilions after the French', but was less taken with its situation, on 'soil dry, barren and miserably sandy, which flies in drifts as the wind shifts'. Nevertheless he visited several times, on one occasion to attend the marriage of Bennet's only child, Isabella – 'this sweetest, hopefullest most beautiful child', Evelyn sighed – to King Charles's son by Barbara Villiers, Henry FitzRoy, an event which would have attracted less comment had not the bride been five years old and the groom twelve. Evelyn feared for a union with 'a boy that had been rudely bred', but seven years later Isabella and Henry – by now Earl of Euston and Duke of Grafton – renewed their vows. The marriage appears to have been happy enough, although Grafton was only twenty-seven when his eventful and audacious military career was brought to an end by a musket ball which struck him in the chest during the siege of Cork.

Evelyn was a leading light in the Royal Society, and he took the opportunity of his stay at Euston in 1677 to investigate the natural marvel of the locality. He noted in his diary for 10 September that he had inspected 'the Travelling Sands about ten miles wide of Euston, that have so much damaged the county, rolling from place to place and – like the deserts of Libya – quite overwhelmed some gentleman's estate'.

The year after Thomas Wright's account of the disaster had appeared in the Royal Society's *Philosophical Transactions*, he died. His tombstone is in the grass beneath the east window of St Mary's Church, and there are various memorials to his descendants inside and outside the building – the last to the Reverend George Wright, Vicar of Downham, who died in 1814. After the Wrights came other, grander owners. The estate was bought by Charles Sloane, Earl Cadogan, the death of whose son, Henry, fighting the French at Vittoria in 1813, is commemorated in the church; and subsequently by Lord William Powlett – later Duke of Cleveland – who lived at Downham Hall until his death in 1864, and whose widow planted the avenue of limes stretching from the Brandon–Thetford road.

Although the Travelling Sands had long since halted their march, sand remained the dominant feature of this landscape until the Forestry Commission covered it in conifers. It is still there, gleaming golden between and beneath the trees. And somewhere beneath the sand is the village that Thomas Wright knew. There is now no trace of his home, and precious little of the Hall, apart from the walls which once enclosed the grounds. Santon Downham is as quiet and obscure as ever it was, forgotten except as a footnote in the weather books: the village that disappeared, buried because the wind blew from the south-west.*

It is not recorded which member of the Royal Society encouraged Thomas Wright to tell his grim story, but it was in keeping with the Society's role that it should have preserved this unusual example of extreme English weather for posterity, and entirely typical of John Evelyn's curiosity that he should have wished to go and inspect the damage. Thanks to the likes of Evelyn and his friend Samuel Pepys, and a host of lesser lights, we have been left with a vivid, if erratic, picture of what living with our weather was like three hundred years and more ago.

The weather itself was not so different from what it was before our current warming phase got going in earnest around 1970. Summers were sometimes miserable, sometimes hot, mostly a mixture of the two. There were dry springs and autumns, wild ones, wet ones, stormy ones, tranquil ones. Winters were generally more severe, and sometimes very severe indeed. But the dominant motif was familiar: changeability, inconstancy, variety.

What was not at all the same – in fact, so different that we cannot imagine it – was the experience of the weather. The discomforts were, of course, felt most keenly by the rural peasantry, compelled to spend their working days outside in all weathers, returning at light's fading to their clammy, leaky,

*Actually Santon Downham is also cherished by weather buffs as one of the country's recognised 'frost hollows'. Its situation, protected from the wind by trees and built on sand, makes it unusually susceptible to unseasonable frosts, and it holds the record for a low in June of minus 6 degrees Celsius.

draughty hovels to eat their meatless stews and lie in their damp clothes on vermin-infested straw beds. But even men and women of education and position were exposed to rigours inconceivable in our pampered age. Their houses were unheated, apart from the one or two rooms where a fire was kept, and even there the warmth from the flames was often sabotaged by the icy draughts infiltrating past ill-fitting doors and windows. On 6 December 1678 Katherine Stewkley wrote to her friend Penelope Verney that 'if my love for you were not very ardent, surely this cold weather would chill it, for I do not know that I was ever so sincible of a sharper time, and tho' (even in the Chimney Corner) I am scars able to write'.

To do their business, men of business had to be ready to go out whatever the weather. There was no comfortable, covered mode of transport until well into the nineteenth century. Over short distances you walked. Over long distances you either walked for a long time, or you rode a horse. Either way, if it rained you got wet. Umbrellas had come into fashion as a protection against the sun in the sixteenth century, but without waterproofing were of little use in a downpour, and it was not until the 1820s that Charles Mackintosh began selling the first genuinely waterproof clothing materials. Understanding of insulation and thermal retention was non-existent – in severe weather men wore several layers of clothing and became very cold.

Contrast those harsh times with our own. We do not know cold or wet as anything more than passing inconveniences. Our homes are dry and warm. We travel in enclosed, heated cars, buses and trains. Most of us work in buildings in which the temperature is controlled so that we can be in short sleeves all the year round. The few farmers still farming plough the fields from within heated tractor cabins. There are almost no foresters, charcoal-burners, fence-makers or furniture-bodgers left; and precious few shepherds and turf-cutters. The trawlermen are probably the chief sufferers from the vagaries of the weather, and they are a dwindling band. Those who are compelled, or choose, to expose themselves to the elements can — thanks to advances in waterproofing and insulation — remain reasonably warm and dry in the worst that our weather can throw at them. Men like Evelyn and Pepys were not significantly warmer or drier than the equivalent gentlemen of two centuries before; we, on the other hand, are considerably more comfortable than the pre-central heating generation, very much more so than our Victorian forebears and unimaginably more so than anyone in late seventeenth-century Britain.

So, we suffer much less wretchedness at the hands of our weather than those who have gone before, which is probably something to be grateful for. But it does mean that our experience of weather is superficial and impoverished compared with theirs. To most of us the weather no longer makes the difference between comfort and discomfort, let alone life and death. Instead of being vitally concerned with it, we can afford to be merely curious.

We have also shed the belief, which may well have contributed to a more intense awareness of weather, that it was divinely appointed; and, more particularly, that prolonged bad weather was a punishment for collective bad behaviour. Theologically, the application of this assumption was inconsistent in that no one seems to have regarded benign summers, good harvests and tolerable winters as rewards for national virtue. But the conviction that tempests, droughts and floods were organised as specific responses to the provocations of sin was general, as was the view that a collective display of penitence and self-denial might sway an angry deity to relent. On 15 January 1662 Pepys breakfasted in his chamber with his music teacher, John Berchenshaw, 'upon a collar of brawne'. The collar disposed of, Berchenshaw wondered – rather pointlessly – whether they had committed a fault in breaking the fast 'ordered by Parliament to pray for more seasonable weather – it having hitherto been some summer weather, that is, both as to warmth and every other thing, just as it were the middle of May or June, which doth threaten a plague (as all men think) to follow'.

When Daniel Defoe published his *History of the Great Storm* – an extended piece of dramatic reportage describing the hurricane of 26 November 1703 – he made it clear where the fault lay: 'When the sins of a Nation are very great and provoking, it is God's usual Method to pronounce destruction against the Nation.'

For Ralph Josselin, the Puritan minister of the Essex village of Earls Colne for more than forty years until his death in 1683, the weather was an infallible guide to God's disposition towards himself and his fellows. Josselin combined his religious duties with farming, and kept a diary describing both. The two critical months of the year for him and his family were February – the coldest and most unhealthy – and September, when the harvest was taken in. Josselin ascribed all misfortunes to divine displeasure, which in 1648 must have been very great: 'Among all the several judgements on the Nacion, God this spring in the latter end of April, when rye was earing and eared, sent such terrible frosts that the eare was frozen and dyed.' Evidently this punishment was insufficient, as that summer 'the Lord goeth out against us in the season, which was wonderfull wet,

flouds every week . . . Dayly raines caused a very great floud,
yet man repent not'.

Divinely directed or not, the weather is and always has been
thoroughly democratic. Wealth and privilege can obtain many
advantages, but more comfortable weather is not among them.

In July 1554 Philip of Spain arrived in Southampton to
conclude his marriage with Protestant England's Catholic Queen
Mary. Even by the conventional standards of the English
summer, the weather was atrocious. The rain beat down from
a leaden sky upon the red cloak which Philip wore over his
diamond-studded black velvet surcoat, white trunks and white
doublet. A mile short of Winchester, where he was to meet his
bride-to-be for the first time, he stopped to change his sodden
clothes. His new outfit, of black and white velvet decorated
with gold bugles, was soaked through long before he could reach
the haven of the cathedral. It was an inauspicious start to an
ill-starred relationship. All Philip's attempts to ingratiate himself
with his wife's fellow countrymen failed, while she earned their
hatred by trying to match his devotion to the Catholic cause.
Thirty years after Mary's death, Philip dispatched the Armada
to reclaim England for the Pope, only to have it dashed to pieces
by British storms. He must have wished he had never thought
of trading the blue skies of Castile for the dark, weeping clouds
of Albion.

For Charles II, in contrast, the weather was one of the attractions about his return from exile. 'The English climate,' he
observed, 'is the best in the world. A man can enjoy outdoor
exercise on all but five days in a year.' The holding of so sound
and robust a view is but one more reason to be grateful that
the dismal Philip failed in his intention to take the English

throne. But even Charles must occasionally have had his reservations. Six weeks after the Restoration, he and his Parliament were due to be received by the City of London amid much ceremony and scenes of public rejoicing. On the morning of the day, 5 July, Pepys looked out of his window at the lashing rain and predicted accurately that 'the glory of this great day will be lost'. A few hours later Pepys himself, drenched to the skin, watched 'the King, the Dukes and all their attendants go forth in the rain to the City and bedraggled many a fine suit of clothes'. Evelyn was there, too – 'I saw his Majestie go with as much pomp and splendor as any Earthly prince could do to the great Citty feast . . . but the exceeding raine which fell all that day much eclips'd its lustre.'

The diaries of Pepys and Evelyn are the two great lamps shining their contrasting but complementary lights on the life of post-Restoration England. Through them we are able, not merely to witness events and meet the great, the good, the humble and the sinful, but to taste the flavour of the times, almost to eavesdrop on its conversation. The weather is but one small part of the world they painted so colourfully and haphazardly. Neither man had more than a passing interest in meteorology for its own sake. But both, being busy and active, were out in it and felt it and took notice of it. To their impressions can be added those of a third observer, much less well remembered today.

Pepys found Evelyn 'a most excellent-humoured man . . . and mighty knowing', who must 'be allowed a little for a little conceitedness', while Evelyn described Pepys as 'a very worthy, industrious and curious person . . . universally beloved, Hospitable, Generous, learned in many things, skill'd in Musick, a very grate Cherisher of Learned men, of whom he had the conversation'.

They liked each other and were generally well liked. In contrast no one liked Anthony Wood – or Anthony à Wood, as he styled himself – and with good reason. Wood was born in 1632, the year before Pepys and twelve years after Evelyn (who outlived them both). His father rented an old house opposite the gates of Merton College, Oxford, and made a meagre living from taking in lodgers and hiring out his tennis court. Wood was born in the house and lived there all his life, shut away in a garret at the top compiling his voluminous records of Oxford men and scribbling away in his diary. On the occasions he emerged, he quarrelled with everyone he'd ever known. His judgements on his Oxford contemporaries were vicious. R.B., a chaplain of Christ Church, was 'much given to the flesh and a great lover of Eliz. the wife of Funker'. Exeter College was 'now much debauched by a drunken Governor'. At St John's were four atheistic undergraduates 'who come drunk into chapel and vomit into their hats or caps there'. Of the future Warden of his own college, Wood wrote: 'He is the very lol-poop of the University, a most lascivious person, a great haunter of women's company and a common fornicator.' He accused the Warden's wife of charging to the college the cost of 'a very large looking-glass for her to see her ugly face and body, to the middle and perhaps lower'.

Among those alienated by Wood's remarkably spiteful tongue were his entire family. He describes with relish a scene during which his sister-in-law – 'the melancholy, malitious and peevish woman' – responded to the suggestion that Wood should be the godfather of her next child by saying 'she would rather see it rot etc'. He finally overreached himself by publishing an allegation that the late Lord Chancellor, the Earl of Clarendon, had enriched himself by selling offices after the Restoration. At the instigation of Clarendon's son, Wood was prosecuted for libelling the dead earl. He was convicted by the Oxford vice-chancellor's court, which ordered him to be expelled from the university and the offending pages to be publicly burned.

Pepys, Evelyn, Wood and other followers of the seventeenth-century vogue for journal-keeping noted the weather as they met it, without any regard for historical accuracy or perspective. As a result, superlatives abound. On 7 March 1658 Evelyn wrote: 'This has been the severest winter that any man alive had known in England. The crows' feet were frozen to their prey.' Four years later he recorded a 'storm of hail, thunder and lightning as never was seen in any man's memory'. According to Wood, the heat wave of July 1667 was 'such that it has not been remembered by man . . . severall scholars mad with heat and strong drink'. On the 13th of that month, Pepys noted, 'being mighty hot and I lying that night (which I have not done, I believe, since I was a boy) with only a rugg and a sheet upon me'. The 15th, Pepys recorded, was 'wonderful hot all day and night, and this was the first night I can remember in my life that ever I could lie with only a sheet and one rug'. And a mere two days after that, the weather was 'excessive hot, so as we were forced to lie in two beds, and I only with a sheet and rug, which is colder than ever I remember I could bear'.

Altogether 1667 was a year of extremes, for on 6 March the King was reported by Pepys as having remarked that 'it was the coldest day he ever knew in England', a contention supported by Wood in Oxford, who noted that 'such weather hath not bin remembred by man'. It would have been interesting to compare thermometer readings for this and the next day, which, according to Pepys, 'was reckoned by all people the coldest day that was ever remembered in England'.

We are left with impressions – subjective, haphazard, unreliable and of no use at all from the perspective of the climatologist searching for data to establish trends. But occasionally the accounts do come together to provide a sustained and coherent picture. One such event, documented by a wealth of sources – although not by Pepys, who by then had been forced by failing eyesight to give up his diary and was anyway in Tangiers on the King's business – was the famous winter of 1683–4.

In the judgement of Gordon Manley, this takes the laurel as the coldest winter in modern history. After a few preliminary skirmishes in early December, the main fall of snow occurred in north-east England on 12 and 13 December, in London two days later and in the south-west just after Christmas. It was followed by the bitterest of frosts, urged on by a vicious east wind, and the country was in the grip of snow and ice for well over two months. At Eggleston in Teesdale, Christopher Sanderson, the owner of a modest estate and an assiduous diarist, copied out a passage from the local newspaper reporting that the sea was frozen to a mile out 'which was never known before'. In Oxford Anthony Wood found his bottle of ink 'froze at the fireside, unheedful of the fire's warmth or the heat of academic passions'. According to the register in the village of Ubley in Somerset, snow lay on the upper slopes of the Mendips until midsummer. 'It was so deppe and driven with winde against the hedges and stiles,' wrote the anonymous historian, 'that the next morning men could not go to serve their catell without grave danger of being buried . . . Some that was trav-elling in Mendipe did travell till they could travell no more and then lye down and dye. The sharpness of the season tooke off the aged and them that was under infirmities, the people did dye so fast that it was the greatest part of their work (which was appointed to do that worke) to burie the dead, it being a day's work for two men to make a grave.'

In London, ice had made the Thames unnavigable by boat traffic well before Christmas. According to Evelyn, it was solid by 23 December. On New Year's Day 1684, he reported: 'The weather continuing intollerably severe, so as streets of Boothes were set up upon the Thames etc: and the aire so very cold and thick as of many years there had not been the like.' On 9 January the ice was 'now become so incredibly thick as to beare not onely whole streetes of boothes in which they roasted meate and had divers shops of wares as in a Towne, but coaches and carts and horses passed over.'

As the freeze persisted, making most of the streets impassable, the capital's trading life was transferred wholesale to the river. Evelyn seems to have been torn between delight in the strangeness and vivacity of the scene created by entrepreneurial ingenuity, and distaste for some of its grosser manifestations. His diary entry for 24 January depicted an extraordinary sight:

> The frost continuing more and more severe, the Thames before London was planted with boothes in formal streetes, as in a City . . . all sorts of Trades and shops furnished, and full of Commodities, even to a Printing presse, where the People and Ladys took a fancy to have their names Printed and the day and yeare set down, when printed on the Thames: this humour took so universaly, that 'twas estimated the Printer gained five pound a day, for printing a line onely at sixpence a Name . . . Coaches now plied from Westminster to the Temple, and from severall other staires too and fro, as in the Streetes; also on Sleds, sliding with Skeetes; there was likewise Bull-baiting, Horse and Coach races, Puppet-plays, and interludes, Cookes and Tipling, and

lewder places; so as it seemed to be a bacchanalia, Triumph or Carnoval on the Water.

But while some Londoners made merry and made money, there was a heavy price to be paid, as the virtuous Evelyn — a countryman as much as a metropolitan, and the country's foremost expert on trees — was well aware:

It was a severe Judgement upon the Land: the trees not only splitting as if lightning-strock, but Men and Cattell perishing in divers places, and the very seas so locked up with Yce that no vessells could stirr out or come in: the fowle Fish and birds and all our exotique Plants and Greens universaly perishing; many Parkes of deere destroyed; and all sorts of fuell so deare that there were great Contributions to preserve the poore alive . . . London, by reason of the excessive coldness of the aire hindering the ascent of the smoke, was so filld with the fuliginous streame . . . that hardly could one see across the streete, and thus filling the lungs with its grosse particles exceedingly obstructed the breathe so one could scarcely breathe . . . and every moment was full of disastrous accidents.

Although Evelyn and Pepys, as men about town, suffered their share of weather-induced discomfort, it is highly improbable that anyone has ever experienced more weather in more places than John Wesley. In the course of a life which spanned all but twelve years of the eighteenth century, the founder of Methodism preached forty thousand sermons — most of them outdoors — and travelled 250,000 miles, mainly on foot or horse-back, taking the Word to every corner of the British Isles. Nothing, and certainly not the transitory discomforts inflicted on him by our God-given climate, deterred him or cast him down. 'His cheerfulness was like perpetual sunshine,' his biographer Southey wrote; and Wesley seems to have accepted the hardships of the itinerant preacher's life almost joyfully.

'Can you bear the summer sun to beat upon your naked head?' he asked of aspiring preachers.

Can you suffer the wintry rain or wind, from whatever quarter it blows? Are you able to stand in the open air without any covering or defence when God casteth abroad his snow like wool, or scattereth the hoar frost like ashes? And yet these are some of the smallest inconveniences which accompany field-preaching. For beyond all these are the contradictions of sinners, the scoffs both of the great vulgar and the small . . . What, think you, could induce any man of common sense to continue thereon one year, unless he had a full conviction that it was the will of God concerning him?

Wesley never complained, at least not in writing. Nor, one imagines, would it have occurred to him to alter his programme in any way had he had access to reliable weather forecasts. He simply accepted what came his way and noted it all down in his diary. On 27 December 1742, at Chippenham, 'the wind drove at us like a torrent; at times from east, west, north and south: the straw and thatch flew about my head'. Two days later, at Leigh, 'more than once I was blown off my horse'. On 17 January 1747, Wesley was on his way to Grantham in Lincolnshire: 'We were met in the midst of an open field with so violent a storm of rain and hail . . . it drove through our coats great and small, boots and everything, and yet froze as it fell, even upon our eyebrows so that we scarce had either strength or motion left when we came to our inn at Stilton.' Heavy snow fell overnight, blocking the roads. But Wesley would not be daunted. 'We can walk twenty miles with our horses in our hands,' he urged his comrades. 'So, in the name of God, we set out. The north-east wind was piercing as a sword . . . however we kept on, till we came to the White Lion at Grantham.'

In July the following year Wesley was on his way to address sinners in Derbyshire when his progress was halted by a downpour of tropical intensity:

The rocks were loosened from the mountains . . . several water-mills were clean swept away . . . the trees were torn up by the roots and whirled away like stubble. Two women of loose character were swept away from their own door and drowned: one was found near the place, the other was carried seven or eight miles. Hayfield churchyard was all torn up and the dead bodies were swept out of their graves. When the flood was abated they were found in several places. Some were hanging in trees: others left in meadows . . . some partly eaten by dogs or wanting one or more of their members.

No snowdrift could deflect Wesley from his and God's purpose. In January 1784 the octogenarian recorded an extremity of cold at Bengeworth in Worcestershire which 'I have never felt before . . . it made me downright sick.' Two years later the snow 'lay so deep it was with difficulty we reached Chippenham'. A month after that Wesley was pushing through 'an abundance of snow' to reach Worcester. He preached for the last time at Leatherhead in February 1791, and a week later was dead.

The antithesis to Wesley in almost every way was his contemporary Horace Walpole. Rich, well-connected, witty, gossipy, frivolous and idle, Walpole was a dilettante, a connoisseur of art and literature, a self-consciously amateur writer whose gifts found their ideal expression in the torrent of letters that poured from his pen throughout his adult life. Walpole's chief interest in life, apart from trading tittle-tattle, was his property on the Thames at Twickenham, which he called Strawberry Hill. There he created a celebrated garden in a partly picturesque, partly classical style, to complement the 'little Gothic castle' with its grand parlour and library and its picture gallery and round tower. Into this extravagance Walpole crammed a collection of curiosities and works of art so extensive that it took him twenty years to catalogue it. He also had his own printing press nearby, where most of his own works were published, including his popular Gothic romance, *The Castle of Otranto*.

Although Walpole was in no sense an outdoorsman, his interest in gardening necessarily gave him an interest in the weather, which was intensified by his preoccupation with his own comforts. He tended to treat it – not, in the manner of Wesley, as an aspect of the divinely appointed world to be observed and accepted, not judged – but as one of his circle of acquaintances. During that freezing winter of 1784, while Wesley was plodding through the snow with nothing but his cloak and his convictions to warm him, Walpole's mind was wholly on keeping cosy: 'Since Boreas and Aeolus and all the demons of the air let loose, I shall keep myself as warm as I can and not venture, being compounded in the snow.' In March the following year he was complaining of 'such a succession of vicissitudes as I can remember . . . repeated snows, severe frosts, and assassinating winds'. Occasionally the climate pleasantly surprised: 'I did not use to love September,' he wrote in the late summer of 1777, 'with its betweenity of parched days and cold long evenings, but this has been all lustre and verdancy.' But much more often, Walpole was moved to comment adversely on the disparity between conventional expectation and the reality. After one particularly grim excuse for an English summer, he wrote: 'Every summer one lives in a state of mutiny and murmur, and I have found the reason; it is because we will affect to have a summer and we have no title to any such thing.' June 1791 confirmed all his prejudices: 'It froze hard last night . . . I went out for a moment to look at my haymakers and was starved. The contents of an English June are hay and ice, orange flowers and rheumatism. I am now cowering near the fire.'

Wesley and Walpole were young or comparatively young men when northern Europe suffered possibly the most unpleasant winter in modern history, that of 1739–40. Its chief characteristic was not the quantity of snow, which was modest, or the temperatures, although these were savage enough, but the wind. This began to blow from the east with extreme ferocity on 28 December. On 31 December Doctor Huxham in Plymouth noted in his journal '*dies frigidissima in hominum memorium*', Doctor Jurin of the Royal Society recorded a temperature of 26 degrees Fahrenheit on the staircase of his house in Garlick Hill, and 34 degrees in his study. In Sheffield Doctor Short reported that 'even in a nobleman's library the thermometer was only at 29 degrees'.

When noblemen are troubled by numbed fingers and feet, lesser mortals die. Several passengers crossing the Thames by boat were frozen to death, and a lighterman in Deptford was found dead and fastened in ice to his craft. A woman was found dead from the cold in Barnet, with her infant child, still alive, at her breast. There were a number of cases of sailors perishing as the icy seas burst over their ships, and Thomas Barker noted the deaths of several postboys in Rutland. Along the east coast of England ferocious storms wrought death and destruction. The once thriving port of Dunwich, near Felixstowe, suffered a fatal blow, as the cliffs which had protected it collapsed and the sea surged through the streets into the centre of the town.

After a few days the gales abated but the cold intensified. By February the ice in St James's Park, London, was 10 inches thick, and in parts of Cumberland it was twice that. Horse racing was staged on the River Tees at Barnard Castle, and a printing press did brisk business on the Ouse in York. Over much of western England and Wales, the winter corn, unprotected by snow, froze and withered. In London, which was cut off for seven weeks by the ice floes piled up in the Thames estuary, the price of coal soared to unprecedented heights. When the thaw finally came, in the last week of February, it was succeeded by a cold, dry, pinching spring which exacerbated the shortages of grain and fuel. A phenological record maintained at Marsham in Norfolk by successive generations of the Marsham family shows that in 1740 the hawthorn was in flower on 8 June – the latest in more than two centuries.

Dr Johnson, typically, did not bother to refer to the weather at all. Wesley, more curiously, hardly did so either, although he was disseminating the good news in the Bristol area at the time, and can have hardly failed to notice the distress suffered. Walpole was out of it, as he was in Italy on the Grand Tour. But for many, the Arctic conditions made life hard and comfort impossible, to a degree difficult for us to imagine. The ageing Jonathan Swift, in his deanery in Dublin, took it almost personally. 'It is impossible to have health in such desperate weather,' he complained the day after the east wind set in. 'Our kingdom is turned to be a Muscovy or worse.' The next day he was grumbling, 'I am not yet worse for the cold weather, but I am angry at it.' Towards the end of January Swift protested, '. . . it is now 25 days since we have found nothing but frost and misery and this day is the coldest of them all. The weather is cursed.'

Throughout the nineteenth century, and up to 1963, severe winters occurred at intervals that were irregular but frequent enough to sustain a collective consciousness of snow and ice as familiar components of the British winter scene. January 1814 was the coldest of the century, with the temperature at Richmond in Surrey remaining below freezing day and night for sixteen consecutive days. That year saw the last of the famous Frost Fairs, as the old London Bridge with its twenty narrow arches was replaced by a five-arch affair which allowed much freer movement to the current and tides and discouraged the build-up of ice. The decade between 1812 and 1821 was the coldest since the 1690s, and fixed in the mind of the young Charles Dickens an image of England under a white mantle which recurred repeatedly in his fiction. January 1838 was viciously cold, and between 11 December 1853 and 10 January 1854 the temperature at Greenwich never rose above freezing. In 1878–9 the whole of Ullswater in the Lake District was frozen solid for fourteen weeks, and the average temperature in Wakefield that January was 30.3 degrees. A blizzard in January 1881 paralysed transport over the entire country; icebergs choked the Thames estuary, and twenty-seven people froze to death on Salisbury Plain. At the end of January 1895 blizzards caused by the collision between moist Atlantic air and an Arctic high-pressure system anchored over the British Isles were followed by exceptional cold. At Braemar in the Scottish Highlands a temperature of minus 17 degrees Fahrenheit was registered on the night of 11 February (a record minimum only equalled at the same location on the night of 11 January 1982, and at Altnaharra, in Sutherland, on 30 December 1995). Lakes, rivers and canals across the land were frozen. The Thames was solid above the tidal reaches and blocked by ice floes as far out as Gravesend. One hundred thousand people skated on the Serpentine one Sunday afternoon, and tens of thousands of farm labourers, watermen and other outdoor workers were reduced to living off charity.

Two twentieth-century winters remain stamped in the shared memory: 1947 and 1962–3. The feature of 1947 was the heaviness and persistence of the snow, rather than extreme cold. The blizzards began in earnest late in January, and by the end of the month the snow was at least a foot deep over virtually the entire country. Snow fell somewhere in Britain on every day between 22 January and 17 March, producing the deepest accumulations ever recorded, with drifts well over 20 feet deep in places. Ice floes were a hazard to navigation along the whole of the east coast, ice breakers were used to keep ports open and a war-weary nation endured the wretchedness of fuel and food shortages and power cuts for many weeks.

The snow cover in 1962–3 was not so deep but lasted longer, as a result of the lowest sustained temperatures since 1740. At Thanet, on the Kent coast, the ice extended two and a half miles out to sea. Bristol harbour was solid with ice and a motorist drove across the Thames at Oxford. Hundreds of schools were closed, a hundred thousand miles of roads were impassable and the diesel in buses and trains froze.

There have been other comparatively recent weather events which hold their place in the collective memory. Britain's worst flooding disaster, measured by loss of life, occurred in Lynmouth on the north Devon coast on 15 August 1952, after the East and

West Lyn burst their banks as a result of a 9-inch deluge on Exmoor. Two hundred thousand tons of boulders and mud, mixed with trees, were hurled down on the town and thirty-four people lost their lives. The following winter the sea defences along a thousand miles of coastline between Spurn Head, on the Humber estuary, and Kent were breached by a massive storm surge caused by exceptionally high tides driven on by a wild northerly gale. Canvey Island was evacuated, 160,000 acres of farmland were inundated by seawater and more than three hundred deaths were attributed to the disaster. More recently, the hurricane of October 1987 has been invested with almost mythic status in the public consciousness, and has become the indispensable reference point for any discussion about high winds. Similarly the deluge of October 2000 which sent floods rushing across many low-lying areas of England, causing extensive damage to towns such as Lewes and Uckfield in Sussex, was widely interpreted as a foretaste of what global warming would have in store for us as the twenty-first century progressed.

These instances of extreme weather — extreme by British standards, that is — caused their share of death, destruction, misery, discomfort and inconvenience. But I stick by my contention that, taken in the round, the collective recorded experience of the weather has become progressively less intense over the past two hundred years or so. For Pepys, Evelyn, Wesley, Barker and White (though not, to the same extent, Walpole) there was no escaping it. But as life became easier, so the educated classes — those most likely to leave a written record — increasingly had a choice as to whether or not they wished to expose themselves to cold and wet; and, in the main, they chose to be warm and dry. However, as always, circumstances varied and there were exceptions.

On 12 February 1870, Francis Kilvert, the eager and passionate young curate of Clyro, in the Welsh Borders a few miles from Hay-on-Wye, conducted the services for Septuagesima Sunday. He wrote in his diary:

Very few people in church, the weather fearful, violent deadly E. wind and the hardest frost we have had yet. Went to Betts in the afternoon, wrapped in two waistcoats, two coats, a muffler and a mackintosh and was not at all too warm . . . When I got to the Chapel my beard, moustaches and whiskers were so stiff with ice that I could hardly open my mouth, and my beard was frozen onto my mackintosh. There was a large christening party from Llwyn Gwilym. The baby was baptized in ice which was broken and swimming about in the Font.

For the young Kilvert the weather was a matter not for literary musing but of direct concern; not so much for himself as for the poor, the elderly and the sick among his flock of rural peasants. When it was savage, they suffered. When it smiled, so did they. Thus, two days after the christening we find him visiting Edward Evans – 'ill with cold from this vicious, poisonous east wind' – and organising extra blankets for him. The tenth of March, by contrast, was 'a heavenly day, lovely and warm, real spring. People busy in their gardens planting and sowing. Everyone rejoicing in the unclouded, splendid weather, and congratulating each other on it in their greetings on the road.' Easter Day, 17 April, was 'cloudless, a glorious morning . . . There was a heavy white dew with a touch of hoar frost in the meadows . . . I leaned on the wicket gate by the millpond. Suddenly I heard the cuckoo for the first time this year.' The winter that followed was, again, bitterly cold. On Christmas Day

Kilvert 'sat down in my bath upon a sheet of ice which broke in the middle into large pieces whilst sharp points and jagged edges stuck all around the sides of the tub . . . not particularly comforting to the naked thighs and loins . . . the ice water stung and scorched like fire'.

Kilvert was as alive as any poet to the beauties created by the interaction between weather and landscape, but he was conscious all the time that, for those in his spiritual charge, the changes spelled the difference between contentment and wretchedness. This awareness brought an unusual intensity to his commentary on the weather. On 24 January 1872 Kilvert visited 'the old soldier', John Morgan, who'd suffered an epileptic fit. 'Came home in a wild storm of rain,' he wrote. 'A waterspout of rain burst in the night and the Dulas and Cwmbythog brooks are in full roar rushing through the dark with a wild, strange, stormy, foamy light.' The fourth of March was 'superb . . . almost cloudless, brilliant, hot as late May and the warm south wind blowing sweet from the Black Mountains'. But May itself was 'the bitterest, bleakest I ever saw and I have seen some bad ones . . . This beats them all and out-Herods Herod. The black, bitter wind violent and piercing drove from the East with showers of snow.'

A few weeks later, Kilvert took his clergyman father, a keen angler, on a trout-fishing expedition. It was 'a pouring wet morning. Nevertheless my Father and I started in the rain for the Vale of Arrow, he riding the Vicarage pony sheltered by two mackintoshes and an umbrella, and I on foot with an umbrella only. We plodded on doggedly through the wet for six miles, casting wistful glances at all the quarters of the heavens to catch any gleam of hope. Hope, however, there seemed to be none. The rain fell pitilessly. We reached (the Vale) . . . more like drowned rats than clergymen of the Established Church.'

Kilvert shared with his parishioners a life whose quality was very largely shaped by the elements, and his wonderful diary reflects that central role. None of the celebrated diarists of the twentieth century — Nicolson, Channon, Bruce Lockhart, Beaton, Crossman, Benn, Lees-Milne, Kenneth Williams, Alan Clark — was materially affected by their weather, and therefore had anything interesting to say about it. The weather's removal to the periphery of experience is apparent even in the work of the best of the countryside writers, such as Stevenson, W. H. Hudson, T. H. White, Richard Jefferies, H. E. Bates and John Moore. They certainly studied their weather and knew it well. But they did not live it. It was something to be observed, possibly with a view to being milled into their writing. Here is Stevenson, walking in winter towards a hill in Ayrshire: 'It had snowed overnight. The fields were all sheeted up: they were tucked in among the snow and their shape was modelled through the pliant counterpane, like children tucked in by their mother . . . The effusion of coppery light on the summit of Brown Carrick showed where the sun was trying to look through; but along the horizon clouds of cold fog had settled down . . .'

Hudson, strolling near Land's End, has his notebook out as the sky breaks after hours of heavy rain: 'The rain-soaked dead bracken had now opened and spread out its shrivelled and curled-up fronds and changed its colour from ashen grey and the pallid tints of old dead grass to a beautiful, deep, rich mineral red. It astonished me to think that I had never observed the effect before . . .'

A similar literary self-consciousness pervades an entry in Virginia Woolf's diary for 30 January 1940, in which she described the effects of one of the most peculiar meteorological events ever to occur in Britain. Heavy rain fell on to a landscape where the temperatures were well below zero and froze the instant it touched any solid object. Trees were encased in ice, cats were frozen on branches, birds died in mid-flight as their wings became rigid. Livestock were entombed in ice and the countryside looked as if it had been crystallised. Virginia Woolf captured the visual strangeness of the scene with forensic detachment: 'Everything glass glazed. Each blade is coated, has a rim of pure glass. Walking is like treading on stubble. The stiles and gates have a shiny, green varnish of ice. The grass is brittle, all the twigs are cased in clear, brown cases and look thick, but slippery, crystallised as if they were twigs of fruit as desert.' Threaded through the word picture is a commentary on the bother experienced by the Woolf household: 'Unable to go to London . . . Percy has to dig paths . . . On Sunday no cars could move . . . Trains hours late or lost . . . Cooked breakfast on dining-room fire . . . almost out of meat, but at last the Co-op sent.'

Here, the weather at its most extraordinary is reduced to an inconvenience and a stimulus to the literary impulse, the search for appropriate words and striking images. That is the way it has stayed, and it will require a consistent realisation of some of the more extreme visions of the global warming doom-watchers for the weather to be restored to a central role. For us, the idea of the weather significantly influencing our lives, let alone shaping the destiny of nations, seems implausible. But it happened.

Chapter 6

Making History

THREE GEOGRAPHICAL FACTORS HAVE MOULDED THE HISTORY OF THE village of Findhorn, on the north-east coast of Scotland. One is the river of the same name and its great estuarial bay on whose neck the village stands. The second is its position, looking due north across the Moray Firth. The third is that it, like Santon Downham in faraway Suffolk, is built on sand.

Sand, sea, sky – these are the elements that define the scene. How they look at any particular moment depends on the weather and where it is coming from. If it is from the landward side, south or south-west, it is generally benign enough. But if it blows across the sea, from north, north-west, or east, Findhorn quickly loses its smile and becomes a grimly exposed little place.

On the day I came, the heat wave that gave the summer of 2003 its most unBritish character was just flexing its muscles. A blue sea glittered in the sunshine, lapping pale golden beaches under a blue sky dabbed with white. Children splashed at the water's edge, watched by parents and grandparents sunk in collapsible chairs. Later arrivals parked their cars on sand-strewn roads and trudged between the dunes towards the beach, weighed down by buckets, spades, chairs and cool boxes. A multitude of sailing boats bobbed at their moorings in the bay, the breeze fluttering the flags on their masts. I wolfed down the biggest fried breakfast the café beside the water could provide, for – even though it was still only mid-morning – I had been on the move for many hours without nourishment. Then, as I waited for someone to be found who would take me across the water, I sat and nursed my mug of strong tea and stared over the bay at the dark mass of Culbin Forest, standing like an army on the other side.

I finished my tea and wandered around to the boat yard. A rangy, shaven-headed lad from Elgin appeared and said he would take me across. The tide was coming in, flooding the mud flats fringing the bay and pulling insistently at the tyres along the pontoons where the boats were moored. My pilot, whose name was Bob, circled around in an unwieldy fibreglass craft to pick me up. As we headed for the neck of the bay, with open sea beyond, I could feel the current thrust against the boat. The navigation buoys leaned backwards, straining against it. I asked Bob if he knew the story of Culbin. 'Oh, aye,' he said, smiling, 'everyone knows that. It's in the history books.' I looked back at Findhorn, strung out along the north-eastern side of the bay, the older stone cottages clustered close to the deeper moorings, with a straggle of bungalows and villas at either end. These days, the main businesses here are sailing, tourism and ministering to the requirements of the RAF base at Kinloss, a mile or two to the south-east. Outside the museum, there is not much to recall the dramas and troubles of times past.

Bob and I emerged from the mouth of the bay into open water and then headed for the trees. I looked west along the shore towards Cromarty, where – according to the history books – the catastrophe had come from. Somewhere below me, beneath the blue water and the golden sand, was where Findhorn had once been.

For centuries the fishermen here had lived on and with shifting sands. If I had come this way in July 1650 instead of July 2003, I would have found the river entering the sea some distance to the east, and the village itself precariously placed on a finger of sand and shingle crooked around the river mouth on the western side. Had I returned fifty years after that, I would have found that finger almost washed away by the sea on one side and the river on the other, and the fishermen dismantling their homes and shipping the stones across the water to make a new settlement on a more protected site a mile or so to the south-east. Soon after the new village arose, the river forged its new path to the sea.

They must have been difficult times, even for a fishing community accustomed to hardship and adversity. But it was as nothing compared with the calamity which – so the history books relate – overwhelmed Findhorn's immediate neighbour to the west, which was known as the Barony of Culbin. It was to this that I referred when I asked Bob if he knew the story. It is woven into the fabric of the collective memory: the great sandstorm.

The tale of Culbin was first related in something close to its definitive form in a lecture delivered in the 1860s in the Mechanics' Hall, Forres, by an elderly schoolmaster from Elgin, John Martin. Martin was a keen amateur geologist and natural historian – as well as being a registered weather observer for the Scottish Meteorological Society – and had wandered far and wide through Culbin collecting rocks and fossils and the remnants of weapons and tools left by the early settlers, and sifting through the records. The Barony of Culbin, Martin told his audience, was 'a very fertile and well-cultivated estate', at the heart of which 'stood a well-built mansion . . . and close by was an extensive orchard, rich in fruit-bearing trees'. The laird – 'surrounded by a flourishing tenantry' – was Alexander Kinnaird, who was 'connected by blood or marriage with some of the leading nobility of Scotland'.

'Never had more magnificent crops promised to reward the labours of the husbandmen than those which decked the Barony of Culbin in the autumn of 1686,' declared Martin grandiloquently. A bumper crop of barley was ready for harvesting in the westernmost fields, and the farmer, in preparation for taking it in, summoned friends and family to feast. The hours passed quickly 'and it was far into the night ere the company broke up . . . the plain rang with jocund laugh and cheery farewell'. But hardly had the farmer and his family retired to their beds than 'gusty blasts began to play ever and anon around the chimney tops'. These served as a prelude to the advent of a hurricane from the west. It raged for hours, filling the strongest with terror. When daybreak came, the farmer and his men set off for the barley fields. 'But lo!' John Martin related, 'what was waving yesterday with yellow grain was now a great heap of dry sea sand.' And that was merely the beginning of the tragedy. 'Thereafter, year by year, the storms which came from the west drove on those desolating waves until farm after farm, house after house, the mansion of the lairds and the cottage of the ploughman, were overwhelmed in one fell destruction.'

That, one might have thought, was enough in the way of disaster and devastation to satisfy any man. But not George Bain who for fifty years until his death in 1926 was proprietor and editor of the local newspaper, the *Nairn Telegraph*, and an energetic chronicler of local history. In 1912, Bain published *The Culbin Sands*, in which he took John Martin's already highly coloured account and applied an artist's touch to it. The fertile estate became 'the garden and granary of Moray'. The laird's mansion expanded into 'a large square building of dressed stones, embowered among rows of tall, shady trees, with a beautiful garden, a fruitful orchard, and a spacious lawn'. The sixteen farms of Culbin, according to Bain, produced an annual rental of almost £3000, a colossal income in those days. In addition, the laird derived rich pickings from the valuable salmon fishery in the Findhorn estuary, which sustained rows of fishermen's cottages along its edge.

From the narrative point of view, George Bain evidently regarded the gradual progression of the disaster as portrayed by Martin as unsatisfactory. His solution was to compress the succession of storms which Martin had spread over ten years into one all-consuming tempest. It struck, wrote George Bain, in the autumn of 1694:

> It came suddenly and without warning. A man ploughing had to desert his plough in the middle of the furrow. The reapers in a field of late barley had to leave without finishing their work. In a few hours the plough and the barley were buried beneath the sand. The drift, like a mighty river, came on steadily and ruthlessly, grasping field after field and enshrouding every object in a mantle of sand . . . In terrible gusts the wind carried the sand against the dwelling-houses of the people, sparing neither the hut of the cottar nor the mansion of the laird. The splendid orchard, the beautiful lawn, all shared the same fate.

There was now no restraining the old journalist's creative energy. He introduced a lull in the storm, enough to raise the tenantry's hopes, before stoking it up again to send 'these poor people rushing from their hearths and homes amid the blinding and bewildering sandstorm'. He dispatched it further east, so that the mouth of the Findhorn was choked, 'which now poured its flooded waters amongst the fields and homesteads, accumulating in lakes and pools till it rose to a height by which it was able to burst the barrier to the north and find a new outlet to the sea, in its course sweeping to destruction the old village of Findhorn'.

By bringing the abandonment of the original village forward by ten years or so, Bain neatly set up his pathetic finale. The laird, his wife, their child and a nurse just manage to escape with their lives. Ruined and broken, Alexander Kinnaird dies a few years later, swiftly followed to the grave by his wife. The orphaned child is taken by the nurse to Edinburgh, where – an imaginative touch – 'she supported him and herself on needlework'.

What actually happened to the Culbin estate owned by Alexander Kinnaird was desperate enough, even if it lacked the quality of melodrama conjured by John Martin and George Bain. For an account rather more firmly rooted in reality, I am indebted to a model work of regional history, called the *Culbin Sands: Fact and Fiction*, which was published in 1992 by the Centre of Scottish Studies at Aberdeen University, and written by Sinclair Ross, a retired meteorologist and geologist now living at Forres. As a young man, Mr Ross – like John Martin – used to wander through Culbin searching for arrowheads and flints and other vestiges of its ancient past; and, like Martin, he became fascinated by the stories of the awful fate that had overtaken it. But unlike his predecessors, he was content to rely upon the testimony in the records of the day.

Mr Ross found that the Barony of Culbin actually covered about one-fifth of the area claimed by George Bain. The sixteen farms were sixteen tenants, and the £3000 annual income was the capital value of the whole estate. Far from being 'the garden and granary of Moray', there is no evidence to suggest that Culbin was any more fertile than anywhere else along that dry, sandy and arid stretch of coastline. Moreover, virtually the whole of Scotland was stricken in the 1690s by famine resulting from a succession of poor harvests caused by the atrocious weather associated with the climax of the Little Ice Age; and there is no reason to believe that this little corner of Morayshire should have escaped the fate of the rest of the country. Mr Ross presents convincing evidence to suggest that 'the old baronial mansion of Culbin' was a modest affair, although it was probably built of stone, unlike the other dwellings on the estate, which would have been made of turf placed over a timber frame and which crumbled to dust once Culbin was abandoned; and that the rows of shady trees, the fruitful orchards and the spacious lawn were pure inventions. As for the hapless laird, it is true that Alexander Kinnaird — in common with many other landowners in those desperate times — suffered financial ruin, and petitioned Parliament for relief from land tax. But it seems that, far from dying in 1698, he actually emigrated to South America, where his fate is unknown.

The Culbin tragedy happened, but it was not a single event, as represented by George Bain, nor a succession of events compressed into a few years, as asserted by John Martin. Sand simply will not shift that fast, not even in the most unrelenting gale. Instead, a series of severe storms towards the end of 1694 completed a process of erosion that had begun many decades before and which had been accelerated by the practice of pulling up the marram grass and juniper bushes that held the sand in place, and the removal of turf to build cottages.

What is beyond doubt is that the march of the sands over Culbin, and the erasure of all signs of human occupation, left one of the most remarkable landscapes in the British Isles. For once George Bain's testimony stands:

> A scene of greater desolation and dreariness it would not be possible to conceive. For four long miles and occupying a space two miles wide, you have nothing but a great sea of sand, rising, as it were, in tumultuous billows. The spirit of the scene is its inescapable loneliness – its utter desolation . . . We find nothing in the central track, neither bent nor shrub – nothing but a succession of hills rising sometimes to the height of 100 feet – all of the finest, lightest and most powdery sand – of sand sparkling in its pearly beauty: of sand so soft that its surface is mottled into delicate wave lines by the wind . . . You can fancy yourself in the heart of some arid desert . . . Silence reigns supreme. The solitude is absolute and unbroken.

As with the sandy wastes around Santon Downham, such an affront to progress could not be tolerated, and the solution to the nuisance caused by the periodic sandstorms blowing east from the dunes of Culbin was the same as on the Suffolk–Norfolk border. The Forestry Commission acquired Culbin and in the 1920s embarked upon an epic project of dune afforestation. The sand was so fine and unstable that the only way to secure the dunes was by 'thatching' them with immature birch and broom saplings and conifer brushwood collected from elsewhere, below which the seedlings were able to root comparatively undisturbed. The principal species used was

Corsican pine, owing to its unrivalled ability to tolerate wind and drought. Less exposed stretches were planted with Scots pine and American lodgepole. The strategy was to move slowly from west to east, with the prevailing wind. In the early 1950s, when Sinclair Ross first started searching for relics, the dunes nearest Findhorn were still exposed. But now the dark mantle of forest extends to the water's edge.

Waving a farewell to Bob, I splashed my way through the shallows to the beach, and went into the trees. At once I was enclosed in their claustrophobic company. The sound of the sea was cut off, and the sky was confined to a square of blue over my head. Had it not been for the cries of the gulls and periodic rumbling roar of Nimrods as they passed over on training flights from Kinloss, the silence would have been complete. As it was, I felt far away from the world beyond the forest. My feet scrunched softly on the carpet of needles and desiccated mosses and lichens. Through the mulch, patches of sand gleamed like gold dust. Ahead of me the straight, bare, rough trunks of the pines rose and fell with the contours of the dunes, now tamed for good. I experienced a rushing certainty that if I strayed too far I would wander for hours. I circled around towards the sea and emerged into the sunshine. The forest and the sand reared up high over the beach like a crested wave caught in the instant before crashing down. I sat on a tuft of grass and looked out over the water. A few miles out was the hump of the Black Isle. To my right, lost in haze, was Burghead; to my left the dim blue bulk of Cromarty. The harsh life and harsher fate of this sandy place seemed to belong to another world altogether.

The legend of the great sandstorm of 1694 has proved remark-ably durable, despite the researches of Sinclair Ross and other hard-headed sceptics. It is recycled in a host of guidebooks and is retold in all its glory in David Thomson's wonderful auto-biography, *Nairn in Darkness and Light*. Thomson included all of John Martin and George Bain's liveliest touches, including the reappearance of the laird's mansion a century after the disaster, which moved one daring soul to shout down the chimney, to be answered by an unearthly echo from below.

Perhaps more surprising is the appearance of the legend in sober works of meteorology produced by professionals trained in the rigours of scientific inquiry. It is invariably deployed as one of the rare and cherished examples of extreme weather that this most moderate of countries has managed over the centuries. In that role it takes the stage in several books by the pre-eminent British climatologist Hubert Lamb – among them *Historic Storms of the North Sea, British Isles and Northwest Europe* and his magisterial study *Climate, History and the Modern World* – and in Brian Fagan's study *The Little Ice Age*. More recently, it has a walk-on part in Philip Eden's *The Daily Telegraph Book of the Weather*, where it serves as an example of a coastal settlement being 'buried' as the Little Ice Age reached its climax.

Meteorologists enjoy sinking their teeth into meaty slices of history. It's an innocent enthusiasm, and is often illuminating when restricted to the influence of the weather on specific events – particularly wars and battles. A fine and familiar example is the Norman invasion of England.

When Duke William's force first assembled beside the estuary of the River Dives, near modern-day Caen, in the late summer of 1066, Harold of England was waiting for him on the other side of the Channel with an army at least as strong. In the normal course, William would have embarked at once, and the battle would have been fought on the south coast of England within a day or two. But — most unusually — the wind set in from the north and blew for a month, pinning the Norman knights in their encampment. While William fretted, Harold was first compelled to allow his men to disperse to bring in the harvest, and then to summon them back in order to deal with another adversary. The same northerly air stream that frustrated Duke William gave the King of Norway, Harald Hardrada, his chance. On 18 September he sailed his fleet into the Humber estuary. Exactly a week later he and his men suffered annihilation at the hands of the army which Harold had hastily assembled and marched north; the Norwegian king and his ally Earl Tostig — Harold of England's younger brother — were slain. Two days after that, the wind in the Channel switched to the south, enabling William to make an unopposed landing at Pevensey on the Sussex coast.

On 14 October William carried the day at Hastings. Harold was shot through the eye, then hacked to pieces, beheaded and disembowelled by his conqueror and three others. In less than a month the course of English history had taken a decisive change of direction, and at every turn the weather had played a vital part. It was little wonder that William and his knights took it for granted that they had God on their side; and the actions of Harold himself suggest he may well have accepted that his extraordinary run of bad luck represented divine judgement on his cause.

A later king, Edward IV, owed even more than William I to meteorological assistance. On Palm Sunday, 29 March 1461, the joint army of Edward and his chief ally, the Earl of Warwick, faced the Lancastrian force of the deposed king, Henry VI, at Towton in Yorkshire. From behind the lines of the Yorkists a cruel blizzard blew up, blinding the troops of the Red Rose who were then cut down in their thousands, so that the snow was stained crimson and the River Wharfe and its tributary, the Cock, ran red with blood. Ten years later, at Barnet on 14 April 1471, Edward's foe was that same Warwick who had fought beside him at Towton. Thick fog shrouded the battlefield, and in the confusion Warwick's men mistook the badge of their ally, the Earl of Oxford, for that of the King. Oxford's troops cried 'treason' and departed, leaving Edward to press home his fortuitous advantage.

Napoleon had famously bad luck with the weather at Waterloo, when prolonged heavy rain delivered by a deep, slow-moving depression over Belgium turned the fields to mud and stymied the rapid troop movements on which his strategy depended. 'A few drops of rain . . . an unseasonable cloud crossing the sky, sufficed for the overthrow of the world,' mused Victor Hugo. However, for an earlier catastrophe – his invasion of Russia – Napoleon could blame human folly. His chief scientific adviser, Pierre Simon, Marquis de Laplace, was acknowledged as one of Europe's greatest mathematicians and astronomers, but his grasp of meteorology was less secure. He advised the Emperor with great confidence that the full severity of the Russian winter did not set in until January. In the case of the winter of 1812–13 he was two months out. In early November the French army encountered conditions of indescribable awfulness, and the fate of the invasion was sealed.

In the days before the D-Day landings of June 1944, meteorologists were listened to as never before in military history. Throughout May and into the start of June, conditions in the Channel had been ideal for invasion. But on 28 May the Norwegian meteorologist Sverre Petterssen – who headed a team from the British Met Office – reported that the conditions in the upper air were becoming unstable and that this instability was likely to extend to ground level within days. His view was challenged by the chief American expert, Irving Krick, who remained confident that a ridge of high pressure would continue to protect the Channel from any storms. On the night of 3 June, Group Captain Martin Stagg – who had the unenviable job of moderating between the conflicting forecasts – advised the commander of Operation Overlord, Eisenhower, that the planned invasion day, 5 June, would be too windy for the troops to land and too cloudy for the bomber crews to see their targets. Eisenhower ordered a postponement for at least twenty-four hours. By then the weathermen had agreed that a period of comparative calm between two storm fronts should allow the invasion force on to the Normandy beaches on 6 June. Eisenhower gave the orders to go – 'thank the Gods of war we went when we did', he commented later.

The great, unanswerable question is: would the outcome of any of these military engagements have been different if the weather had not behaved as it did? And would the course of history have thus been changed? If the winds in the Channel had behaved normally in the summer of 1066, William would undoubtedly have launched his invasion earlier. But would Harold have beaten him, and England been spared Norman domination? Conceivably – but, given all the other imperatives at work, probably not. Much effort has been expended on working out the weather patterns that unleashed the storms in which Philip II of Spain's Armada was smashed in August and September 1588, but it is clear that the Spanish navy was already a beaten force before Atlantic depressions took a hand. Similarly, Napoleon's army was already withdrawing from Russia when it was ambushed by the onset of winter, so it is difficult to argue that the Tsar's lands escaped French subjugation because of its intervention. But what if the 250,000 men Napoleon lost in Russia had been available to him later? And had the sun shone at Waterloo, would his empire have lasted significantly longer? It's a fair bet that, had the D-Day landings gone wrong, Germany's resistance and Europe's agony might have been prolonged; but no one suggests Germany would have won the war.

Meteorologists enter much trickier territory when – wearing the robes of historical climatologists – they set about reconstructing the climates of the distant past, and attempt to forge causal links between weather patterns and such matters as population dynamics, migrations and the rise and fall of empires. Much of the pioneering work in this field was done by Professor Hubert Lamb. Having exhaustively investigated every available source of data – including contemporary chronicles, administrative and estate records, manorial rolls, personal journals and correspondence, and proto-scientific observations – Lamb identified three overarching climatic sequences for Europe after the Dark Ages. These were the Medieval Warm Period from roughly AD 900 to 1200, a period of cooling from 1250 which culminated in the Little Ice Age at the end of the seventeenth century, and a gradual and erratic warming from about 1850 onwards.

Lamb's climatic phases have been very widely accepted, and the evidence he deployed has been extensively, not to say slavishly, reproduced. But in their keenness to establish the credentials of the new discipline of historical climatology, Lamb and his followers unwittingly stretched it well beyond its reliable application. For instance, to support his assertion that a dramatic increase in storms in the North Sea in the early thirteenth century heralded the end of his Medieval Warm Period, Lamb quoted a number of accounts of devastating inundations of low-lying areas of the Low Countries and north-western Germany. Neville Brown, in his imposing and scholarly study, *History and Climate Change*, demonstrated convincingly that the estimates for the number of deaths caused by these disasters were unsubstantiated and enormously exaggerated.

Lamb also contended that the amiable weather conditions prevalent in northern Europe during the Medieval Warm Period encouraged the colonisation of Iceland, and then Greenland, by Norsemen; and that the abandonment of the Greenland settlements in the middle of the fourteenth century was precipitated by the comparatively sudden deterioration in the weather. Without going far into what is an immensely complicated subject, I think it is fair to say that subsequent research – carried out by the Climate Research Unit at the University of East Anglia, which Hubert Lamb founded – has shown conclusively that much of the data on which he relied was flawed, incomplete and unreliable. It is clear that if Lamb's Medieval Warm Period did indeed exist it was very much more erratic, imprecise and complex than he realised; and, further, that many of the satisfyingly definitive connections he made between climatic conditions and human affairs simply cannot be substantiated.

The fault at the heart of Lamb's methodology was identified a very long time ago by an American of great intelligence and perception, the lexicographer Noah Webster. 'Men are led into numberless errors,' he wrote, 'by drawing general conclusions from particular facts. "Lady Montague sat with her window open in January 1718 and therefore there is little or no winter in Constantinople" is very bad logic.'

Nevertheless, the approach that Lamb pioneered has its uses. The well-documented expansion of Europe's population in the thirteenth century could not have been sustained had not the climate been generally favourable to increasing crop yields and permitting settlements to spread on to higher ground. Similarly, the social upheaval that overtook and transformed England in the fourteenth century had at least some of its roots in the agrarian crisis triggered by a sequence of appallingly wet years and consequent bad harvests between 1314 and 1317. The drastic decline in the population obviously owed most to the arrival in 1348 of the Black Death (itself materially assisted by the weather). But well before that, the onset of harsher conditions had led to privation, a steep decline in life expectancy and the abandonment of marginal farmland in many parts of the country.

With the later and climatic phase of the Little Ice Age, the climatologists are on firmer ground, thanks to the comparative wealth of data, even if the interpretation – witness the Culbin story – is sometimes not as straightforward as it first appears. The already Arctic disposition of the weather was intensified by several volcanic eruptions in various parts of the world – one of them of Hekla in Iceland – which produced a massive dust-loading in the atmosphere, further restricting sunshine and warmth. Although there were harsh winters and some wet, miserable summers in England, the main impact of the most severe period – between 1690 and 1710 – was on the more northerly band of European countries.

Finland was brought to its knees: in one winter, 1696–7, one-third of the entire population died of starvation or disease. In Scotland, the agrarian crisis which had developed progressively through the seventeenth century deepened into catastrophe. Winter after winter the snow lay deeper and longer than anyone could recall, while the summers were summers in name only. Livestock perished wholesale, and the crops on which the rural peasantry depended – mainly oats – would not ripen. Starving peasants fought for the nettles growing in churchyards, and famine stalked the land. The population of many parishes fell by between a third and two-thirds. Whole villages were abandoned and previously viable upland estates reverted to the wild.

These were known for evermore in Scotland as The Seven Ill Years, and they had far-reaching social and political consequences. By 1691 one-tenth of the population – 100,000 people – had left to start a new life in Ulster, and the legacy of that influx is with us still, even though it should be remembered that the initial stimulus was not the weather or the resulting hardship but the decision of James I and his ministers to use colonisation to subdue the unruly native Irish. Scotland's economic woes also undoubtedly contributed to the mood of national resignation in which the union with England in 1707 was pushed through. As for Ireland, its tragedy reached its own climax much later with the famine of the 1840s, in which at least a million people died. The weather played its malign part, the abnormal humidity and subsequent drenching rains providing perfect conditions for the multiplication and spread of the potato blight fungus.

The difficulty with all of this lies not in accepting that climate has played a part in determining the fate of nations but defining to any useful degree what that contribution was. It is a truism that without the weather we wouldn't be here; that it has been the indispensable condition for our existence and development since our ancestors evolved into an upright position and began growing crops and domesticating animals. When the sun shone and the rain fell in moderate abundance, societies prospered and multiplied. When the rain or the sunshine persistently failed, they struggled and disappeared, or went in search of somewhere more favourable, or devised ways of accommodating what was thrust on them from the skies.

But the task of accurately assessing climate's role in human history is formidable, and very likely impossible. A wise, if now unfashionable, British historian, Sir Ernest Barker, observed:

> History is a tissue of many factors and a web of many threads; and though a prudent historian will do well to keep his weather-eye open, and to allow for the possible influence of climate change when it is historically certain, he will also be wise to consult meteorological records . . . In the sphere of general history, we can hardly allow any weight to the influence of climatic cycles.

Although Hubert Lamb was bold occasionally to the point of rashness in his mission to shape climatology into a series of coherent, almost architectural, sequences, he was cautious about drawing grand historical conclusions. He may have exaggerated and even – unwittingly – distorted the data in his eagerness to arrange it so that it would back his case, but he could not be accused of endorsing the doctrine viewed so disdainfully by Ernest Barker: that climate had been THE dominant force in shaping the course of history.

Faith in the creed of climatic determinism had been strong among French intellectuals from the sixteenth century through the Enlightenment and onwards, and remained in vigorous health into the twentieth century. It was first articulated by the social philosopher Jean Bodin, who died of the plague in 1596, and was revised and extended in its application by several of his eighteenth-century followers, principally the Abbé du Bos and – most influentially – Montesquieu. The crucial underlying assumptions were that the climate of non-Mediterranean Europe had warmed significantly since classical times as a direct result of the clearance of the forests which had previously shaded the earth from the sun; and that as the environment of northern Europe became more congenial, so did the balance of power on the continent shift its way.

This beguilingly simple chain of cause and effect received a new lease of life in the twentieth century from an American geologist, geographer and – ultimately – racial supremacist, Ellsworth Huntingdon. In a succession of fat books, stuffed with the fruits of his tireless statistical exertions, Huntingdon – the son of a Congregationalist minister in Illinois – expounded his thesis about climate fluctuations and the fate of civilisations.

His starting point was rainfall, and he developed a majestic sequential structure in which the abundance or dearth of rain shaped the fortunes of ancient cultures. The decline of classical Greece was attributed to water shortages exacerbated by an expansion of marshes which bred malaria. The preceding Egyptian civilisation had gone the same way for much the same reasons. Palestine at the time of Christ enjoyed abundant water, prosperity and stability, but slipped downhill as it became more arid. The Roman Empire was progressively undermined by diminishing rainfall, and was brutalised and enfeebled by malaria from the swamplands. The rise of Islam followed a prolonged period of instability, enforced migration and dissatisfaction with existing religions, all fuelled by progressive crop failures. 'When there is plenty of water and grass,' Huntingdon observed, 'there is very little raiding and fighting.'

Huntingdon's mission was to explain the northward shift of what was to evolve into modern civilisation. In *Principles of Economic Geography* he wrote:

As recently as the time of Christ, mankind had not learned to live comfortably in what are now the most stimulating climates. At that time forest covered practically all the cyclonic regions. These could not be conquered until man discovered cheap and easy ways of making iron axes and learned to utilize beasts of burden, prepare warm clothing and build warm, dry, and well-lighted houses. Thus in those ancient periods, the Mediterranean offered the best climate among the parts of the world which man had hitherto been able to conquer.

The thrust of the argument was that once the peoples of northern Europe had gained mastery over the various discomforts and inconveniences caused by the cooler and more variable climate, they secured an advantage over the south which they never surrendered. Central to it was the belief that the temperate climate possessed intrinsic virtues which favoured those under its sway over others, the chief of these being that it promoted the energy to work efficiently out of doors throughout the year. In a book called *Climate and the Energy of Nations*, published in 1942, one of Huntingdon's British disciples, the politician Sir Frank Markham, defined the ideal zone as one with a temperature range between 60 and 76 degrees Fahrenheit, with humidity varying between 40 and 70 per cent, gentle breezes and 'agreeable sunshine'. 'The nation that enjoys these conditions,' Markham wrote, 'will have an immense advantage over its rivals.'

Ellsworth Huntingdon expended enormous effort trying to identify the parts of the world most conducive to human endeavour. He developed a 'standard climograph' to compare the merits of the great cities. New York and Philadelphia came out on top for temperature, rainfall and humidity. London was in fourth place, with Paris and Berlin below. Moscow was low down on account of its winters, while Tokyo, Osaka and Shanghai were at the bottom because of their oppressively hot and humid summers.

It does not appear to have occurred to Huntingdon that the familiarity of the Japanese and Chinese with their own climates might – as had presumably happened in northern Europe and the United States – enable them, in time, to devise the means of coping with the inherent shortcomings. In fact, he had already extended his thesis to its logical conclusion, which was that, as a result of climatic influence, one racial group – his own, the white, Protestant, north European/North American stock – had acquired a hereditary genetic superiority over all others. From there, it was one short step to embrace the cause of selective breeding, or eugenics, a step Huntingdon took eagerly.

The belief that superior climates make for superior people had been central to Aristotle's Hellenocentric world view. He stated that the people of Thrace and the Balkans – 'the cold places' – were full of spirit but short on intelligence, and therefore not fit to rule others. Asians, in contrast, were bright and skilful, but their exposure to excessive heat made them defective in spirit and thus liable to be conquered and enslaved. In the middle, with the advantages of both and the shortcomings of neither, was Greece, which was thus qualified to rule over everybody. Hippocrates was more specific about the influence of climate. Variability in temperature, rainfall and wind stimulated spirit and prevented its stagnation. Those who lived in well-watered, changeable mountain areas were big, strong and brave, if somewhat uncouth. Where the soil was bare and waterless, the men were 'hard, thin, sinewy and hairy . . . self-willed, with an inclination to be savage'. Both had the edge over the inhabitants of the moist, warm valley country, who were not well made but tended 'to breadth and be fleshy and dark . . . of less native courage and endurance'.

As so often, Aristotelian precepts displayed remarkable staying power. Jean Bodin adapted them to his own ends, dividing Europe into three zones of which the middle – containing his native France – was the most favoured. Montesquieu – who in his own day and for long afterwards exercised an unrivalled influence over political and social philosophy in Europe – went much further. Book Fourteen of his monumental *De l'esprit des lois* dealt entirely with the role of climate in human development, presenting a succession of bald statements on the subject with barely a shred of evidence to back them up. Men are more vigorous in cold climates because the fibres that form the surface of their bodies are shorter and more elastic. For the same reason, their hearts are more powerful, their strength and courage greater, with the result that they have been free. In contrast, Montesquieu declares, 'the cowardice of the peoples of hot climates has almost always made them slaves'. In Europe, strong nation faced strong, and all were free, whereas in Asia the brave and active people of the cooler countries lived immediately next to the 'effeminate, lazy and timid' people of the hot countries, and conquered them. This, said Montesquieu, accounted for 'the servitude of Asia'.

What seems fairly innocuous in Aristotle and slightly absurd in Montesquieu becomes sinister and repellent in the racial judgements of Ellsworth Huntingdon. This is Huntingdon on the Bushmen of the Kalahari: '. . . very short . . . dirty-yellow faces . . . rather unattractive . . . crafty expressions . . . animal-like appearance . . . Very clever in their methods of catching animals . . . extremely cruel . . . the mode of life makes it impossible to

have anything but a very loose type of political organisation . . .
no interest in either peace or agriculture . . .' Eskimos are on
the same lowly rung on the human ladder: 'They gorge themselves until they regurgitate and even then go on eating . . . They
stuff good fat blubber into their mouths and cut it off with knives
wielded dangerously close to their noses.'

Huntingdon was much exercised by the problems faced by
his Anglo-Saxon model workers when transferred to the unsuit-
able environment of the tropics. The trouble with such places,
he reflects, is that 'the lazy, indolent type of man' can support
himself and his family just as easily as the more industrious,
because everything grows so fast. Indeed the layabout may do
better as he does not exert himself, whereas the hard-working
white man wears himself out and is undone by exhaustion and
disease. Too often the unhappy fate of the white man marooned
among lazy natives in the tropics is to descend into sexual
immorality, drunkenness, loss of drive, fits of rage and apathetic
idleness. Huntingdon attributed the survival of slavery in the
southern United States to the fact that the climate there made
the white man's labour worth no more than that of 'such incompetent people as the negroes', whereas in the more vigorous
north it profited the whites to do the work themselves rather
than delegate it to an inferior race.

For Ellsworth Huntingdon the explanation of how the US
and its allies and friends in Europe had come to dominate the
world was simple. As a consequence of economic migration, the
best people had found the best climate. At the time of his death
in 1947, he could see no reason why this dominance should ever
be challenged. Even so, he experienced continuing difficulty in
pinning down the location of the absolute climatic ideal.
Patagonia, for example, excelled in matters of temperature,

hours of sunshine and changeability – but was too dry. Ireland was well favoured in most respects, but too wet. The whole of Asia was eliminated as being too hot in summer and too cold in winter. The equatorial region was too hot, humid and monotonous. In the end, despite the competing claims of various American cities, he plumped for south-east England. It comes, he wrote, 'nearer to the ideal than almost any other place. The climate is stimulating at all times, both by reason of abundant storms and because of a moderate seasonal range. It never reaches such extremes as to induce the nervous tension which prevails so largely in the United States.'

Huntingdon's method for settling these issues was to conduct comparative analyses of the data he had compiled on key indicators such as factory output and the rates of births, deaths, suicides and mental breakdown. He was thus able to demonstrate to his own satisfaction – if not to that of many other reputable judges – that the Anglo-Saxon triumph was directly attributable to the happy union between the innate virtues of the stock and the weather. For his spiritual predecessor, Montesquieu, the great riddle was not the economic and cultural achievements of the English – which were no greater, and in many respects palpably inferior to those of the French – but their success in gaining and defending their political liberty. Montesquieu spent two years in England studying the workings of Parliament and the courts, the writings of John Locke, the laws, the social life of the privileged and other pertinent factors. His verdict was that the strengths of the nation were directly related to the awfulness of the climate. Weather that made life so intolerably uncomfortable must, he argued, breed a corresponding intolerance of tyranny and a determination to preserve liberty.

Like many French intellectuals, Montesquieu was fascinated and mystified by the English. He did his utmost to rationalise the distinctions between them and the other civilised nations of Europe. But his conclusion – that a good legislator will resist the vices of the climate while a bad one will succumb to them, and that England was well supplied with good legislators – seemed hardly adequate to explain the Anglo-Saxon phenomenon. The suspicion took root that the British not merely behaved differently from other nations – they WERE different, spiritually and physically; and that the geography and climate of the islands must somehow be responsible. The key to the riddle became that nebulous, potent, invisible property: the national character.

Chapter 7

Hard Grey Englishmen

AT A LITTLE OVER 2900 FEET CROSSFELL IS THE HIGHEST OF THE PENNINE hills which wind north from Edale in Derbyshire to the Scottish Borders. But you hardly notice how high it is, because of the way it fills the landscape from side to side, like a giant sleeping on its side, with its hipbone as the summit. Approached from the south-west, it is wholly revealed, a great inescapable lump, its crest sometimes sharply defined against the sky, but more often hidden in cloud.

This was April and one of the usual days, the hipbone mantled in grey wool. A brisk, moist wind blew from the south-west. This did not really suit me, but the sheep were comfortable with it. A number were nibbling their way around the graveyard of the little church of St Lawrence at Kirkland. They had their noses down beneath the thick sandstone walls, munching right up to the foot of the squat, square tower, at the top of which the bell swayed in the wind.

I turned up the lane past a row of stone cottages with heavy slate roofs. It ended beyond the dark, sturdy walls of Kirkland Hall, in a glade of trees where daffodils were showing in the grass. From there the path wound up at a gentle incline through fields of tussocky grass and crisp brown bracken. The south-west face of Crossfell is cut with dark scars, as if a finger had been drawn firmly downwards through the volcanic rock and limestone to mark the courses of the becks which drain the soggy upland. In time these waters find their way to the Eden, the broad, big river whose fertile valley skirts the base of the hills. To my left, as I plodded uphill, was the cleft containing Ardale Beck, which is born as an insignificant trickle in the slope beneath the summit of Crossfell, and then issues forth as a sprightly stream at the bottom of a tumble of little cliffs and steep screes squeezed between High Cup and Brown Hill.

I stopped when I reached a spot level with the source of the beck. The wind cuffed my head and hissed through the grass, flattening it. Below me stretched the Eden valley. Its vivid green pasture and rich, dark red fields, dotted with farms and settlements, broken by copses and plantations of conifers, seemed a world away from the bare, tawny fellside. Up here, wandering lines of rough, wind-battered dry-stone walls enclosed irregular shapes of ungrazed pasture. There was nothing by way of human dwelling if you discounted the odd ruined bothy where the sheep drivers sheltered in the old days when their flocks roamed up to the fell tops. Above me, the cloud pressed down and over the giant's hipbone. I sat looking at the emptiness around, listening to the wind and the gurgling of the infant stream hidden among the sprays of rock and smears of coal-black mud, trying to imagine what it was like when the Helm wind blew.

The Helm is the only wind in Britain considered worthy of a name of its own: our little-known cousin of the Bora, which tears down the southern side of the Dinaric Alps on to Trieste and the northern Adriatic, and the Mistral, which funnels through the Rhône valley between the Alps and the Cévennes.

The Helm is generated when the prevailing surface air stream is from the north-east, and it encounters the obstacle of Crossfell and its companion, Great Dun Fell, lying at right angles across its path. The slope facing the wind is smooth, and there is no gap through which it can funnel its way. So it thrusts up against the crest, clamping a band of cloud on it which appears to be solid and unmoving, but which is actually being continually created on the windward side and dispersed on the leeward. Squeezed between the rising ground and a layer of warmer air above, the air stream becomes cooled and denser as it breasts the summit. The effect is similar to that of water coming over a weir. The stored energy gives the flow a sudden, downward impetus. It tends to leapfrog the comparatively steep upper slopes close to the top, before coming down against the land where it assumes a gradient of about one in six. It charges down the fell until the slope begins to flatten out, then takes off to form a second cloud – known as the Helm Bar – anything between three and six miles to the south-west.

That, shorn of many intimidating complexities, is the genesis of the wind as far as I am capable of understanding it. We owe this account mainly to the indomitable perseverance of Gordon Manley, who in the late 1930s spent two years investigating the intimate secrets of the Helm from a small hut which he had transported to the top of Great Dun Fell. He resolved most of the outstanding questions about a phenomenon which had excited a good deal of fanciful speculation over preceding centuries, much of it originating with various clergymen whose duties in the isolated villages scattered about the westerly and southwesterly approaches to Crossfell left them with plentiful leisure to indulge their curiosity about natural history.

Among them was the football-loving rector of Ousby, the

Reverend Thomas Robinson, whose theories about the genesis of wind were endorsed with such enthusiasm in the Reverend John Pointer's *A Rational Account of the Weather*. A whole chapter of Mr Robinson's *New Observations on the Natural History of This World*, published in 1696, is devoted to 'Wind, Helms and Arches', in which Crossfell's wind is included in a mighty continental network of 'Grand Helms' extending from 'the mountains of Germany', and across 'the gibbosity of the eastern seas . . . where the flux and reflux breaketh', until 'the Grand Pabulum is spent'.

Gordon Manley's rather less grandiloquent exposition has been modified subsequently in the light of research into the intricate and subtle interactions between air currents of different temperatures and humidity levels. But as far as I can gather, its broad outline still holds good. In any case, what concerned me was not the abstrusities of geostraphy but the impact of the Helm wind on those living and working under its harsh and unpredictable sway.

The assault of the Helm is attritional rather than destructive, and it cannot be said to compare in violence with its continental relatives. Its wind speed rarely gets above 50–60 mph, a level the fell people learned by experience to accommodate. They built their cottages low to the ground, if possible in protected hollows, and at right angles to the slope to offer the minimum exposure. They used weighty slabs of sandstone for the walls, and a double layer of sandstone tiles along the eaves and the edges of the roofs to hold down the slates.

For the sheep farmers and their shepherds, the Helm made the working day wearisome, noisy and uncomfortable. But it was rarely hazardous, apart from the odd instance of men being blown over walls on their way to tend stock. The sheep had the worst of it. In times past, the late winter and early spring Helm often kept company with heavy snow. The fences and dry-stone walls would disappear with remarkable speed, leaving the animals buried in their lee, where they might have to survive for two weeks or more until either the farmer managed to dig them out or the snow melted. In 1917 a shepherd from Renwick, towards the northern extremity of the Helm's territory, found one of his animals which had survived forty-two days' entombment by eating its own wool. It was an unlucky beast, for — having been nursed back to health with the aid of a feeding bottle — it was hardly back on its feet before it was trampled to death by some stampeding calves.

Inevitably, the Helm figures prominently in the oral history and folklore of the district. There are stories of waterfalls being blown upwards, of crops of turnips being blasted out of the ground, of a householder having to retreat from his garden to avoid a fusillade of brussel sprouts which had been stripped from their plants. Locals refer to the wind being strong enough to 'bla t'nebs off t'stegs' [beaks off the geese] or 't'tail off t'coo'. My hope was that a place culturally and geographically distinct, and subject to a unique and potent meteorological phenomenon, would provide a laboratory to test the various assertions and theories about the influence of weather on human nature. But I was too late. For one thing, the Helm in recent years has been a shadow of its old, rough self, confined to making infrequent and fleeting appearances. And for another, the old way of life built around a pattern of hill-farming that had persisted for centuries has all but disappeared. It was already precarious enough before the foot-and-mouth outbreak of 2001, which persuaded many sheep farmers that it was time to give up the wearying struggle to make a half-decent living, take the compensation and sell up. This set off an influx of retired people and professionals with jobs elsewhere, and the farmers who do remain are no longer prepared to risk sending their flocks on to the higher slopes to wander at will.

So where I was sitting I had no sheep for company, though there were plenty in the fenced pastures below, and snatches of bleating were carried to me on the breeze. I could not see another human being, although had I taken the trouble to get to the top of Crossfell I would certainly have encountered dedicated ramblers marching the 250-mile Pennine Way. But the ridge was shrouded in the cloud and further away than I cared to walk.

Instead I circled around the upper edge of the screes and rocks above Ardale Beck, passing the ruins of a bothy that would never see another shepherd arriving in search of a night's shelter, and strolled down the slope of Brown Hill and Man At Edge. I met a path called the Maiden Way, which the sign said was a Roman road, although it was not easy to imagine what business would have brought the centurions here. I arrived back at Kirkland through a meadow crowded with sheep which followed me, bleating with passionate intensity, their sharp little hooves rustling as they cut through the grass.

Later I asked David Uttley about the folk of the fellside. Mr Uttley came to live on the outskirts of Skirwith – which is about a mile from Kirkland and right in the path of the Helm wind – after retiring from his career as a neurosurgeon. He became very curious about the wind, and eventually published a comprehensive history of it, called *The Anatomy of the Helm Wind*, from which I have taken much of the factual information in this section. Mr Uttley interviewed a large number of locals in the course of his research, and at the end of the book he wrote:

The people who inhabit the fellside villages often seem to be a race apart. They are, for the most part, modest and seemly in their ways, cautious and rightly shy of strangers . . . They have not forgotten the virtues of self-reliance and the value of close-knit family and life-long friends . . . The people are honest and straightforward and always ready to help if the need arises; these are the Cumbrian 'statesmen' whose sturdy independence of thought and action have been respectfully recognised for many centuries by those who know them.

Did that assessment, I asked Mr Uttley, amount to an acceptance that this place and its peculiar weather bred a type to match, with a shared character? He was positive that it did not: that these were common responses to environment, and that the variations in the nature of individuals was as wide in the fell villages as anywhere else.

What else did I expect? Well, nothing, really. The title of this chapter is adapted from the 'Ode to the North-east Wind' by the same Charles Kingsley who refused to read out a prayer in his church appealing to God for fine weather:

> 'Tis the hard grey weather
> Breeds hard English men.
> What's the soft South-wester?
> 'Tis the ladies' breeze,
> Bringing home their true-loves
> Out of all the seas:
> But the black North-easter,
> Through the snowstorm hurled,
> Drives our English hearts of oak
> Seaward round the world

While Kingsley himself doubtless saw plenty of hard grey weather while tending to the parishioners of his impoverished living, and when off pursuing his passions for fishing, hunting and natural history, a hard Englishman he was not. In fact he was neurotic, sensitive, incurably restless, a martyr to ill health, a stammerer, addicted to tobacco, the author of daringly experimental novels, a social and religious radical. He could be said almost to exemplify the contradictions within the John Bull stereotype which foreigners are so fond of seizing upon: bluff, athletic and vigorous in demeanour and action, a nervous wreck within.

The German-born architectural historian Nikolaus Pevsner claimed that, as a result of his many years' residence in England, he could identify the two distinct racial types. One was John Bull, 'of ruddy complexion and indomitable health, busy in house and garden and garage with his own hands . . . devoted to outdoor sports'; the other 'tall with a long head and long features, little display and little gesticulation'. In a book called *The Genius of Europe*, Henry Havelock Ellis — who, although English, was driven throughout his life by a most unEnglish passion and curiosity about sex, science and art — asserted that the John Bull model was most commonly encountered in 'the Danish regions of the east':

He is fair and high-coloured, large of stature, of fleshy texture and rounded outlines . . . a little irritable, if not suspicious and defiant, though tender and emotional underneath . . . sometimes he may be merely bucolic and sometimes he has the high intelligence and character, the gravity and firm decision of the finest Englishman, but always there is a certain personal consciousness, a burden of responsibility, whether the burden is his own health or the burden of ruling a province . . .

In the early 1950s, the poet and novelist Geoffrey Gorer compiled a book called *Exploring the English Character*, which was based on a survey of readers of the *People* newspaper. Gorer enumerated a considerable list of supposedly common traits, including 'a great resentment at being overlooked or controlled, a love of freedom; fortitude; a low interest in sexual activity compared with most neighbouring societies; a strong belief in the value of education for the formation of character; consideration and delicacy for the feelings of other people; and a very strong attachment to marriage and the institution of marriage'.

Half a century later, in his book *The English*, Jeremy Paxman was much more cautious about identifying enduring components of the 'national character', and generally confined himself to recording ways in which the conventional apprehension of Englishness had been erased, sabotaged or corrupted; or, simply, had never existed in the first place. Looking at Geoffrey Gorer's list, it would be contentious to suggest today that other European nations were innately less attached to freedom than us, and ludicrous to assert that our belief in the value of education, our consideration for the feelings of others, or our attachment to family were more powerful than anyone else's. As for our attachment to marriage, the fact that we have one of the highest divorce rates in the world indicates this may not have been as deeply rooted as Geoffrey Gorer believed. All that is left is the enduring assumption that foreigners are both much more interested in sex than us and more adept at getting it. I have never seen any evidence to support either of these contentions, and I strongly suspect that they are not, and never have been, true.

One of the difficulties with supposedly common traits is that as soon as you focus on one, the faces of a dozen people who do not share it spring into the mind's eye. Tolerance is frequently advanced as a British virtue; yet intolerance of immigrants, blacks, Muslims, Jews, gypsies, homosexuals, supporters of hunting, opponents of hunting, Church of England liberals, liberals in general, Conservatives, Americans, single mothers, people on benefit and representatives from a thousand other groups is rampant. In the end, the best you can say, perhaps, is that this is a society in which tolerance and intolerance are at war, and the balance tilts this way and that without ever threatening a final resolution.

Because 'we' – the English, the British? – feel instinctively that we are different from 'them', we assume that there are elements in us which define that difference. But as soon as an attempt is made to identify them, the exercise degenerates into the dumping of stereotypes into a rubbish skip of prejudice. The Scots are mean – well, they are, aren't they? And did you ever meet an Irishman who couldn't talk the hind legs off the proverbial beast of burden? The Welsh – untrustworthy. The English – arrogant. Germans – overbearing. Italians – cowardly. Americans – vulgar. French – full of themselves, unable to resist tryants. Australians – oafish. And so on.

Paul Langford, in his acute and entertaining study, *Englishness Identified*, observed that in the past the notion of 'national character' enjoyed a general and unthinking acceptance, but had become 'repugnant to the liberal conscience' in our own time. It is also surely true that two of the dominant forces of the age – economic and cultural globalisation, and the dilution of racial stocks resulting from mass migration – have combined to make it untenable. If the concept of a national character did have some application in the pre-globalisation era, the question is: where did this common heritage come from? One obvious answer lay in the two permanent, individual, constant physical influences on any country: its geography and its weather.

The horror registered by Montesquieu upon encountering the British climate echoed the incomprehension of a fellow countryman of his from an earlier age — albeit one enlisted to serve William Shakespeare's dramatic purpose. In *Henry V* the Constable of France offers his reflections about their English opponents, their weather and their beer to his King and others:

> . . . Where have they this mettle?
> Is not their climate foggy, raw, and dull,
> On whom as in despite, the sun looks pale,
> Killing their fruit with frowns? Can sodden water,
> A drench for sur-rein'd jades — their barley-broth —
> Decoct their cold blood to such valiant heat?
> And shall our quick blood, spirited with wine,
> Seem frosty?

From the time of Tacitus, abusing the climate of Britain was an almost automatic response among foreigners moved to ponder the place and the peculiarities of its people. The Roman historian never actually visited these shores, but was assured by those who had that the climate was 'objectionable' on account of the frequent winds and rains. His Greek predecessor, Strabo, initiated what was to become a favourite theme: the rarity and feebleness of the appearances of the sun. 'In a whole day,' Strabo stated, 'the sun is only seen for three or four hours around mid-day.' A late eighteenth-century tourist, Henry Meister — a Swiss who introduced himself to readers of his popular *Letters Written During a Residence in England* as 'correspondent and literary agent for the Empress of Russia, the Duke of Brunswick and Margrave of Anspach and other sovereigns' – wrote: 'A sky in which no cloud is to be seen is so great a novelty that it takes the place of all other news; and it is impossible for a foreigner not to remark on the joyful congratulations which he hears on all sides, when the sun condescends to show himself ever so little – "*a very fine day – very fine weather indeed!*".' Meister regarded England as 'the land of mists and vapours', where the sun was reduced to impotence by having 'to force a passage through such a dense atmosphere'.

Others, echoing Charles II's feelings, were more favourably disposed. One exotic enthusiast was Mirza Abu Taleb Khan, a Persian raised in northern India whose travels brought him to England in 1799, where he became something of a pet of London society. Abu Taleb said he had feared his health would suffer 'in the severity of the climate . . . but on the contrary I found I had a keen appetite and became every day stronger and more active'. He listed the virtues of the climate: that it rendered men vigorous in mind and body, and women fair and handsome; that it obliged men to take exercise 'which hardens and invigorates the constitution and inspires them with that valour'; that it made them 'open-hearted and sincere, steady in the pursuit of knowledge and not led away by flights of fancy or sallies of imagination'. Abu Taleb also applauded the necessity of wearing several layers of clothing 'which are troublesome and very inconvenient for taking off', on the grounds that it discouraged indolence, and caused nights to be spent in 'harmless sleep' – as opposed to India 'where the day is frequently devoted to sensuality and repose and the night to business and conviviality'.

A German historian, Johann Wilhelm von Archenholz, spent ten years in England at about the same time as the so-called

'Persian Prince', and came to very similar conclusions about the maligned weather. It was true, von Archenholz reflected, that it was very varied; but it could not 'with any justice, be called intolerable'. It promoted 'the happy temper, intrepidity and continual activity of the people', bestowing good health on 'all the carpenters, blacksmiths, farmers, miners, porters and peasants'. The grass in England was 'of incomparable beauty . . . the finest green colour and extremely delicate', while the women were not far behind — 'the fairest in Europe', von Archenholz enthused. He noted an admirable corollary: 'The English women are so beautiful that unnatural pleasures are held in great abhorrence by the men. In no country are such infamous pleasures spoken of with greater abhorrence.'

Generally speaking, the British themselves have been more cautious than foreigners in ascribing common aspects of behaviour or shared characteristics to the climate. In *The English Climate* Hubert Lamb claimed there was 'plenty of evidence that being accustomed to alternations of warmth and cold that are not too extreme, and of storm and sun, is beneficial to health, gives zest to live, and affects character', although he did not actually say what the evidence was. Gordon Manley, in his *Climate and the British Scene*, was slightly more forthcoming. He suggested that the principle characteristic of our climate — its variability — encouraged a general flexibility, a readiness, as he put it, 'to change the plan and to refrain from placing all the eggs in one basket'. He wondered if this unpredictability might not have helped make Britain 'a country in which irregularities of pattern of every sort are not only experienced but esteemed', and to have nourished our tolerance of varieties of opinion. But Manley also identified a reverse of the coin. 'Life becomes too easy,' he complained. 'The vicissitudes of our climate are scarcely more than an inconvenience that upsets the football match or the Sunday picnic.'

In his series of lectures on national character Sir Ernest Barker accepted that there might be patterns of behaviour associated with particular nations. But he dismissed the idea that these might be hereditary. 'Nations pride themselves on racial purity,' he commented wisely, 'when if they were more discerning, they would pride themselves with greater propriety on racial impurity.' He pointed out that to sustain the theory of race characteristics in the case of the British would require not merely the disentangling of the Nordic stock from later Scandinavian influxes, but the separation of the disparate elements within them – Nordic Celts, Angles, Jutes, Saxons, Danes, Latinised Normans and so on.

Barker dismissed the geographical determinism promoted by Ellsworth Huntingdon – 'the conception that the territory of a nation becomes its destiny and the climate of a given territory becomes the special genius which presides over the formation and development of national character'. The fact that Britain was an island, he argued, had clearly been a considerable factor in our history, and might even have influenced the way we think. But he equated the belief that mist and cloud and rain could exercise an influence on the collective disposition and temper with astrology. 'We are not dealing here with a branch of science,' he wrote. 'We are hardly dealing here even with a matter for speculation, in the strict sense of the word. Speculation may one day be verified; but a guess which remains a guess admits of no verification.'

However, nothing deters foreign commentators from taking what Barker termed 'a walk through an unknown country in the dark' in order to pronounce boldly on the peculiarities of the species. One of the most celebrated verdicts on the myth-ical Britisher was delivered by the Anglophile American Ralph Waldo Emerson: 'In short, every one of these islanders is an island, safe, tranquil, incommunicable. In the company of strangers, you would think him deaf. He is never betrayed into any curiosity or unbecoming emotion . . . he does not give his hand. He does not let you meet his eye.' An American philosopher of a later generation, George Santayana, drew on a meteorological parallel to generalise: 'His [the Englishman's] character is like his climate, gentle and passing from dull to glorious and back again; variable on the surface, yet perpetually self-restored and invariably the same.'

But the French — jealous and uncomprehending in equal measure — had no time for such mellifluous generalities. Following obediently in the tracks of Montesquieu, a succes-sion of historians bent on cracking the enigma of perfidious Albion deployed the determinist approach in both its geographical and climatic guises with impregnable certitude. Jules Michelet, revolutionary enthusiast and author of the monumental twenty-four-volume *Histoire de France*, constructed his Theory of the Two Seas to explain the impressive bodily vigour and military prowess of the English — 'the one surrounding the island, and the other pressing down upon it from the louring skies'. According to Michelet, this 'profound and perpetual humidity' should have had the most enervating effect on the constitution. But in fact, by encouraging the raising of cattle and 'the unparalleled consumption of meat', the English had turned it to their advantage.

Michelet's successor as the dominant figure among French historians, Henri Taine, was almost as exercised by English history and literature as by that of his own land. Where and when Taine encountered his 'typical Saxon' are matters for speculation:

> Huge white bodies, cool-blooded, with fierce blue eyes, reddish flaxen hair, ravenous stomachs filled with meat and cheese, heated by strong drink, of a cold temperament, slow to love, home-stayers, prone to brutal drunkenness – these are, to this day, the features which descent and climate preserve in the race . . . there is no living in these lands without abundance of solid food; bad weather keeps people at home; strong drinks are necessary to cheer them; the senses become blunted, the muscles are braced, the will vigorous.

All these themes – dreary weather, gross meat-eating, largeness of body, lack of sensitivity and imagination, preference for hearty outdoor sport over the sophisticated game of seduction – were synthesised in a book called *The English People: A Study of their Political Psychology*, which was written at the turn of the nineteenth century by Emile Boutmy, another distinguished Academician and the founder of the School for Political Science in Paris. Boutmy was in no doubt that the key factor in explaining Britain's success in preserving political liberty, winning wars and securing the economic edge over its civilised neighbours was its awful climate. He pondered the same conundrum as Montesquieu: how could weather so oppressive to the spirits promote this appetite for greatness? Boutmy agreed with the master that the required qualities had developed IN REACTION to the appalling weather. His exposition of this unusual chain of cause and effect was extremely thorough.

He began with the matter of physique: 'The atmosphere,' he wrote, 'is charged with moisture to a degree which, at times, renders respiration difficult and the enfeebled body can only maintain its normal temperature by a large amount of exercise; for this reason England abounds in big, vigorous men.' The professor turned his attention to the land itself – 'moistened by fog and drowned by showers' – and found that only by 'incessant drainage and clearing' could it be prevented from reverting to marsh and forest. But when the Englishman keeps to the task, 'the labour is crowned with admirable results'. Similarly, 'the constant presence of moisture in the atmosphere, the feebleness of the sun, whose rays are softened by the mist and the gloom . . . makes the task of clothing, housing, warming and lighting himself peculiarly laborious.'

Nature, the professor continued, offered the English the choice between 'an imperious ultimatum and a seductive invitation: a rich harvest if they persevere in their efforts, inevitable decay if they relax'. The secret lay in the national obsession with sport – 'the satisfaction of a physical need as imperative as hunger or thirst'. Everywhere he went, he found the manifestations of this passion – 'in Lancashire boxing has the preference of the majority', whereas in Northumberland 'the working man devotes himself to quoits whenever he has a spare moment'.

The difference between the English worker and his Gallic counterpart, Boutmy observed, was striking. The Englishman works and keeps working and is not prone to the temptation to 'raise his head, as a Frenchman would, to watch a fly'. This was all because of the climate. 'The sensibilities of the English are less acute . . . In these big, white-skinned bodies, bathed in an atmosphere of perpetual moisture, sensations are experienced far more slowly.' This, in the professor's judgement, gave them further advantages: 'Their physical imagination is lethargic and dull. This is one of the reasons why surgical operations are much more successful on an Englishman than on an Italian . . . The imperturbability of the English Grenadiers under fire, in Spain, at Waterloo, at Inkerman, has extorted the admiration even of their enemies.' The prevalence of mist and moisture also accounted for the style of English landscape painting – 'the clamour of red and green alone resist the deadening influence, and these are the colours for England', Boutmy stated. As for the poets and playwrights – Shakespeare, Wordsworth, Shelley and the rest – it had been the very paucity of external visual stimulation that had driven them inwards to explore their imaginations. Thus the inner life of the spirit was, perversely, nourished into high art by the dismal conditions prevailing outside the window.

Compared with the historians of today, so tentative in their conclusions about anything, Boutmy's supreme confidence in himself and his thesis seems valiant and rather splendid. Did it ever occur to him, one wonders, as he peered through the murk at quoit-playing Geordies and pugilistic Lancastrians, that the notion of a climate restricted to these islands, arrested at the white cliffs of Dover or midway across the Channel, might be meteorologically unsound? Did he not notice that the weather here is the same in its essentials as in Normandy, Brittany and the rest of northern France, including the city where he instructed his pupils in the principles of political science? One presumes not, otherwise the professor would have to be written off as a fool, a charlatan or a joker.

My own view, for what it is worth (no more than anyone else's), is this. The concept of a national character – in the sense of a complemetary set of deeply ingrained, inherent traits and attitudes shared by a people – is extremely seductive. We do not know what it is like to be French, or German, or Italian, but we assume that it feels different from being British, and that the ways in which we feel different reflect the components of the national character. The difficulties arise when an attempt is made to separate and identify those components.

Furthermore, if this elusive commonality exists, where is it to be found? Is there really a broad, overarching sense of shared identity binding the peoples of these islands, which accommodates the ancient suspicions and hostilities between, say, Highland and Lowland Scot, southern and northern Walians, Lancastrians and Yorkists, town and country dwellers, natives and immigrants? At a local level, the residents in a particular street may be united in their dislike of vandalism, their suspicion of a proposed mobile phone mast, their affection or distrust of their MP or parish council, even their inclination to complain about the weather. But they will be divided, house by house, by politics, religion, income, aspiration, age, fertility, sociability, temperament and a host of other potent factors. Even within ourselves, impulses are in conflict. I would like to think of myself as a tolerant Englishman, yet I am well aware that a tendency to the opposite persists in me; even, occasionally, has the upper hand.

As for the role of the weather and geography in all this, the waters are muddy indeed. Charles Nevin argued in his sparklingly witty and idiosyncratic study of his native county, *Lancashire: Where Women Die of Love*, that the warm, moist westerly winds had created a romantic, whimsical race, whereas on the other side of the Pennines, exposed to the bitter blasts off the North Sea, lived 'a sad and surly people unable to understand why they haven't been let in on the joke'. The urge to make such connections is potent. The Scots work harder than the English and are more careful with their money because their climate is harsher. The people of the flatlands of East Anglia are inclined to melancholy because there is nothing around them to surprise them or divert them from contemplating this vale of tears. The Puritan ethic prevailed under the sombre skies of northern Europe but withered in the sunshine of the south.

The contention that our weather has assisted in making us the people we are can be argued indefinitely without a resolution coming into sight. But what very many of us undoubtedly do share is an attitude towards our weather, and a way of talking about it. As I suggested earlier, this is often represented as a national obsession, when in fact it amounts to little more than a habit: to complain endlessly, ritualistically, repetitiously and tediously about something over which we have no control, and which is of very little practical significance to us. It is also frequently stated that we are unusual among European nations in the closeness of our interest in our weather. This is a moot point. The prominence given to weather forecasts in newspapers and on television in the countries I know best – Italy and France – suggests that this may well be wishful thinking. On the other hand, an Italian acquaintance who was sent to school in England and knows it well told me his fellow countrymen and women did not talk about the weather because there were many more interesting matters – principally food – to occupy their minds. Our response to that would probably be that the reason we talk more about our weather is that there is more of it, and therefore it is more interesting.

However, it is open to doubt whether our conversations on the subject are that interesting; or, indeed, whether they qualify as conversations at all. In some ways our meteorological exchanges – so dear, so familiar – are closer to the model of morning prayer: 'The Lord be with you / and with your spirit /

Lord have mercy upon us / Christ have mercy upon us' etc. The weather liturgy might go: 'Horrible day, innit? / You can say that again. You wonder if it's ever going to stop / Too true. Whatever happened to summer? / Summer? Don't make me laugh. Still, the ducks are happy' etc etc. Or: 'Another lovely day, innit? / Suppose so. Bit hot for me, though. Could do with a decent drop of rain. Garden's parched / Not much chance of that, according to the forecast. Mind you, when did they ever get anything right? / You can say that again. Remember the big storm, '87 was it? That Michael Fish' etc etc.

It is most unusual for a casual weather chat between strangers to rise much above this level. Nevertheless, a large proportion of the population continues to trade these banalities on an almost daily basis, and shows no sign of getting tired of doing so. Our attitude to our weather recalls the relationship between many dog lovers and their pets. Their gripings about the animal's eating habits, uncertain temper, unattractive smell and appearance are a guise for their affection. I would not suggest that we are united in love for our weather, but we are grudgingly attached to it. It is ours and it suits us. We like to think that no one else has weather quite like it; and, at a deeper level, we feel it is on our side.

Shakespeare's friend Michael Drayton attempted a triumphant celebration of its virtues:

. . . of Albion's glorious Ile, the wonders whilst I write,
The sundry varying soyles, the pleasure infinite;
Where heat kills not the cold, nor cold expels the heat,
Nor calmes too mildly small, nor winds too roughly great;
Nor night doth hinder day, nor day the night doth wrong,
The summer not too short, the winter not too long.

The bathetic quality of Drayton's lines indicates that moderation, the avoidance of extremes, a bit of this and a bit of that and not too much of either, do not make the ideal raw material for heroic, declamatory verse. Perhaps nearer the mark is Gordon Manley's wry, affectionate, deprecating – dare I say it, typically British – tribute in *Climate and the British Scene*: 'The astringent mildness of our dominant maritime-polar air is one of the few unalterable comforts we possess, however much we may personally deplore its harassing benevolence. Truly the air that reaches us, in the words of Shakespeare's Ariel "suffers a sea-change / Into something rich and strange".'

Chapter 8

Airs Wholesome and Pestilential

TOWARDS THE END OF AUGUST 2003 THE LATEST IN THE SERIES OF HIGH-pressure systems that had kept Britain panting under a burning sun for two months and more quietly drifted off. There was no fuss about it, no dramatic coda of thunderstorms and floods as in 1976. The heat wave just quietly packed up, as if to say: I'm off now, but not to worry. As it turned out, the weather remained generally fine right into October. The twenty-ninth of August was a Friday, the last of the holidays. In the morning it rained on and off for an hour or two on to the straw-coloured grass, and the wind backed into the north-west, pushing bands of grey cloud at a brisk pace across the sky. It was an English summer's day as they used to be, and it reminded me of English summer holidays by the sea. So I took myself off to Weston-super-Mare to see what the weather was like and how the seaside holiday was bearing up.

Weston-super-Mare, Weston-above-the-Sea: something of a hyperbole if you are feeling charitable, downright misleading if you are not; particularly if you reach the seafront when the tide is almost out. I took a circuitous route from the station along streets of large, comfortably ugly stone residences. Although some were still private houses, most seemed to have been turned into hotels, guesthouses, or old people's homes. I asked a woman of mature years who was sweeping the steps of one of these establishments her opinion of Weston. She had been born in the town, she said, had moved away to the Midlands when she got married, and had moved back when her husband died. She liked the place, although she couldn't really explain why. 'Me husband, he's gone now,' she said reflectively, 'he was in the army in Cyprus and he said the best thing about coming home was seeing the green of England again.' He'd have been disappointed today, I thought.

Next door two ancient men and two ancient women were sitting outside the St Agnes Residential Home warming their brittle bones in the sunshine that had broken through the cloud. 'Too hot, too many old people,' grumbled one of the elderly gents churlishly when I asked him about the place where he was seeing out his days. One of the ladies chided him. 'It's nice, you can enjoy the bracing sea air,' she said gallantly.

There was a cheerful scene in Clarence Park, where the Clarence Bowling Club's open week was drawing towards its close. It was the Mixed Fours, and across the flat, well-watered greens, black spheres were making smooth, leisurely journeys. Everyone was in white, except me: white skirts and blouses, white flannels and sweaters, white cardigans and windcheaters, white caps and sun visors; and the effect of the white against the green of the grass and the foliage of the trees was very pleasing. The salty air was filled with politeness and goodwill, banter, friendly rivalry, and commiseration, restrained urgings of the bowls and muted bursts of applause. A most English scene.

From the park I walked down to the seafront, or Marine Parade as it is officially designated. My spirits sank. For some time I stared out at the Bristol Channel, trying to spot the sea.

But it wasn't there, having left in its absence a vast expanse of khaki mud, glistening stickily like the surface of a flypaper. A ship sailed from left to right, apparently across the mud, with the blue hills of south Wales on top of it. I presumed that if I walked straight out I would reach water sometime; except that to do so would be to die, unless I could assume the form of a wading bird. 'DANGER – SINKING MUD' warned the yellow signs placed where the brown sand, wet from the night's rain, gave way to the wet ooze.

I went down onto the sand. To my left lay the lump of Brean Down, to my right the long, low line of Worlebury Hill, with rows of late Victorian and Edwardian villas and terraced houses splayed out across its slopes; and between the two, the town of Weston, and the mud. I was assailed by the peculiarly poignant melancholy which hangs over a seaside resort on its uppers. I strolled between the flattened vestiges of the previous day's sand-castles past a dismal concrete oval bowl filled with brown water which advertised itself as the Model Yacht Club. Two middle-aged couples from Bromsgrove were unfolding collapsible chairs and arranging cool boxes. I asked them if they were Weston regulars. It turned out that they had been once, before cheap foreign holidays had raised their siren faces. Now they were seeing if they could recapture something of the magic they had found in Weston long ago. But the consensus was that a day would be plenty.

A little way on, thrust out on stilts over the sand, was the first of Weston's extensive collection of derelict monuments to its departed splendour. Once the Tropicana was the biggest and best outdoor swimming pool in the South-West, resounding all summer long to the shrieks of children hurtling down its cele-brated water chute. Now it stood silent, boarded up, crumbling.

Outside, a sign promised its early transformation into 'an exciting new entertainment complex', but there was no sign of any progress towards that rebirth, and I was told later that the company involved had gone bust, or pulled out, or both.

A mother and daughter were buying cups of tea at a kiosk, while keeping a watchful eye on two boys playing on the sand nearby. They had last been to Weston twenty years before, when the mother of the children was herself a child. This was another revisiting of the precious past. So how was it going? 'Never again,' the younger woman said tearfully. Was it the children, I asked? Did they think it was boring? No, no, they were fine, they loved playing in the sand. It was her husband, accustomed to holidays under the southern sun, golden beaches, shimmering blue seas. What were they doing in a flat in Weston-super-Mare, for Christ's sake? She sniffed dolefully.

On the other side of Marine Parade the monumental façade of the Grand Atlantic Hotel looked out over the mud flats, perhaps recalling better days. A pair of elderly donkeys with whitened noses were standing motionless on the beach, heads down, while some children tried to decide if it was worth pestering their parents for the slow plod along the sands. In the irredeemably tacky town centre youths thrust and yanked at the squealing games machines in the amusement halls, while couples trudged behind pushchairs along the pedestrianised route between M&S and H&M. A smell of batter and frying fat mixed with seaweed and sludge wafted through the streets. I had a plate of fish and chips and a mug of strong tea at an extraordinarily low price in the Regent Restaurant, then made my way inland to the Town Library to find out something about those better days.

*   *   *

So thorough has been the redrawing of our collective mental landscape by the package foreign holiday and budget airline ticket that it is difficult to recall a time when the English seaside resort and the English seaside holiday were not a sad joke. As a boy I spent at least one summer holiday with assorted brothers and cousins at Middleton-on-Sea in Sussex. For some reason, the foundations of our rented house had been built above ground so as to be accessible, and we spent as much time crawling around these tunnels, unravelling string from a ball so as to be sure of the route back to the outside world, as we did on the beach. Middleton was reckoned to be a step above Bognor, just to the west, which was thought very plebeian.

Yet Bognor had once basked in royal approval – bestowed on it and other seaside places because of the belief of royal doctors in the health-giving properties of seawater, sea air, sea weather. The movement began in the 1730s in Scarborough, where it was the custom for men to plunge naked into the water from boats, while the ladies emerged decorously covered from dressing rooms along the beach. It received decisive impetus from the publication in the 1750s of a dissertation by a well-known London physician, Richard Russell, recommending the use of seawater to treat a medley of ailments, including scurvy, leprosy, consumption, cirrhosis, scrofula, gonorrhoea and gout.

To avail himself of unlimited quantities of the healing fluid, Doctor Russell relocated his practice to a seaside village in Sussex called Brightelmstone. The metamorphosis of this insignificant place into Brighton was sealed by the visit in 1783 of the young Prince Regent, who was in search of relief from glandular discomfort. The Prince made it his favourite pleasure ground, and gathered around him there a band of those who shared his notion of what pleasure was. Sea-bathing was one of their more proper pursuits and was jointly presided over by the Prince's personal swimming tutor, John 'Smoaker' Miles, and the daughter of a well-known local family of fishmongers, Martha Gunn.

Other previously unregarded fishing villages began to blossom under royal patronage. The Prince Regent's father, George III, became a regular at Weymouth, where the royal bathing machine was accompanied by a second containing fiddlers, who played the National Anthem while the monarch frolicked in the water. The status of Worthing was much enhanced by the championship of one of George's daughters, Princess Amelia. Another daughter, Princess Charlotte, preferred the air at Bognor.

All this time, the village of Weston remained unnoticed beside the turbid waters of the Bristol Channel. The coming of the railway changed that, just as it brought about the fall of Brighton from aristocratic grace. Once the professional classes started pouring on to the platforms, it was time for persons of distinction to retreat. Queen Victoria came to Brighton in 1843, pronounced its people to be 'very indiscreet and troublesome', and never returned. The ease of access to Weston from Bristol made it an ideal destination for the new breed of day-trippers, while it soon became the resort of choice for families from the emergent industrial powerhouse of Birmingham.

The early promoters of Weston's attractions could not disguise the awkward fact that twice a day the sea disappeared out of sight. Ingeniously, they decided to make a virtue of its muddiness. On the principle that if you say something often enough and with sufficient conviction it will be believed, they spread the message that the air blowing over the mud flats was infused with unusually health-giving qualities. The first guidebook to Weston, published in 1822, commended the air as being 'bracing and peculiarly efficacious to those constitutions with which the Devon coast disagrees . . . so balmy that even when blowing a hurricane it imparts strength to the invalid'.

To be able to persuade visitors that they were deriving unique benefits even when the weather was at its foulest was a potent selling point for a resort subject to the usual vagaries of the English summer, and not blessed with many obvious natural advantages. The 1850 Guide spoke of the 'rapidity with which lacklustre eyes, pasty features, attenuated limbs and listless gait are exchanged for a robust frame, activity of body, and chubby cheeks stamped with the rosy tint of health'. Gradually the health pitch acquired pseudo-medical trappings. The 1877 Guide referred to 'remarkable cures of nervous exhaustion and spinal disease', and added sagely that 'a modern man of science will probably say that ozone is especially abundant here'. By 1907 this theme had been further developed: 'Weston winds are proverbial and the vast expanse of salt mud exposed at low tide is considered to be the prime contribution to its well-known salubrity. The Medical Officer of Health says breezes blow across the mud and catch up large amounts of ozone and iodine and discharge their loads into the lungs of visitors and residents alike, making the weak as strong as giants.'

Medically, the question of whether sea air is imbued with curative powers is contentious, and ozone and iodine are not generally acknowledged as treatments for spinal disease. Nevertheless, millions upon millions who have holidayed by the sea, and in many cases have been moved to migrate permanently to the coast, would testify to the positive effect of moist, salty breezes on body and mind – even if they could not measure it. At the same time, the medical profession accepts that to feel better is often a considerable step towards getting better, although it may struggle to account for the phenomenon epidemiologically.

Ever since physicians invented their profession, they have been advising the more affluent among their patients to take themselves off to milder, warmer climes to escape the detrimental effects of the British weather. As recently as 1935 an article in the *British Medical Journal* spoke of the 'vital importance' of climatic treatment for patients suffering from 'arterio-sclerotic hypertension', and recommended wintering in Bournemouth, Torquay, Sidmouth or Paignton; or — for those who could afford it — Madeira, the Canaries, Egypt or Algiers. The benign climate enjoyed by Nice was a prime attraction for the affluent English seeking escape from the miseries of our winter, who in time turned the city into an Anglo-Saxon stronghold. But even Nice could not be relied upon. In 1763 Tobias Smollett bloomed under its blue Mediterranean skies, and enthused: 'There is less wind and rain in Nice than in any other place in the world I know . . . This air, being dry, pure, heavy, and elastic, must be agreeable to the constitutions of those who labour under disorders arising from weak nerves, obstructed perspiration, relaxed fibres, a viscidity of lymph and a languid circulation.' The following winter Smollett returned to Nice, experienced fifty-six days of rain between November and March, and was less effusive about the benefits of wintering in the south.

The corollary of the belief that some climates are 'better' for us than others — which, even now, is widely held — has been the belief that some are very much worse. The worst of all, to the point of being ruinous and frequently fatal, was that to be found in 'the tropics' — which covered European colonial possessions in India, South-east Asia, Africa, the West Indies and Central America. It was, of course, essential that the white man go to these places to supervise their useful exploitation. But it was an article of faith among colonial administrators, experts in tropical diseases, and the public at large that to do so was to run a high risk of succumbing to one or other or several of a host of malign influences. The heat, the humidity, the violence and abundance of the rainfall, the warmth of the winds – the opposite of bracing – were the obvious propagators of ill health.

The most authoritative nineteenth-century textbook on the subject was *The Influence of Tropical Climates on European Constitutions*, first published in 1812 and written by an Irish-born medical practitioner, James Johnson. Johnson based his analysis and recommendations on his own extensive experience of conditions in Egypt, India and China, gained while serving on various Royal Navy vessels. He attributed the 'gradual degeneration' of the European man in such places to the meteorological factors mentioned above, working in concert with another sinister agency: miasmas, the emanations from damp, swampy, insect-ridden lands. According to Johnson, the only hope of survival for the pale skinned was to observe a regimen as temperate as the weather at home. He advised the wearing of a turban to protect against the heat, and a cummerbund to guard against dangerous cooling in the abdominal region, and vigorously attacked the 'tyrant custom' of arranging formal events during the heat of the day, and requiring those attending them to wear civil dress or military uniforms. In particular, Johnson urged in the strongest terms the avoidance of indulgence in alcohol, spicy foods and licentious behaviour. Some found abstinence easier than others, and some did not try. One of the latter was the Duke of Wellington's elder brother, the Marquis of Wellesley, who wrote from India – where he was Governor-General between

1797 and 1805 — that 'this climate excites one sexually most terribly . . . as for sex, one must have it.'

A century after James Johnson's cautionary words, Charles E. Woodruff of the US Army Medical Corps, astounded and appalled by the incidence of disease and death among troops guarding the Panama Canal, came to the conclusion that it was physiologically impossible for the white man to acclimatise to the ultraviolet rays poured down by the sun in tropical regions, though the effects could, he advised, be mitigated by the wearing at all times of orange-red underwear. A rather more sober assessment of the medical risks associated with the American presence in Panama, issued in 1929, concluded that 'by far the larger part of the moribundity and mortality formerly attributed to tropical climates was due, not to climate *per se*, but to isolation, tedium, nostalgia, venereal disease, alcoholic excess, poor municipal conditions and — most important of all — to infection with specific parasites whose invasion is now almost wholly preventable'.

Today, following the general retreat of the White Man from the tropics, and the development of specific medicines, the notion of an inherent antagonism between the climates of such regions and the constitutions of visitors from more temperate parts has faded. Images of grey-faced, shuddering malaria victims and pitiable neurasthenics — fine men whose nervous systems had been shot to pieces by miasmic influences — have lost their potency. Even so, a faith in the salubrious and curative effects of 'good air' — particularly sea air — quietly persists.

From Weston's Public Library I walked across to a prosperous looking medical practice on the other side of The Boulevard, with the names of at least six doctors inscribed on a polished brass plate beside the entrance. I wanted to ask one of them if they would endorse the view that Weston's air was unusually beneficial to health, but they were all out tending to the sick. However the female receptionists were in no doubt that the town's reputation was deserved. One said she had been advised by experts at Great Ormond Street Children's Hospital in London to bring her ailing son to the seaside, and he was now a picture of health. Another, who had lived in Weston for twenty-nine years, gave all the credit for her hale and hearty condition to 'the air', although she admitted that in all that time she had never once been to the beach.

Back on Marine Parade, the sun was out. The view across Weston Bay to Brean Down — the sheeny, metallic grey-brown mud now lapped by the incoming brown tide — struck me as astonishingly unappetising. But no one else seemed bothered. A big Irish woman paused between mouthfuls of scone, clotted cream and jam to tell her companions that she never had the appetite to eat like this at home. A couple from Birmingham, trim and fit in old age, spoke approvingly of the flatness of the sea front; and were delighted that their week — including coach ride from home, bed, breakfast and evening meal in a hotel, plus 'entertainment' each evening, plus bingo — was costing them less than £200. It's a cheap place.

I descended some stone steps to a concrete slipway which led over greasy rocks to the water. Ahead were the rusting bones of another abandoned relic of Weston's past, Birbeck Pier. Water resembling stewed tea was surging around its supports and slapping against the slipway. Two girls and two boys, in shorts and T-shirts and armed with hand lines, were hauling small, inedible green crabs out as fast as they could prise the claws off the bait, drop the beasts into their bucket and lower the hooks back. They were shouting and squealing with excitement. One of the girls got into a tangle, and thanked me graciously when I unravelled it for her. 'We love it here,' one of the boys shouted in response to my question as he swung another crab in. Cloud was beginning to spill in from the north and the wind was picking up.

I walked back along the slipway, and then along a wet wall separating a deserted concrete paddling pool from the sea, to Knightstone, a rocky outcrop on which stood the decaying remains of what had once been Weston's most splendid attraction: a grand complex of theatre, dance hall and indoor swimming pool built towards the end of the nineteenth century. It is doubtful whether, even in its heyday, many would have regarded this neo-classical/imperial riot of pillars and porticoes and turrets as beautiful. But Knightstone did express, with great eloquence, a civic pride and confidence so long departed that no one – certainly not the successive local councils that have presided over Weston's apparently irreversible decline – can remember what they felt like.

On the Grand Pier, built in the 1930s in an endearingly brash art nouveau style and unique among the town's marine adornments for still being open and not falling into dereliction, the cacophony of fruit machines and daredevil driving games filled the amusement hall. I wasted several pounds feeding ten pence pieces into one of those seductive machines that deliver them down a chute on to a shining field of coins, overhung at the near end so that occasionally – very occasionally – a cataract of winnings collapses with a clatter into the receptacle below. Then I went and stood at the end of the pier. The tide, though advanced, was still well short of the metal legs. I looked down at the mud and wondered how many people, overcome by sadness at their own condition or that of their species or of

Weston-super-Mare, had let themselves topple over the railings. I wondered how far into the mud I would penetrate if I went in feet first. Would I be stuck, half in, half out, to await ignominious rescue? Or would I disappear, sucked down, the ooze closing silently over my head? I made for the station, feeling rather melancholic, though in good physical fettle, the ozone and iodine coursing through my veins.

In 1702 Charles Leigh, a physician at Lymm in Cheshire, was called to treat a most unusual and distressing case. A boy of thirteen, John Pownel, was speechless and wracked with convulsions so powerful that it required three people to lie on him so that the doctor could examine him. In a letter to the Royal Society, Leigh described the other symptoms: 'The jaws clashed together with that violence that several of his teeth were beaten out . . . There came a great foam from his mouth. He snarled, barked like a dog and howled like a hound . . . At other times he roared like a Bull, made a noise like a Hog, and sometimes that of a Gosling . . .'

The boy's family were convinced that he was possessed by demons. But Doctor Leigh, evidently a level-headed medical man, disagreed, and treated John with his usual remedies for 'distemper'. After six weeks, the boy's powers of speech returned and the dreadful convulsions lessened and then stopped. 'The boy,' reported Doctor Leigh to the learned men in London, 'is now very cheerful.'

Sixty years later the residents of the hamlet of Wattisham, between Ipswich and Bury St Edmunds, were disturbed and distressed by the shrieks of pain coming from the hovel of 'a poor labouring man' called John Downing. His eldest girl, aged fifteen, was suffering unendurable agonies in the calf of one leg.

Over the next few days every member of the family, with the exception of the father, was afflicted in the same way. The limbs blackened and then mortified, at which point the pain lessened. Two of the girls had legs amputated below the knee without suffering any discomfort. In one case 'the feet separated from the ankle without any assistance from the surgeon'. The baby died, its lower limbs quite black. Otherwise, the victims made complete recoveries, once they had shed the putrified parts. The vicar of Wattisham, the Reverend James Bones, reported that 'one poor boy . . . looked as healthy and florid as possible, and was sitting on the bed, quite jolly, drumming with his stumps.' As in the Cheshire case, the father was convinced that demons were to blame. Mr Bones recorded: 'The man is so possessed with notions of witchcraft that I cannot excite in him even a desire of attributing this disease to any other cause.'

In fact, neither the Devil nor the distemper diagnosed by the good Doctor Leigh were to blame, but the weather. The boy, John Pownel, and the wretched members of the Downing family, were victims of a form of poisoning known for centuries as *Ignis infernalis*, or St Anthony's Fire, which attacks the central nervous system and — in its gangrenous form — kills the tissue surrounding the bones. The poison is produced by an almost invisible parasitic fungus which, in very specific and unusual meteorological conditions, attacks the flowers of cereal crops, chiefly rye, causing cells to divide and enlarge into swollen nodules, or *sclerotia*, where the poison resides. The fungus is called ergot, hence the name by which the condition is known today, ergotism. It has always been much more prevalent on the Continent than in Britain, because rye is much more widely grown there, and there are many gruesome accounts in French history of whole villages being ravaged by poisoning accompanied by mass hallucinations and followed by gangrene and death. The most recent case occurred as late as 1951 in the small, one-bakery town of Pont St Esprit, on the confluence of the Ardèche and Rhône rivers, where most of the residents were suddenly afflicted by severe burning sensations in their legs, many of them hallucinating that they were flying. Ergotism remained common in eastern Europe until comparatively modern times, several outbreaks having been recorded in Russia during the twentieth century. Of the very few authenticated cases in Britain, the last appears to have been in Manchester in 1912 among Jewish immigrants from eastern Europe who bought their rye bread made from an infected crop grown in Yorkshire.

The first requisite for an outbreak of ergot fungus is a very wet and abnormally warm spring, to encourage the *sclerotia* to germinate. The crucial time is the flowering of the crop. The reason rye is much more susceptible than other cereals is that, unlike them, it depends on cross-fertilisation, and opens its glumes to receive pollen. Normally this stage lasts no more than a week, after which the glumes close. But if the warmth that encouraged the *sclerotia* to germinate is followed by a period of wet and cold, the flowering time can be extended, leaving the glumes much more vulnerable to infection. And if the weather then turns warm again, the growth of the *sclerotia* is nourished, and the toxicity of the poison enhanced.

Ergot poisoning is an exceptional example of a bizarre and terrible assault on the human body triggered by a particular combination of meteorological factors. The potato blight that precipitated the Great Hunger in Ireland owed much of its impact to the singular wetness of the autumn of 1846, and to the savagery of the winter that followed, which laid waste a people enfeebled by starvation. There have long been arguments about the supporting role played by the weather in the overwhelming catastrophe of the fourteenth century, the Black Death, with Hubert Lamb — among others — suggesting that massive floods in the Far East may have driven disease-bearing rats into a westerly migration. Certainly, the early writers regarded wet, warm springs as certain portents of plague. Thomas Short, writing of the arrival of the Black Death in Europe in 1347, referred to 'earthquakes, thunders, tempests etc . . . Chasms in the earth sent forth blood . . . in France blood gushed out of the graves of the dead . . . In England it rained from Christmas until mid-summer.'

'The south wind,' asserted John Worlidge, a popular seventeenth-century authority on husbandry and allied matters, 'is the worst for the bodies of men . . . It dejecteth the appetite, it bringeth pestilential diseases, increaseth rheums. Men are more dull and slow than at other times. The north wind makes men more cheerful and begets a better appetite for meat.' Worlidge shared with virtually all educated men and women the belief that the elements exercised a constant influence on mental and physical health. It went back a very long way — far beyond Aristotle, even — as did the efforts to understand it.

According to Frederick Sargent's study *The Hippocratic Heritage*, the idea that human beings were microcosms of the universe around them, and that their physical and mental states were determined by the forces loose within that universe, was first set down in a Chinese text of the third millennium BC, the *Nei Ching*. This provided the basis for Taoist teachings about the necessary harmony between humankind and the natural world, and the tension between Yang — with its qualities of sunshine, heat and dryness — and the murky cold and wet of Yin. The fundamental medical precept was this: 'The sage does not wait for men to become ill before caring for them.'

The Greeks came to similar conclusions. Hippocrates taught that good health was not merely the absence of illness, but a positive condition to be actively promoted so that people could carry out their social responsibilities. Ill health resulted when the balance between the four humours in the body – yellow bile, blood, phlegm and black bile – was disturbed as a consequence of alterations between the elements of fire, air, water and earth in the atmosphere. These disturbances were often linked with changes in the weather. But they could also be associated with different geographical locations. Thus people from 'the southern exposure' had poor appetites, and were prone to bowel trouble, intestinal disorders and fevers. Those facing east experienced disease less severely, and the women had less trouble in giving birth.

The relationship between organism and environment, and the effect of 'air' on health, were the fundamental concerns of Marcus Aurelius's Greek physician, Galen, whose mass of original treatises and commentaries on Hippocrates shaped medical orthodoxy in Europe between his own death in about AD 200, and the eighteenth century. The leading light among the medical men in London in Robert Hooke's day was Thomas Sydenham, a friend of Robert Boyle and John Locke, who became famous throughout Europe for his *Method of Curing Fever*, which he wrote after retreating from London with his family in the summer of the Great Plague.

Sydenham's methods were innovative and his understanding of disease was acute. He was one of the first to use so-called 'Peruvian Bark' – the *cinchona* from which quinine was later derived – as a treatment for malaria and gout. He introduced an effective cooling method for treating smallpox, and wrote accurate accounts of chorea and gout. But when it came to the causes of illness, Sydenham's approach was purely Hippocratic. He regarded exposure to cold as the single most important factor, because it closed the skin pores, resulting in the retention of harmful exhalations. Similarly, the heat of summer was to be avoided at all costs, since it served only to heat the blood to 'inordinate action and effervescence', with potentially disastrous consequences.

Robert Boyle himself had speculated about a direct connection between air pressure and health. He wrote that he was 'prone to suspect that the very Alterations of the Atmosphere in point of weight may in some cases have some not contemptible Operations even on men's Sickness or Health'. The notion of the body as a 'human barometer' was widely adopted by medical theorists, among them the Scottish-born physician and wit John Arbuthnot. Arbuthnot's reputation as a healer was made by a singular stroke of good fortune, which was that he happened to be attending the races at Epsom one summer afternoon in the early 1700s and was on hand when Queen Anne's husband, Prince George of Denmark, was suddenly taken ill. Having treated him successfully, Arbuthnot was appointed Physician Extraordinary to the Queen herself. He gained great favour at court, and became doctor, confidant and friend to a wide circle of literary men. Swift and Pope were devoted to him, and he wrote a great many satires, parodies and spoofs, including a pamplet in 1712 entitled *The Law is a Bottomless Pit; or, the History of John Bull*, which was intended as an assault on the foreign policy of the ruling Whigs.

Arbuthnot did not, as is frequently claimed, invent the persona of the 'typical Englishman', which was already current.

But the development of John Bull's peculiar qualities — his honesty, plain-speaking, choleric nature and tendency to quarrel, particularly 'if they pretended to govern him' — was Arbuthnot's work; as was the variability of Bull's mood 'which depended very much upon the air — his spirits rose and fell with the weather-glass'. Arbuthnot's serious, professional side was much taken up with this subject, and in 1733, two years before his death, he published his *Essay Concerning the Effects of Air on Human Bodies*. In it, he stated: 'I have observed very sensible Effects of sudden falls in the Mercury in the Barometer in tender people, all the symptoms they would have felt by the Exsuction of so much Air in an Air-pump.' Arbuthnot also observed that 'ladies and other tender people' were particularly at risk if they inhaled air 'tainted very much with the steams of Animals and Candles'.

Arbuthnot's younger medical contemporary Thomas Short claimed to have identified specific links between atmospheric pressure and disease. High pressure was associated with 'Quinzies, Pleurisies, Peripneumonies, ardent Fever', low pressure with 'Hysterics' and 'putrid, slow, nervous eruptive Fevers'. Other eminent medical practitioners of the day — including John Huxham of Plymouth and John Fothergill of London — maintained their voluminous weather journals with the express purpose of identifying connections between the weather and the condition of their patients. The most sustained attempt to organise these principles into a coherent whole was undertaken by a Dublin physician, Doctor John Rutty, and published in 1770 under the title *A Chronological History of the Weather and Seasons*.

Rutty was actually born in Wiltshire but went to Ireland as a young man and stayed there the rest of his life. For many years he kept what he called his 'spiritual diaries and soliloquies', in which he reflected at great length on his imperfections — the chief of which he considered his irritability and greed, and excessive fondness for the study of meteorology and the *materia medico*. The most important conclusion he drew from his extremely detailed chronology of ill health in Dublin between 1725 and 1766 was that more people die in dry weather than in wet. He was particularly wary of the effects of a cold, dry spring after a warm, damp winter – as in 1762 when 'catarrhs prevailed greatly to the end of March . . . various disorders of the lungs, pleurisies, pleuro-peripneumonies, pulmonary consumptions, coughs and quinzies greatly prevailed and often proved fatal . . . About the middle of May began in Dublin the catarrhal fever or feverish cold, scarcely sparing a family . . . Those who, after taking a puke, threw up much bile generally found great relief.'

Doctor Rutty's advice to 'valetudinarians . . . those of weak or distempered lungs . . . the asthmatic and consumptively disposed' has a familiar ring: 'Take special care NOT ONLY in the winter but MORE ESPECIALLY the spring season, whose north and easterly blasts are not less noxious to the lungs of such as they are to the tender rudiments of fruits; wherefore they ought studiously to counteract the pernicious effects of these blasts by GOOD FIRES, WARM CLOATHING, AND A PROPER REGIMEN.' He was a good advertisement for his own prescriptions, living until the ripe old age of seventy-seven. John Wesley visited him shortly before his death in 1775, and found him 'tottering over the grave, but still clear in his understanding, full of faith and love, and patiently waiting till his change should come'.

All these efforts to establish direct links between the state of the weather and the state of physical health achieved very little of practical use. Even today, this branch of medical science is not much further forward than it was when the *Nei Ching* was first set down; indeed the holistic approach of the ancient Chinese is only now finding echoes in the growth of 'alternative' treatments. We know little more than Doctors Rutty, Fothergill and Huxham knew: that extremes of cold, heat and damp are bad for those in a vulnerable condition. Old people in uncertain health without the means to keep themselves warm in cold weather die in large numbers. Old people in uncertain health without the means to keep themselves cool in sustained hot weather die in large numbers. People with bronchial and other chest problems suffer more when it is damp and chilly, as do those with arthritis.

The belief in connections between specific weather conditions and certain minor ailments is durable. Only this morning our cleaner arrived complaining about having a cold. I commiserated, whereupon she replied that it was her own fault 'because I went out without any socks on'. The notion that having cold feet makes you more vulnerable to the virus which causes the common cold stands alongside the myth that standing in the way of a draught from an open window is a sure way of 'catching a chill'. Both have more to do with superstition than science, but remain popular; even if another warning often delivered on dank, chilly winter days at my boarding school in Northamptonshire – that leaning against radiators stimulates an unhealthy loosening of the bowels – is perhaps heard less often today.

When it comes to the influence of the weather on our state of mind, we are pretty well united in agreement with the sentiment expressed by Montaigne more than four centuries ago:

The minds of men do in the weather share,
Dark or serene as the day's foul or fair.

Dr Johnson naturally dissented loudly from this attitude. He was just about able to understand the compulsion to talk about the weather, even if he was disdainful of it: 'The Englishman's notice of the weather is the natural consequence of the changeable skies and uncertain seasons . . . In our island every man goes to bed unable to guess whether he shall behold in the morning a bright or cloudy atmosphere; whether his rest shall be killed by a shower or broken by a tempest.' But for beings endowed with reason to allow their state of mind to be dictated by such inconstancy was, in Johnson's eyes, intolerable: 'Our dispositions too frequently change with the colour of the sky; and when we find ourselves cheerful and good-natured, we naturally pay our acknowledgments to the power of sunshine; or if we sink into dullness and peevishness, look around the horizon for an excuse and charge our discontent upon an easterly wind or a cloudy day.' This feebleness enraged him. 'To call upon the sun for peace and gaiety,' he fumed, 'to deprecate the clouds lest sorrow overwhelm us, is the cowardice of idleness and the idolatry of folly.'

Johnson urged reasonable men to see every day as bright, and every hour as 'propitious to diligence', and to struggle against 'the tyranny of the climate and refuse to enslave his virtue or his reason to the most variable of all variations, the changes of the weather'. But his command was a denial of human nature – not least his own, since Boswell observed of him that 'the effects of the weather . . . were very visible'. Like most of us, Johnson remained a creature of impulse and feeling, which is why the version of the relationship between our weather and our mood proposed by one of his favourite writers, Robert Burton, was and remains much more in tune with human nature than his own noisy fulminations.

Johnson said of Burton's *The Anatomy of Melancholy* that it was the only book he would get out of bed early to read. Of its eccentric and solitary author not a great deal is known. He was born in Leicestershire in 1577, schooled in Nuneaton and Sutton Coldfield and sent to Brasenose College, Oxford, and subsequently Christ Church. In 1616, by which time he was already immersed in his labours on *The Anatomy*, Burton was presented with the living at St Thomas's, on the west side of Oxford. The first edition of his great work appeared in 1621, and he continued to devote himself to revising and expanding it for later editions, the sixth of which was published shortly after his death in 1640. Burton died – as he had predicted many years before – on 25 January; the ungenerous Anthony Wood suggested he had 'sent up his soul to heav'n thro' a noose around his neck', in order to fulfil his own prophecy.

Burton's life was spent shut away among books, reflecting on human nature. *The Anatomy* – a vast bran tub of autobiography, soliloquy, self-analysis and speculation, larded by quotations from earlier poets, playwrights, historians, quacks, travellers and impostors – is organised into three sections, dealing with the causes and symptoms of melancholy, its cure and the two strands of amorous and religious melancholy. Among the causes, one had a special significance: 'Such is the Aire,' wrote Burton, 'such be our spirits: and as our spirits, such are our humours.' He quoted 'Bodine' – Jean Bodin – as the authority for identifying 'hote countries' as the most troubled with melancholy – which was why 'in Spaine, Africke and Asia Minor ... they are compelled in all cities of note to build peculiar hospitals for them'.

But even in the colder countries there was no escape. Burton identified the conditions most favoured by the melancholic mood: 'In a thicke and cloudy Aire (saith Lemmius), men are tetricke, sad and peevish: and if the westerne winds blow, and there be a calme or a faire sunshine day, it cheares up men and beastes: but if it be a turbulent, rough, cloudy, stormy weather, men are sad, lumpish and much dejected, angry, waspish, dull and melancholy.'

Inevitably, observers from continental Europe found an abundance of melancholy in Britain to correspond with the depressing condition of the skies. Merely to arrive at these shores was said to be enough to deprive the Frenchman of his *joie de vivre* and the Italian of his singing voice, while the German 'is depressed down below the suicidal point in the mental barometer but has not energy enough to lift a pistol to his head'. The Swiss authority on all matters English, Henry Meister, stated that 'constantly to look up to a sky obscured with cloud and vapour . . . disposes the mind to gloomy thoughts and melancholy ideas'. The Abbé Le Blanc, who visited England in the first half of the eighteenth century, claimed in all seriousness that there were English families which had not laughed for three generations.

Over the past century there have been more systematic attempts to identify links between mental health and meteorological and seasonal factors. Several studies have focused on the well-authenticated tendency for suicides to increase in the spring and summer, exploring on a statistical basis the proposition that variations in quantities of sunshine, rainfall or barometric pressure might trigger the self-destructive impulse. No firm conclusions have been reached, which may reflect a failure to take into account a more straightforward explanation

– that many people are gloomy in winter and cheer up in the spring, whereas truly self-destructive types do not, and thus feel more isolated than ever when the blossom appears and the nestlings take to the air. An analysis of suicides and murders in Switzerland showed a significant increase when the foehn – the warm, dry wind of the Alps – was blowing, which merely corroborated the advice given to Mercutio by Benvolio some centuries earlier:

> I pray thee, good Mercutio, let's retire.
> The day is hot, the Capulets abroad,
> And if we meet we shall not escape a brawl,
> For now, these hot days, is the mad blood stirring

Occasionally, earnest efforts to produce statistical backing for hypotheses had ludicrous results. Ellsworth Huntingdon, in a highly characteristic exercise, collected figures which showed a marked rise in the numbers of people visiting public libraries during storms. He speculated that this phenomenon was due to the 'psychologically energising' effect of falling pressure – in other words that people were inspired by a sudden surge in appetite for enlightenment, rather than a desire to get out of the rain. Similarly, an exhaustive analysis of motor accidents in Germany in the early 1950s purported to identify a firm link with electro-magnetic pulses associated with storms. The banal fact that driving becomes more hazardous when roads are wet appears not to have occurred to the researchers.

I suspect that most of us would accept the existence of a direct causal relationship between our weather and our mood. But, again, it has proved problematic to analyse the links and pin them down. And anyhow, without the means to fix the weather, what would be the use? Better to submit, to make the best of it; or, in Longfellow's words:

> Be still, sad heart, and cease repining;
> Behind the clouds is the sun still shining;
> The fate is the common fate of all,
> Into each life some rain must fall,
> Some days must be dark and dreary.

Chapter 9

Into Each Life

TWO-THIRDS OF THE WAY UP THE PATH LEADING TO THE WETTEST PLACE in England, I was puffing hard, acutely aware of protesting calf and thigh muscles, a little damp on the inside of my coat as a result of perspiring, but worryingly dry on the outside. One does not take considerable trouble to get to the wettest place in England in order to stay untouched by the stuff. I paused by the tumbling waters of Styhead Ghyll to catch my breath. Below, the fell side dropped down to the flat meadows at the head of Borrowdale, which stretches in the shape of a crooked finger due south from the bottom of Derwentwater. Squeezed between the hills is Seathwaite Farm, a cluster of whitewashed cottages under dark slate roofs, and grey stone barns under sheets of corrugated metal, surrounded by fields and livestock pens, with a stream running through which sustains a tiny trout farm.

To my right rose Green Gable, with the Great Gable ahead, still dabbed with snow on this late February day. Beyond, hidden, was the pass leading to Wastdale Head and the dark, stern depths of Wastwater. Somewhere over to the left were the crags of Scafell, obscured by the modest bulk of Seathwaite Fell in the foreground, and somewhere in the bowl between the Great Gable and Scafell was the wettest place in England. The forecast that morning had assured me that it would live up to its name. The barometer was dropping, a low-pressure system was bringing rain from the Atlantic across Ireland and the Irish Sea, heading for the Lake District. The sky looked full of promise: heavy grey cloud was marching purposefully over my head towards the north-east. But it was now early afternoon and I was still dry. I pressed on, thinking about the man whose trail I was following.

This had taken me, the day before, to the port of Whitehaven, which stands on that long, unprotected curve of coast pushed out into the Irish Sea by the clenched fist of the Lakeland mountains. With its straight streets of tall, stately Georgian houses, Whitehaven is a strikingly good looking place, but palpably down on its luck and uncertain what to do with itself. The spring of wealth that nourished its splendour ran dry a long time ago. At the harbour the fine stone Customs House faced a trashy metal and plastic octagon called The Hub. A little further along was a hideous building of concrete, glass and grimy panelled cladding, housing the Social Security offices. Beyond was a sturdy red sandstone block, once the public baths, now a desperate looking pub 'n' disco called The Park. On the morning of my stroll, there were a handful of small fishing boats tied up to the harbour wall, with fish boxes stacked among the strands of seaweed on the quayside. A rusted crane was frozen in movement, its grabber half lowered, swaying slightly between its chains. There was no sign at all of commercial activity.

How different it had been when Gilbert White's friend Thomas Pennant came this way to gather material for one of his popular travelogues. 'About a hundred years ago,' Pennant wrote in 1772, 'there was not one house here except for Sir John Lowther's and two others, and only three small vessels. At this time the town may boast of being one of the handsomest in the north of England, built of stone, and the streets pointing straight at the harbour with others crossing them at right angles. It is as populous as it is elegant, containing twelve thousand inhabitants, and has a hundred and ninety great ships belonging to it.'

The Lowther referred to by Pennant belonged to one branch of a great and ancient Westmorland dynasty, and it was he who – having secured grants of land from Charles II – built the harbour to transport the great coal deposits hidden within the bleak hinterland. By 1700 the Lowther pits were producing 27,000 tons of coal a year, and by the middle of the eighteenth century Whitehaven had established itself as one of the most important ports in the country. At about that time the mines came into the ownership of the head of the other main branch of the family, Sir James Lowther, later the first Earl of Lonsdale, known throughout the North-West and far beyond as the Bad Earl.

Few public figures have attracted such general dislike as Lonsdale. He was described by Alexander Carlyle – a leading Scottish Presbyterian and a great friend of Smollett – as 'more detested than any man alive, as a shameless political sharper, a domestic bashaw, and an intolerable tyrant over his tenants and dependants'. Boswell, whose attempts to ingratiate himself with Lonsdale brought him endless insults and humiliations – including the theft of his wig at Lowther Castle – termed the Earl 'a brutal fellow'. His gross manners and readiness to pick a quarrel were legendary, and were exhibited with equal lack of restraint in his public and private lives. Lonsdale's chief passion was politics – which, in his view, meant the winning of elections by any means and the deployment of his influence to cause as much mischief as possible. At one stage he had no fewer than nine of his placemen in Parliament – known as the

Ninepins — who represented constituencies from Cockermouth to Haslemere.

While Lonsdale was away causing trouble and making enemies, his power base on the windswept north-west coast prospered. Pennant was not alone in finding the spectacle of mineshafts sunk all around Whitehaven exciting and romantic. A local poet, James Eyre Weeks, enthused:

> Wher'e'er you look, on ev'ry side around,
> The coal-mines num'rous in the hills abound.
> There down the Pits descend the *human moles*
> And pick their passage thro' the Veiny Coals,
> Maintain thro' ev'ry obstacle their way,
> And force their entrance ev'n beneath the sea.

The moles dug and the town boomed. In his book *The Lakers*, Norman Nicholson wrote of those times that there was 'a stirring of the imagination, a new credulity, a sense of Cumberland as part of the greater world, a queer hope, too, that it might be a leader in that world'. The queer hope did not last, fading as the coal ran out. But its echo can still be half heard, blowing with the wind about Whitehaven's broad, straight streets.

John Fletcher Miller, the man who located the wettest place in England, was born in Whitehaven in 1816. His father was a well-to-do tanner and a Quaker, and the family lived at Number Seven, High Street, a double-fronted stone residence which faced south-west and offered from its upstairs windows an uninterrupted view of the harbour and its outer walls, the lighthouse on North Head, and the open sea across which the prevailing west and south-west winds blew. I have been unable to find out anything much about Miller's personal life, except that he hoped for a career in medicine but was prevented – presumably by delicate health – from pursuing it. It seems reasonable to guess that, as a boy, he watched the weather come in from the sea, and that his vantage point played its part in arousing what became a consuming meteorological passion.

The fruits of that passion are stored in the vaults of Whitehaven's Public Records Office: six weighty leather-bound volumes, each containing six hundred pages, each page divided into its columns, the columns crowded with readings and observations written in black ink in a sloping, flowing script of hypnotising evenness and precision; a silent and forgotten monument to an expenditure of time and effort so enormous as to challenge comprehension. These are the meteorological journals of John Fletcher Miller.

He began early. In November 1832, aged fifteen, he was already recording daily details of barometric pressure, temperature and rainfall on the left page, complemented by his observations on the right. His summary of January 1833 gives a taste of the boy's prose style: 'The barometer has, during the whole of this month, been unusually high and has not manifested any sudden variations; but with one exception, viz. on the 25th when the mercury fell nearly half-an-inch in 24 hours.'

Little by little, the scope of his project broadened. Miller began to include maximum and minimum thermometer readings as well as meteorological titbits from other parts of the country, and – at the end of each year – a lengthy analysis of the weather of the previous twelve months. He clearly shared the confidence of the age that, through the accumulation of statistics, light would one day be shone into the meteorological darkness around. He looked forward to a time 'when the weather may be portended to an almost mathematical certainty'; and in the meantime it was his mission to collect the data. By 1836 Miller was recording pressure and temperature three times a day and rainfall twice, and making observations on wind, cloud formation and the motions of the moon. In 1843 he ventured into print for the first time with his *Abstract from a Meteorological Journal Kept at Whitehaven for the Year 1842*. 'After a long series of wet years,' Miller wrote with the easy confidence of the expert, 'we have now to record one of a totally opposite character – a year memorable for its cloudless skies, its dry and balmy climate, the abundance of fruits of the earth and luxuriance of the whole vegetable creation.'

There is no reason to suppose Miller's little pamphlet attracted much attention either in Whitehaven or outside. But matters of great meteorological moment were afoot in the wider world, and the ambition of the young man to make his mark beyond his pleasant, balmy, breezy home town was stirring.

The process leading to rainfall starts when the water vapour within clouds is cooled to a point at which it condenses into droplets around specks of dust, pollen, sea salt and other microscopic particles. The droplets freeze into crystals which stick together as they collide until they are heavy enough to descend, melting as they do so; or coalesce into larger droplets which eventually form raindrops. The process is intricate and elusive, and it is only within the past seventy years that scientists have gained a proper understanding of the dynamics of clouds and precipitation. It is hardly surprising that the Victorians should have been content – in the words of the hymn 'We Plough The Fields And Scatter' – to count the 'soft, refreshing rain' among the 'good gifts . . . sent from Heaven above' and leave it at that. But the prevailing ignorance about how much of it fell on different parts of the kingdom is, perhaps, more puzzling.

Although Wren, with Hooke's assistance, had devised a workable, self-tipping rain gauge, no one at the Royal Society had the inclination or perseverance to make proper use of it. The first methodical rain measurer was the Lancastrian Richard Towneley whose ingenuity was so warmly praised by the great Robert Boyle when he presented his law on air pressure. Although Towneley was well known in scientific circles, as a Catholic he was barred from openly participating in scientific debate. As a result his activities were largely confined to his family seat, Towneley Hall, where, in 1677, he installed his rain gauge and embarked upon a record of measurements which lasted until 1704, three years before his death.

Towneley's gauge was an individual affair. According to his own description, published in the Royal Society's *Philosophical Transactions*, the rain was received into a tunnel 12 inches in diameter fixed into the roof of the north-east wing (which was demolished around the time of Towneley's death). From there it was fed downwards via a sealed lead pipe into vessels placed near Towneley's chamber, where it was weighed and converted into depth. The readings were communicated to William Derham in Upminster, who conflated them with his own for presentation to the Royal Society. The tables showed that, on average, roughly twice as much rain – 40 inches as against 20 – fell each year on to Towneley Hall as on to the rectory in Upminster. It was clear that Lancashire was wetter than Essex, but the rest was a mystery.

In 1769 William Heberden, a well-respected London physician with an enthusiasm for experimental science, reported to the Royal Society the results of a year-long study of rainfall in the capital. He had obtained three rain gauges, placing one on the ground outside his house in Pall Mall, another beside the highest chimney and the third on the roof of Westminster Abbey. Heberden informed the Society that the total rainfall on the Abbey was – at 12.099 inches – little more than half of that recorded at ground level in Pall Mall. Heberden himself was evidently flummoxed by what he termed 'this extraordinary difference'. 'What may be the cause,' he wrote, 'has not yet been discovered.' Gilbert White's friend Daines Barrington – an acquaintance of Heberden's – may have had his doubts, for he arranged to have two gauges placed on a mountainside in Wales, one 1300 feet higher than the other. Barrington found the rainfall measurements to be much the same. Even so, no one challenged Heberden. Nor does it seem to have occurred to anyone that there was a simple explanation as to why the top of Westminster Abbey should catch less rain, which had nothing whatever to do with the amount of the stuff coming down from the sky and everything to do with the exposure to greater windiness and dispersal.

Instead, it became an accepted truth that less rain fell on the tops of the hills than in the valleys, and great and ingenious were the efforts to provide a meteorological explanation for this phenomenon. One – still favoured when John Fletcher Miller went to work – was *The Theory of Rain*, written by a Scottish geologist, James Hutton. Hutton had been the first scientist to observe that the earth's crust was subject to a continuous process of decay and formation – 'I can,' he wrote, 'find no traces of a beginning, no prospect of an end,' which in the religious context of the age was both visionary and courageous. But his speculations about the origins of rainfall were not so firmly rooted in sound observation. Put as simply as possibly,

Hutton believed — guessed might be nearer the mark — that rain resulted from the mixing of saturated or nearly saturated air currents at different temperatures, and that since this mixing declined with height, it followed that the higher you were, the less the quantity of rain.

This misapprehension may seem laughable to us, but it is no more so than the various explanations in vogue at the time of what rain was and how it was made. All that anyone knew for sure was that it was wet and came from the clouds. But how was it — just to take the first, baffling riddle — that water, which was heavier than air, could be suspended within air? Aristotle suggested that the droplets were held up in the same way that specks of dust floated on the surface of water, although he was vague about whatever it was that persuaded them to descend. One theory, popular in the seventeenth and eighteenth centuries, was that vapour consisted of droplets of water filled with fire, which ascended through the air until they reached a height where their specific gravities were equal, at which point they stopped. An alternative was that the droplets contained tiny bubbles of air which enabled them to remain aloft. These were known as vesicles, and Upminster's rain man, William Derham, asserted in a series of lectures delivered in 1711–2 that he had observed them through a microscope 'as they swim about in the rays of the sun'. Support for the vesicle theory came seventy years later from a Swiss physicist, Horace Bénédict de Saussure, who stated that — while investigating the rainfall question in the Alps — he had observed the minute bubbles burst against a piece of black card.

Hutton and Saussure were subjected to violent verbal assault by another Swiss scientist, Jean André deLuc. DeLuc had acquired a lofty reputation as a geologist on the Continent, before coming to settle in England in 1770 following the failure of his family business. He secured a position as scientific adviser to George III's wife, Queen Charlotte, and since she had no perceptible interest in science this left him free to pursue his great purpose in life, which was to reconcile his geological findings with the account of the Creation in Genesis. But deLuc was a man of formidable energy, and he had plenty left to advocate his own unshakeable belief in the 'water and fire' theory of rain. In his thousand-page epic, *Idées sur la météorologie*, deLuc maintained that he had not merely proved the theory to be true, but had discovered that that vapour had the ability to hide itself in the atmosphere disguised as a 'gaseous fluid', ready to resume its watery form to produce rain. He is characterised in W. E. Knowles Middleton's exhaustive *A History of the Theories of Rain* as 'a formidable controversialist' equipped with 'remarkable powers of self-deception'.

Occasionally a shaft of sound sense penetrated the fog of theoretical muddle. In 1686 the astonishingly brilliant and versatile Edmund Halley presented a paper to the Royal Society in which he referred to vapours descending 'towards the earth and in their fall meeting with other aqueous particles, they incorporate together and form little drops of rain'. In the middle of the eighteenth century, Benjamin Franklin, who, as well as helping write the Declaration of Independence, was America's first true meteorologist and the first man to achieve a proper understanding of electricity – described how 'where there is great heat on the land . . . the lower air is rarefied and rises', even though his further deduction, 'that the colder, denser air above descends', is faulty. Another glimpse came not long afterwards from an Irish natural philosopher, Hugh Hamilton – later Bishop of Ossory – who suggested that air acquired vapour by 'rubbing against water and dissolving into itself those particles with which it is in contact'.

But no one was able to come up with a coherent account of rainfall which could both overcome the ignorance about how much fell and where, and accommodate the assumption that it decreased with elevation. The trouble was that well-intentioned observers kept coming up with more evidence to bolster the fallacy. One was John Gough, the celebrated sightless sage of Kendal. Gough was blinded by smallpox at the age of three, but trained himself through his sense of touch to become a formidable mathematician as well as one of the foremost botanists of the age. He was a friend of Wordsworth and was introduced to Coleridge, who found him 'amiable and estimable' and reported that 'the rapidity of his touch appears fully equal to that of sight, and the accuracy greater'. One of Gough's many interests was the weather of his native Lake District, and he had two rain gauges, one set in his garden and the other well up the nearest hillside. He reported that the higher received significantly less rain than the lower, which confirmed his faith in Hutton's theory.

Among Gough's disciples in Kendal was a young Quaker of exceptionally sober character, John Dalton. Years later Dalton was to gain an international reputation as the discoverer of the atomic nature of matter, but his first scientific calling was to meteorology. Encouraged by Gough, he began keeping a journal of the weather which he maintained until the day before his death at the age of seventy-eight. In 1793 Dalton, then aged twenty-seven, accepted the professorship of mathematics and natural history at New College, Manchester, where he spent the rest of his life and was a familiar figure in his Quaker uniform of black knee-breeches, black tunic, grey stockings and buckled shoes. Dalton never married, did not approve of reading for its own sake and had no amusement beyond a game of bowls every Thursday afternoon outside the Dog and Partridge, and an annual walking holiday in his beloved Lake District.

In the same year he arrived in Manchester, Dalton published his *Meteorological Essays*, which included an account of the behaviour of water vapour and the phenomenon of condensation much nearer the mark than Hutton's. But even though he realised that moist air currents were pushed upwards by mountains, and that condensation then occurred, Dalton did not follow through his observations to challenge the belief in rainfall decreasing with elevation. Indeed, he produced readings from his own rain gauges in Manchester – one on the ground and the other on top of a nearby church – which appeared to confirm it, and as late as 1819 was still proclaiming his loyalty to Hutton's theory of rain.

Against this background there was some surprise at the Royal Society in London when news reached them from distant Westmorland that in the course of 1836 a Mr Beck, resident near Esthwaite Water, had measured 50 per cent more rain in his garden than that recorded at Kendal, which was only ten miles away but considerably lower. This deepened to something like disquiet seven years later, when a Mr Jefferies announced that no less than 90 inches of rain had fallen on to his garden in Grasmere, a quantity four times greater than that in London, and far in excess of anything recorded before. John Fletcher Miller noted that the Grasmere figures 'were received with astonishment by meteorologists, not unaccompanied by some degree of suspicion as to their correctness. Indeed, it was with a view of removing all doubt in the matter that in the year 1844 I was induced to begin the present series of experiments.'

The experiments Miller had in mind represented a formidable undertaking. His daily commitments in Whitehaven already extended to multiple readings of barometer, thermometer, anenometer, hygrometer, evaporation gauge and rain gauge. But he had come to realise that the weather of Whitehaven, fascinating though it was to him, could reveal little about the great mystery of rainfall. The key to that lay in the cloud-shrouded hills to the east. During the summer of 1844 Miller established rain gauges at various locations in the Lake District, including Buttermere, Ennerdale, Loweswater, Grasmere and Wastdale Head, at the head of Wastwater. In October he installed gauges at Keswick and Cockermouth; and a little later he rode his horse up the path along Borrowdale to the hamlet of Seathwaite and placed a 5-inch gauge in the ground beneath the gaze of Scafell and the Great Gable.

Miller relied on a network of volunteers to take the regular readings on which the whole exercise depended. The name of only one is recorded: John Dixon, curator of the celebrated Seathwaite gauge. He was one of a long line of Dixons who – for 150 years and more – managed the mine at Seatoller from which the finest quality graphite in England was dug. This mine, about halfway along Borrowdale, was opened in Elizabeth I's time and was so valuable that the graphite was transported to London in a six-horse waggon under armed guard, while the entrance to the mine itself was watched day and night by men with guns.

At the end of 1845 Miller received extraordinary tidings from Mr Dixon. It had been a wet year. Nearly 50 inches of rain had fallen on Whitehaven (though no more than 33 of them were recorded in Miller's gauge 78 feet up on the steeple of St James's Church). Keswick had reported 62, Crummockwater 87,

Grasmere a splendid 121 and Gatesgarth 124. But the gauge at Seathwaite eclipsed them all, with 151.87 inches of rain, of which almost 25 inches — equal to London's annual average — fell in December alone. Such amounts were unheard of, undreamed of. More than 100 inches of rain? This was England, not Madras or Java.

Miller realised he was on to something important. More and more columns sprouted across the pages of his journal to accommodate the swelling stream of statistics. He published the collated results for 1845 in Whitehaven, and sent them to the *Edinburgh Philosophical Review*. Interest, mixed with scepticism, stirred in London. In March 1848, at the request of the Royal Society, Miller completed his paper *On the Meteorology of the Lake District of Cumberland and Westmorland, with the Results of Experiments in the Fall of Rain at Various Heights*, which was read to the Society that May. As it turned out, 1848 — the year of revolution across Europe — was even more excitingly watery than 1845. Almost 161 inches of rain fell at Seathwaite, 30.55 of them in February — 'by far the largest amount ever measured in any month in this country', noted the proud Miller.

By now he had more than a score of rain gauges dotted around the North-West. His volunteers did the daily checks but Miller himself regularly inspected his instruments, on one occasion completing a seventy-mile round trip from Whitehaven, on horseback through the wildest country, to ensure they were working properly. There were hazards, too. In his 1850 paper for the Royal Society, Miller wrote:

In severe winters . . . I find it difficult to get parties to attend to these instruments for almost any pecuniary recompense; indeed, so great is the risk of fractured limbs, and the sacrifice of life itself, that even the hardy shepherds shrink from the task of ascending such elevated and rugged peaks as Sca Fell Pike and the Gabel . . . On the 31ˢᵗ January, as the person who has charge of the gauges was ascending the Gabel with two large, empty copper receivers fastened together, his foot slipped and he slided down the precipice, a distance of several hundred yards.

Miller's man escaped serious injury, but the gauges were 'literally dashed to pieces'.

Despite the odd mishap, Miller pursued his great enterprise with unwavering determination. And now an even greater prize beckoned. Mr Dixon had told him that there were occasions when Seathwaite itself was dry, while the rain was bucketing down on higher ground not far away. Miller soon had a gauge in place. The results were, by meteorological standards, sensational. 'The most interesting and important circumstance connected with the experiments of 1850,' he reported to the Royal Society, 'is the discovery of a mountain station which promises to yield nearly one-third more rain than the celebrated hamlet of Seathwaite . . . hitherto, and with good reason, considered to be the wettest spot in Great Britain. The new station is about a mile-and-a-half distant from Seathwaite in a south-westerly direction and 580 feet above it . . . it is on the shoulder of Sprinkling Fell, or The Stye, about 100 yards south of the road leading over the Stye Pass to Wastdale.'

Miller could not be exact as to how much rain had fallen on his new favourite place because the gauge had only been put in position at the end of January, and had overflowed four times. The amount measured for the eleven months was 174 inches, and he calculated an annual total of 190 inches – as against 144 for Seathwaite. Miller further estimated that during the year of deluges – 1848 – Stye Head would have collected 211.62 inches. There was, he enthused, no other place in the land to match it for wetness.

The tanner's son from Whitehaven had proved his case, and the mutters from the sceptics were silenced. Miller continued his inquiry for another three years, but the additional data merely confirmed what he had already demonstrated. In the spring of 1854 he finished preparing the last of his meteorological papers for publication. Running to almost thirty large pages, and crammed with tables recording every drop of rain collected in his gauges for three years, it amounted to little more than a reiteration of his earlier work; and, indeed, Miller stated in the first paragraph that the investigation had been brought to a close at the end of 1853 'when its main objects were considered to have been satisfactorily answered and attained'. The paper eventually appeared, not in the journal of the Royal Society of London, which may have grown weary of the statistical torrent flowing from the north-west, but in that of the Royal Society of Edinburgh. By the time it did so, in 1857, its author was dead.

Miller was only forty. The cause of his death is not recorded, but it is tempting to speculate that his exertions in the Lake District may have had something to do with it. Certainly the journals hint at a drastic decline in energy or interest, or both. Through 1854 the entries become increasingly sparse, and although the columns for 1855 were ruled, and the headings written, the pages are otherwise blank. It may well be that, after completing his great endeavour, Miller found that he had tired of the duty of recording Whitehaven's pleasant but unexceptional climate.

A great endeavour it had certainly been. For Miller there was no difficulty in answering the question thrown through the ages by condescending outsiders at train-spotters, plane-spotters, weather nuts and other amateur accumulators of statistical information. 'I am often asked by persons unacquainted with such matters,' he wrote, 'what beneficial end I expect such a series of experiments to lead to, and what information I have gained in return for my time and trouble. To this question, I may reply that they have shown us that at least sixty more inches of rain is deposited in England than we were previously aware of; that 150 inches sometimes descends on the Lake District in a year, more than falls in most parts of the tropics with which we are acquainted, and sufficient to drown standing two of the tallest men in England, one on top of the other.'

Moreover, Miller had demolished the nonsense that the hill-tops were drier than the lowlands, and had illuminated another wholly unappreciated facet of the mystery: the extraordinary disparities in the amounts of rain falling on places very close to each other. What he was not equipped to do was make sense of what he had found. He had stumbled upon the critical clue, which was the interaction between moisture-bearing clouds and very particular, localised geographical features. But rather than search out an explanation, Miller retreated into conventional piety:

I am unable to offer any satisfactory reason for the great excess of rain at Seathwaite over all the other valleys; judging from its position, I should, *a priori*, have looked for the greatest fall at Wastdale Head, as it is surrounded by the highest mountains and the valley opens out fairly to the south-west. But the maximum quantity is found to obtain, not where theory would indicate, but in the identical spot where it is most required – the Vale of Borrowdale, which affords the principal supply of water to the extensive and

207

picturesque lakes of Derwent and Bassenthwaite; thus adding one more to the multitudinous instances which surround us, of the wonderful adaptation of external nature to the physical wants and requirements of man.

I continued to think about Miller and his quest as I resumed my trudge up the path towards Styhead. How many times must he have come this way, stopping to get the latest news from Mr Dixon at the graphite mine, before tethering his horse below and scrambling up beside the foaming brown waters of the ghyll, excitement tugging at his heart at the thought of the marvels that might be revealed by the copper container in the boggy wastes above? The gradient flattened and the going became easier. I looked ahead, hoping to see the little tarn beyond which the path curves right towards Wastdale. My plan was to stand as close as I could to where Miller's top-scoring gauge had been installed, then to cut south-east to Sprinkling Tarn, where he had another, and then around the lump of Seathwaite Fell to strike north back to the farm. Alas for plans!

The weather remained extremely dark and threatening. Then I became aware of a speckling of moisture on the lenses of my glasses. Ahead, nothing much had changed. The Great Gable was as before, Scafell was just showing its head. There was still no sign of the tarn. Then everything disappeared behind a curtain of rain. The wind struck at the same time, rattling my spectacle frames on the bridge of my nose. The water, blown horizontally, stung my face. In my enthusiasm for standing in the footsteps of John Fletcher Miller, I had temporarily forgotten how unpleasant rain in February usually is. Now I was reminded. I put my head down, hitched up my trousers and forced myself forwards into the downpour. The trousers, a pair of heavy corduroys, rapidly became saturated and developed an annoying habit of slipping down over my hips, requiring me to stop every few yards and lift my coat to pull them up. My boots, which were not at all waterproof, squelched dispiritingly with each step, and produced amusing gouts of water through the lace holes.

Blinded and sodden, I plodded on for a while until I spotted a jumble of big granite rocks ahead which promised some shelter. Already huddled in their lee was a party of proper walkers in proper waterproofs with proper maps sensibly protected inside plastic wallets. With them was a bedraggled terrier. I asked them where they were heading. 'Wastdale' one shouted cheerily over the din of the gale. I asked how far that was. Only a couple of hours, another said casually. They left, and within twenty yards had vanished into the rain. That made me think. With visibility almost nil, what were the chances of my reaching my objective and knowing that I had done so? Low, came the answer. And what were the chances of my becoming entirely lost, and being left to wander around in circles while the current gloom deepened into full darkness? Correspondingly high, came the answer.

A little (but not very) ashamed of myself, I turned back. With the wind and the rain now thrusting me along, I made good progress, interrupted only by the frequent halts to attend to my sagging corduroys. Once I got below the lip of the bowl leading to the pass, the wind dropped and the rain, instead of flying horizontally, resumed the more conventional practice of falling vertically. Below me, Borrowdale revealed itself in classic Lakeland dress, the grey rain cloud pressing down on the dark roofs of the barns and the cottages, the sheep, still and dripping in the meadows, the air filled with a soft hissing.

That evening, as I toasted myself before the fire at the Shepherds Inn at Melmerby, below the great bulk of Crossfell, awaiting my steak and chips 'wi' a' t'trimmings', the rain still beat down outside. It was a night that the man whose mission had brought me here would have relished.

Miller's rain gauge at Seathwaite did not perish with him. For a time after his death the faithful John Dixon continued to take the measurements, and in 1863 Miller's nephew, Isaac Fletcher, arranged for several new gauges to be installed about the place. In time, the care of the Seathwaite weather station was absorbed into a much larger enterprise, set up and led by a man in the grip of a weather obsession quite as powerful as John Fletcher Miller's, and with an even keener appetite for accumulating statistical data.

Even as a boy, George James Symons' ruling passion was the weather. In 1860, at the age of twenty-two, he got a job in the new meteorological department set up within the Board of Trade, but he resigned three years later to devote himself to what had started as an extension of his boyhood hobby – the collection and collation of information about rainfall. Symons' first published compilation was *English Rainfall 1860*, which was succeeded by the more ambitious *British Rainfall 1861*. By then he was receiving readings from more than five hundred volunteers. Unwittingly, Symons had tapped into a spring of pure enthusiasm which – once opened – gushed stronger and stronger. Year by year, more and more rain-watchers enlisted, so that by 1885 he was able to state, without any exaggeration, that 'there is scarcely a spot in the British Isles from which, were I suddenly dropped from a balloon, I should not be within walking distance of one of my correspondents'. Symons turned himself into a one-man production line of weather facts. Apart from the appearance each year of his grand compilation, he published *Symons' Monthly Meteorological Magazine* and contributed a steady flow of papers to learned journals – the last of which, on the Wiltshire Whirlwind of 1 October 1889, was read to the Royal Meteorological Society in May 1900, two months after his death. By then his volunteer army numbered over three thousand, and the crusade went on. For another twenty years *British Rainfall* continued to be produced from Symons' house in Camden Square, London, until it was eventually taken over by the Meteorological Office.

Comparatively early on Symons achieved his primary objective, which was to create a firm statistical basis for understanding patterns of rainfall across the country. The pressing questions were answered: it rained more in the west than in the east, more in the north than in the south, more in late summer, autumn and winter than in spring and early summer. Thereafter the accumulation of facts became an end in itself, a source, no doubt, of satisfaction to the accumulators themselves and of interest to other enthusiasts, but of limited use in a scientific context.

Symons himself made no grand claims for his work, expressing the modest hope that it 'might serve the development of agriculture, sanitation and the water supply'. The fact was that he – in common with many before him and since – simply loved the weather for itself, and cherished information about it for information's sake. There was no great goal, no high ambition – just the innocent enjoyment of an inexhaustible subject. Symons must surely have pondered the great mystery of rain, how it was made. But he does not seem to have felt any compulsion to join the ranks of the theorists. Perhaps he enjoyed himself so much bringing in the harvest of facts that he did not worry over much about the meaning of it all. Perhaps, being a modest man, he realised that the task of explanation was beyond him. Perhaps he even recognised that it was beyond the capability of his age altogether. For, although the study of the weather became a serious business in the course of his lifetime, the great objective of reliable prediction remained remarkably elusive.

Chapter 10

The Dancing of Atoms

JOHN FLETCHER MILLER — LIKE HALLEY, FRANKLIN AND DALTON — HAD glimpsed one facet of the behaviour of clouds. That was meteorology's problem: it advanced piecemeal, one isolated discovery at a time. Well into the nineteenth century it remained something far removed from a scientific discipline. It was, instead, a vast stockpile of more or less reliable data which had never been organised according to the principles of rigorous inquiry and which was kept company by a sackful of speculations, the sensible hopelessly jumbled up with the nonsensical, and almost none of them verified or capable of being verified. Because there was no discipline of meteorology, there were no true meteorologists in the sense of trained and qualified men working from a foundation of tested knowledge and principles. There were just enthusiasts, pursuing their enthusiasm in isolation, unrestrained in their theorising except by the limits of their imaginations.

Pitmaston is a district of the city of Worcester chiefly associated with two unusual and distinctive varieties of apple. The Pitmaston Pine Apple and the Pitmaston Russet Nonpareil were both displayed for the first time at an exhibition organised by the London Horticultural Society in the early nineteenth century. The grower was a Mr John Williams, of Pitmaston

House. In 1806 a book called *The British Climate* was published, its author a Mr John Williams, of whom no personal details are revealed beyond that he came from 'Pitmaston, Worcestershire'. It may be that there were two John Williamses of Pitmaston venturing into the public arena at the time; or, as I prefer to think, that there was but one John Williams, pomologist and meteorologist.

The title of *The British Climate* is reassuring, promising a solid, sober, factual account of the wonder of our weather. Its opening premise was that in the thirty years after 1770 summers had become significantly wetter than before, and the records suggest that this was, indeed, the case. But the explanation offered by Pitmaston's weather-watcher was curious. It lay, Williams stated authoritatively, in the 'great power which vegetables have in depriving floating vapour of its electricity'. He continued: 'From the first dawning of spring, when the grass starts, till the autumnal frosts prevail, our highly manured pastures are constantly exhaling a large portion of vapour; and this vapour is much deprived of its electricity; consequently the sun has less power in dissolving it into transparent air.' This dangerous exhalation of vapour had greatly increased of late because of '. . . the enclosing of the open fields and wastes; the multifarious intersections of them with fences, especially with hawthorn, the increased luxuriance of our crops; the late increase in pasturage . . . the numerous plantations, more especially of foreign trees and such whose exhaling power is prodigiously great, and the immense bodies of nearly stagnated water in the numerous canals that have been cut within the assigned period'.

John Williams was not a man to wring his hands over a looming crisis without having a ready solution to hand. The measures he urged were extreme, beginning with the felling of all unnecessary trees and the removal of all hedges; or, if that turned out to be impractical, the replacement of hawthorn with holly, which exhaled much less of the pernicious vapour. To support this strategy, he called for the construction in all parts of the kingdom of large buildings equipped with 'cylinders or plates of glass filled up with rubbers etc for exciting electricity', so that the recharged vapour might dissolve itself as in the old days, instead of falling as rain and ruining the summers.

Williams was certainly ahead of his time in grappling with the great issue of climate change. Other dedicated amateur weather-watchers preferred to remain in the quiet tradition of Thomas Barker and Gilbert White, and more often than not their records of observations and measurements stayed out of the public domain. One that did achieve publication was the modestly titled *Observations on Meteorology*, published in 1858, and written by Leonard Jenyns, an interesting and attractive member of that now long extinct breed, the clergyman/amateur scientist.

Jenyns was born in 1800, the grandson of the same Dr Heberden whose interest in rainfall had innocently sown the seeds of so much misunderstanding. Always intended for holy orders, he went to Eton and then Cambridge, where a shared passion for natural history brought him the friendship of Charles Darwin. A few years later, on the strength of his researches into botany, ornithology and zoology, Jenyns was offered the position of naturalist to the *Beagle* expedition. By then vicar of St Mary's, Swaffham Bulbeck, in the flatlands of Cambridgeshire, he felt unable to accept, but warmly recommended his friend Darwin in his place. Subsequently, at Darwin's request, he edited the volume of the *Beagle* papers dealing with fish. Jenyns also wrote a *Manual of British Vertebrate Animals*, and an enormous number of contributions to various scientific periodicals. His hero was Gilbert White; as a boy he had copied out the whole of *The Natural History of Selborne*, and at the age of ninety-one he read a paper to the Gilbert White Society entitled *Records of a Rookery*.

For all Leonard Jenyns' scholarship and his status – according to the *Dictionary of National Biography* – as 'the patriarch of natural history studies in Great Britain', it is difficult to imagine that anyone who did not have a keen interest in what the weather was like in east Cambridgeshire between 1820 and 1849 can have got much pleasure or benefit from his *Observations on Meteorology*. He introduced its four hundred pages as 'simply an attempt to give a general character of the weather and its seasons in that part of England in which the observations have been made and to point out the ordinary conditions under which weather changes take place'. Much of it consists of entries from his journal – such as this, for 31 October 1838: 'Steady rain with N. Wind from before sunrise until after 3pm. Sky then clearing and stratus beginning to form. Soon afterwards the temperature, which had risen to 44-and-a-half during the day, falling to 35 degrees at sunset and the air very chilly. Fine and clear throughout the evening but sensibly warmer three hours after sunset and the thermometer risen to 38-and-a-half.'

Occasionally the tempo is raised. There is a lively account of a thunderstorm on 9 August 1843 during which 'the straw was chopped to pieces by hailstones as big as pullet eggs'; and an interesting, though uncorroborated, report of a white ox losing its spots as a result of being struck by lightning. Overall, however, the book is trivial, parochial and pointless, as well as being as dull as the water in a Cambridgeshire ditch. Neither it, nor the implausible speculations of the Pitmaston apple-grower, have any scientific value whatever, beyond illustrating the condition of meteorology at the time. There was no intelligent understanding of how the weather worked, while the prospect of reliable weather forecasting seemed as distant as when the Venerable Bede had stated that dolphins jumping in the sea was a sure sign of a gale to come.

But it is also fair to say that between the appearance of the two books the mood of the times had changed. A breakthrough came with the foundation in 1831 of the British Association for the Advancement of Science. This was stimulated by a growing impatience among a new generation of clever, serious and public-spirited men of science with what they saw as the elitism, lethargy and amateurishness of the Royal Society. Among the pioneers were two Scotsmen of high-minded and severe disposition — David Brewster, famous for his investigation of polarised light and for the invention of the kaleidoscope, and his much younger friend and colleague, James David Forbes. Forbes, who was born in 1809, was a man of exceptional and precocious brilliance whose early work in physics had won him election to the Royal Society of Edinburgh when he was only nineteen. His chief claim to lasting renown came from his studies of the movement of glaciers, but climate was a competing interest. In the first full year of the British Association's existence, Forbes presented to it a report on 'the infant science of meteorology', which rang loud with a young man's impatience and intolerance:

As few persons have devoted their whole attention to this science alone, or the whole exertions they *did* bestow, to one branch of so wide a field — no wonder that we find strewed over its irregular and far-spread surface, patches of cultivation upon spots chosen without discrimination and treated in no common principle, which defy the improver to inclose and the surveyor to estimate or connect them . . . Meteorological instruments have been for the most part treated like toys, and much time and labour have been lost in making and recording observations utterly useless for any scientific purpose.

Not long afterwards, much the same sentiment was expressed more charitably – as well as in more expansive language – by another revolutionary in a hurry. To John Ruskin, the treatment of the weather was fundamental to the aesthetic of landscape painting, and he retained a close practical interest in meteorology throughout his life. In 1838 he contributed a paper to the newly formed Meteorological Society in which he identified with great accuracy the defective condition of the science:

A Galileo or a Newton, by the unassisted working of his solitary mind, may discover the secrets of the heavens and form a new system of astronomy. A Davy in his lonely meditations on the crags of Cornwall or in his solitary laboratory might discover the most sublime mysteries of nature, and trace out the most intricate combination of her elements. But the meteorologist is impotent if alone; his observations are useless, for they are made upon a point, while the speculations to be derived from them must be in space . . . It is of no avail that he changes his position, ignorant of what is passing behind him and before; he desires to estimate the movements of space and can only observe the dancing of atoms; he would calculate the currents of the atmosphere of the world, while he only knows the direction of a breeze.

Ruskin saw that there was only one way in which this amateur's pastime could mature into a legitimate branch of science. There had to be a great pooling of effort and knowledge, a coming together of the enthusiasts and the evangelists to form one 'multitudinous Power . . . which will be capable of solving the most deeply hidden problems of Nature . . . and reducing to principle and order the vast multitude of beautiful and wonderful phenomena, by which the wisdom and benevolence of the Supreme Deity regulates the course of the times and seasons, robes the globe with verdure and fruitfulness, and adapts it to minister to the wants and contribute to the felicity of the innumerable tribes of animated existence'.

Ruskin's eloquence appeared to invest his programme with visionary quality. But, in fact, he was signalling the end of the age of the gentleman virtuoso and the dawn of the age of the professional meteorologist. Although Ruskin envisaged an essential role for the gatherers of data, it was a subservient one. The task of organising the harvest of their labours must be undertaken centrally, by men qualified by the strictest scientific training. The volunteers – as Ruskin characterised them, the pastor on the Alps, the voyager on the surface of the sea, the solitary dweller on the American prairies – must be encouraged to persist in their drudgery but dissuaded from obscuring the pure air with their useless speculations.

There was one essential, practical condition for the great cooperative enterprise to succeed. Ruskin referred to it obliquely: 'It was necessary that the individuals should think, observe and act simultaneously though separated from each other.' A fundamental truth was gradually revealing itself: our weather was not ours at all, it merely belonged temporarily to our part of the planet and the atmosphere above it. It was born far out over the oceans and distant lands and moved along great paths, organising and reorganising itself as it went. The weather in Cambridgeshire one afternoon had been born of the weather in Cornwall, Cumberland or Copenhagen that morning. It was becoming clear that to work out what 'our' weather was up to, it was necessary to track it along its paths; and that the only way to do this was to have access to information gathered along those paths, and for that information to travel faster than the weather itself. The invention by Samuel Morse of the electronic telegraph made this possible.

By 1840 Morse's telegraph had matured into a workable system for rapid communication. Its potential in weather forecasting was recognised by a young scientist working at the Royal Observatory, James Glaisher. He had been recruited by the Astronomer Royal, Professor (later Sir) George Airy, a formidable specimen of the emerging breed of professional scientist, and put by him in charge of a new magnetic and meteorological department. By 1848 Glaisher had recruited a network of sixty volunteers — mostly doctors and clergymen — to record temperature, pressure and other weather observations, and to telegraph them to him. These observations were made at nine o'clock each morning, and used to compile a national weather report which was published in the next morning's *Daily News*. On 8 August 1851 visitors to the Great Exhibition at the Crystal Palace were able to buy the first weather charts, composed by Glaisher to show wind direction, barometric pressure and the general conditions at each of his stations.

What he did not attempt — knowing full well the limitations of his project — was forecasting. But the pressure in this direction was growing, as a result of the enormous expansion in commercial ocean traffic, particularly between the United States and Europe, and the need to protect valuable trading vessels from storms and to speed their passage. An American naval officer, Matthew Maury, had begun publishing charts of Atlantic winds and currents, and in 1853 he organised an international conference in Brussels at which the ten leading maritime nations agreed on common standards for weather observations. In Britain, the Board of Trade decided to establish a meteorological department to put the Brussels agreement into effect. A fateful choice was made when Vice Admiral Robert FitzRoy was approached to become its first head.

FitzRoy was then forty-nine, with an extraordinary and turbulent career of public service behind him. Descended on his paternal side from that Duke of Grafton whose nuptials John Evelyn had witnessed a few miles from the Travelling Sands of Santon Downham, and on his mother's side from the first Marquis of Londonderry, he was an English aristocrat to the marrow of his bones: autocratic, arrogant, highly strung, intensely religious and extremely touchy. He went to sea at the age of fourteen, was made lieutenant at twenty, and in 1828 – when he was twenty-three – was appointed to the command of the survey ship *Beagle*, then charting the coasts of Patagonia and Tierra del Fuego.

In December 1831 the *Beagle* left Portsmouth at the start of a five-year voyage, with FitzRoy in command and Charles Darwin as official naturalist. FitzRoy's temperament, clouded by his obsession with duty and recurrent fears for his own sanity, made him an uncomfortable mess table companion. Years later Darwin wrote of him: 'I never in my life knew so mixed a character. I once loved him sincerely; but so bad a temper and so given to take offence that I gradually quite lost my love . . . But certainly there was much noble and exalted in his character.'

FitzRoy brought all his high-mindedness, high-handedness, passion, moral conviction and prodigious capacity for hard work to his position at the Board of Trade. He rapidly became convinced that it was his destiny to ride to the rescue of the Royal Navy and the merchant fleet by developing a reliable system of weather forecasting. His first initiative was to commission new and accurate instruments of measurement, write a detailed manual of instruction on how to use them and have them distributed to ships' captains. In October 1859 the whole country was shaken by the news that the *Royal Charter*, one of the new generation of fast ironclad steamships, had been driven by a storm on to the rocks off the north-east coast of Anglesey, and smashed to pieces, with the loss of more than four hundred lives. The weather system responsible for the disaster had developed over the Azores, then tracked over Brest in northern France, then Plymouth, then north over Wales. FitzRoy studied the charts showing its progress over and over again. He became convinced that the route of the storm could have been predicted in time for the *Royal Charter* to have been advised to stay in port in southern Ireland, where she had arrived the previous day. At the same time the British Association was urging the setting up of a national system for gathering weather data. FitzRoy saw his chance.

He enlisted informants around the shores of the British Isles, equipped them with modern instruments and the telegraph, and instructed them to transmit their readings to London daily. By the end of 1860 he had established more than twenty weather stations in Britain and five on the Continent. On 5 September of that year *The Times* published the first official Board of Trade weather summary, and early the next year FitzRoy began issuing storm warnings to coastal stations. That August his office produced the first daily weather forecasts, which were published in *The Times*, and − subsequently − other newspapers.

FitzRoy took a grave risk in committing himself so early and so publicly, and it was a strategy which was to rebound on him with tragic results. He was, in effect, appealing over the heads of the experts to the public to support him. The scientists – even those, such as Matthew Maury, who were initially supportive – were sceptical, regarding FitzRoy's network as far too sparse and erratically positioned, and the readings too few and far between, to permit anything resembling a reliable synoptic analysis. Repudiated by the scientific community, the Admiral had to rely upon the accuracy of his forecasts. But – as many, much better resourced than him, have found out subsequently – the weather of Britain owes no loyalty. In April 1862 an editorial in *The Times*, written in response to a swelling chorus of complaints about the forecasts, pointed the finger directly at FitzRoy: 'While disclaiming all credit for the occasional success,' the newspaper said, 'we must however demand to be set free of any responsibility for the too common failures which attend these prognostications. During the last week Nature seems to have taken special pleasure in confounding the conjectures of science.'

FitzRoy's position was becoming irreparably undermined. He himself saw it as his duty to pursue the goal of forecasting in order to save lives, protect ships and serve the nation's interests. It was his great misfortune that his efforts to realise that lofty ambition became fatally confused in the public perception with the prophecies of a rival gaggle of cranks and charlatans known as the astro-meteorologists. Chief among these was Lieutenant Richard Morrison – like FitzRoy a former Royal Navy officer – who was better known under his astrological pseudonyms of Zadkiel and Tao-Tze.

Morrison had joined the Navy in 1806, when he was eleven, and had seen extensive action during the Napoleonic Wars and afterwards, eventually leaving the service to devote himself to soothsaying. The first of Zadkiel's Almanacs, containing his predictions on all aspects of human affairs as well as a monthly weather forecast for the year ahead, appeared in 1831. Within a few years, the Almanac was selling in sufficient volume to keep The Seer – as he preferred to be known – and his large family in some comfort, and it continued to appear each year until his death in 1864.

Morrison became something of a national celebrity in 1861 when his prediction that Prince Albert would suffer ill health was followed within months by the Consort's death from typhoid. Two years later, The Seer brought a libel action against yet another naval officer, Rear Admiral Sir Edward Belcher, who had written to the *Daily Telegraph* alleging that Morrison had gulled several members of the nobility into parting with cash in return for being put in touch with their dear departed via Zadkiel's crystal globe. Although The Seer won his case, he received negligible damages and no costs, and the publicity given to his methods did little to advance his own reputation or that of his calling.

Back in 1837 Morrison had joined the Meteorological Society of London, whose secretary, William White, held similar views to his own about the influence of the planets and stars on our weather. When, some years later, the sober and wholly orthodox James Glaisher became the first secretary of the newly founded British Meteorological Society, White initially challenged its authority, then attempted to infiltrate it, and finally broke away to form the Astro-Meteorological Society. Glaisher and his colleagues regarded this as no more than a charlatans' talking shop. The fact that FitzRoy shared this view of White and Morrison did nothing to help his cause. The perception of Glaisher and the other experts was that FitzRoy and the stargazers were essentially in the same business and that the good name of legitimate science was being exposed to ridicule.

Relentlessly mocked in the newspapers, disowned by his peers and abused by the astrologers, FitzRoy went to pieces. The publication of Darwin's *Origin of Species* and the ensuing public uproar distressed him deeply. He himself was an undeviating fundamentalist who had maintained in his own book about the *Beagle* voyage that the dinosaurs and mastodons had been doomed to extinction because they were too big to get through the doors of the Ark. The warfare raging around his office at the Board of Trade deepened his depression. In April 1865 he roused himself from his lethargy to go to London to meet Matthew Maury. He returned home incoherent with excitement. Early next morning he left his wife in bed, kissed his sleeping daughter and cut his throat in his dressing room.

Within a few weeks of FitzRoy's suicide, a joint committee from the Board of Trade and the Royal Society had begun an investigation into his work. Its conclusion was damning: 'We can find no evidence that any competent meteorologist believes the science to be at present in such a state as to enable an observer to indicate day by day the weather to be experienced in the next 48 hours.' The committee recommended that the daily forecasts should be discontinued. The Royal Society itself implemented that recommendation and took charge of FitzRoy's network. This, in time, became a model for government-funded scientific research and eventually metamorphosed into one of the great, familiar institutions of our public life: the Met Office.

The professionals had prevailed and they would never relax their grip. The amateur weather-watchers — the clergyman tapping his barometer in the rectory hall, the retired medical man consulting his thermometers, the country gentleman inspecting the contents of the rain gauge so carefully positioned on the southern wall of the kitchen garden – were ushered to the margins and told in condescending tones that their observations (if made with approved instruments according to prescribed standards) were still considered valuable, even if their opinions were not. The age of the layman, the enthusiast with his speculations and theories, had come to a quiet close.

As it turned out, the progress of scientific meteorology under the direction of the scientific men of the Royal Society was snail-like. With FitzRoy's ignominious end, the whole notion of forecasting had taken a severe knock. The professionals were well aware that they were simply not equipped to unravel the mysteries of how weather systems generated far away over the seas were delivered. The Royal Society's response was to return to basics, which meant accumulating more mountains of information about the weather as it happened. But the imperative that had inspired Robert FitzRoy would not disappear. Sir George Airy, an implacable critic of the Royal Society, had put his finger on the dilemma in a letter to FitzRoy in 1860: 'As a matter of abstract science,' he wrote, 'I think meteorology desperate; but as a matter of practical use, in the proper hands, its value may possibly be great.'

It was also what the public wanted. Under pressure, the Royal Society resumed daily forecasts in 1879. But their accuracy had improved very little in the period since FitzRoy's suicide. The problem – as John D. Cox has pointed out in his book *The Storm Watchers* – was that meteorology still could not organise itself into a proper discipline. Important advances had been made since James D. Forbes' disdainful dismissal of the dilettantes and their toys, but they had been achieved haphazardly, without any structure of principles. By the end of the nineteenth century, 'the government agency men', as Cox characterises them, had spent thirty years extending the geographical range of the data-gathering, without managing any corresponding extension of intellectual grasp. The main work of the rapidly burgeoning meteorological service was to plot the course of weather systems according to the observations telegraphed to them by the volunteers. But the dynamics dictating how this weather was created were, quite simply, beyond the horizons of their thinking.

To be fair to them, those conceptual horizons were exceptionally wide, and the kind of mind that could span them did not come along very often. The intractable character of meteorology had two dimensions: the processes by which weather was made were inconceivably complex; and they took place in a region inaccessible for observation. For those reasons, the significant advances in understanding tended to occur at infrequent intervals, and were often not recognised for what they were because no means existed to corroborate them.

As long ago as 1688 Edmund Halley drew a chart illustrating the direction of wind flows over the tropical and sub-tropical oceans, and hypothesised a general circulation of air over the earth's surface. Fifty years later Halley's concept was refined and expanded by another English scientist, George Hadley, into a coherent explanation of the trade winds which took account both of thermal convection and the rotation of the planet. Hadley's brilliant piece of deduction was ignored in England; indeed, long after his death, John Dalton arrived independently at the same conclusions and was somewhat surprised and put out to discover that he had been beaten to it. However, aspects of it were picked up on the Continent by, among others, the prodigious Swiss-born mathematician Leonhard Euler, who developed the first mathematical explanation of fluid flow, which in time enabled the American William Ferrel to formulate equations of atmospheric motion above a rotating earth.

The impact of these theoretical landmarks was, in their own time, negligible. Nor was progress in practical understanding of the weather much more coherent. In the 1820s the German meteorologist Wilhelm Heinrich Dove realised an important truth about storm systems in the northern hemisphere, which was that they were generated by the collision between warm, moist air from the tropics and cold, dry air from the polar north. Robert FitzRoy was much influenced by Dove's work, but his experience illustrated graphically the difficulties that inevitably arose when one facet of a complex whole was put to work in isolation from all the others. FitzRoy's failure rammed home the message that there were no simple solutions to the mystery of what was happening in the atmosphere. James Glaisher was fully conscious that the answers lay in the region of the clouds, and he made a series of pioneering balloon flights during the 1860s to look for them (on one of these flights he lost consciousness at 30,000 feet, and the balloon's accelerating ascent was only arrested when Glaisher's companion used his teeth to pull the valve cord). Glaisher made some useful discoveries about the height and behaviour of clouds, but was not equipped, either in terms of knowledge or technology, to penetrate further.

In the view of most of those who know what they are talking about, the father of modern meteorology was the Norwegian physicist and mathematician Vilhelm Bjerknes. In 1898 Bjerknes published what became known as his circulation theorem, which made the link between dynamic and thermo-dynamic forces on atmospheric motions, and in the years that followed he became a passionate advocate of the need to bring physical theory to bear on the practice of weather forecasting – in other words, to make meteorology an exact science. A giant stride towards that goal came in the early 1920s, when Bjerknes, his equally talented son Jacob, and a colleague of theirs, Halvor Solberg, produced an entirely original model to explain the growth and decay of weather systems, in which the concepts of cold and warm fronts were introduced. The impact was enormous. For the first time meteorologists were given a reasonably clear idea of what they should be looking for: the movement and development of frontal systems. Moreover, the development of aviation was making it possible to gain the information necessary to track these systems at high altitude. During the 1930s the technology became available to dispatch unmanned balloons into the upper atmosphere, equipped with instruments to measure pressure, temperature, humidity and wind speeds, and transmit the data by radio back to the ground. The ability of radar to detect areas of rain was put to use in the 1950s to track belts of precipitation, and the last important piece in the jigsaw of the atmosphere was fitted with the launching from Cape Canaveral in 1960 of the first weather satellite, Tiros One. At last it was possible to observe the laboratory in which our weather was created from below, from within and from above.

One massive obstacle remained, however, and it took the advent of computer power to overcome it. Although the data was being made available, the quantity of it was so vast that it simply could not be processed quickly enough for the meaning to become apparent. The fantastic, almost nightmarish scale of the enterprise was grasped by an extraordinarily brilliant and visionary English mathematician-cum-meteorologist Lewis Fry Richardson. Richardson was a Quaker, a lifelong pacifist, a loner, misunderstood or ignored by his contemporaries, so far ahead of his time that it had still not quite arrived when he died in 1953. Richardson's peculiar genius lay in his ability to deploy differential equations to predict the course of things that change. While in charge of the Eskdalemuir Observatory in southern Scotland just before the outbreak of the First World War, Richardson had the vision of a great 'forecast factory', in which an army of human computers – he whimsically suggested 64,000 would be needed to keep up with the weather around the world – tabulated atmospheric pressures at certain altitudes, latitudes and longitudes so as to 'give a general account of the state of the atmosphere at any given instant over an extended region'.

It was pure theory, but – in Richardson's view, at least – very far from being a daydream. War came, and Richardson's conscience took him from his peaceful laboratory in the Scottish lowlands to the Western Front. For two years he drove an ambulance and worked on the equations which – in the absence of 64,000 assistants – he had to do himself. Making use of data relating to a single day in May 1910 which Vilhelm Bjerknes had published in one of his books, Richardson set himself the task of calculating pressure changes and wind speeds for a six-hour period. When, after months of toil, he came to compare his results with what really happened, Richardson found his figures wildly out. But he was not deterred. He knew that what mattered were his methods, and he proceeded with the publication of his *Weather Prediction by Numerical Process* in 1922. The book was politely received but not at all understood. No one – with the possible exception of Richardson himself – could have foreseen that he had opened the way to what became known in the 1950s as Numerical Weather Prediction; thanks to the ability of computers to handle the millions of calculations per second that are needed to make sense of the data, this has remained the cornerstone of weather forecasting ever since.

The mind of Lewis Richardson was certainly one of the few capable of spanning those wide horizons. He offered no apology for the complexity of his work, which rendered it inaccessible to even the ablest meteorologists of the 1920s. 'The scheme is complicated,' Richardson wrote, 'because the atmosphere is complicated.' He also, rather wistfully, expressed his regret that Einstein and the other great theorists of his age had not tackled the subject. Had they done so, he speculated 'they would have had to abandon the idea that truth is really simple'.

In the end, of course, Robert FitzRoy's vision of meteorology as a public service prevailed. His tragedy was that the science in his day was in no state to sustain that vision. It was not until Bjerknes broke through into the vaporous world of the atmosphere that the science could come of age. In Britain, the state-funded agency that had seized hold of meteorology after FitzRoy's downfall contributed very little to advancing the understanding of the genesis and fate of weather systems, and was laggard in recognising the achievements of others and putting them to use. Eventually, however, the Met Office woke up to the realisation that, without knowing what to look for in the creation of our weather, there would be no finding it; and that the great goal of accurate short-term forecasting would remain out of reach. Prediction had to be the primary point in studying the weather. It was not enough, and never had been enough, to follow Francis Bacon's advice that 'men must pursue things which are just in the present, and leave the future to the divine Providence'.

Chapter 11

The Wisest Prophets

WHITBY ON A BOISTEROUS, BREEZY APRIL DAY WAS FULL OF STRANGE-looking people with white faces wearing black clothes. I met one in the library of the Whitby Literary and Philosophical Society, which is inside the town's handsome museum. Her face was as pale as porcelain, her hair, make-up, top, miniskirt and tights as black as a raven's feathers. I asked her what she and her fellow Goths – for such they were – found so congenial about Whitby. She enthused about the place, its history, its pubs, its hospitality. 'And we really like the Goths,' the spinsterly library assistant said with a smile. 'They're so polite. You should see them all in Safeway's. They're no trouble. Only once, someone found some black wax on a gravestone in the churchyard.'

The Goth lady was in the library to research for a dissertation about Whitby Abbey, the ancient ecclesiastical institution that once stood above the town looking out over the pewter waters of the North Sea. It was here or hereabouts that Caedmon, the first English poet, became a monk under the rule of the saintly Abbess Hilda; and here that the bishops gathered for their Synod in 664, which decided that England should adopt the Roman form of Christianity and forsake the Celtic. No more than a few Saxon stones survive from the abbey that Hilda built and the

Vikings burned. But the shell of its medieval successor is still upright, and it is a good place to stand and feel the wind blowing in over the cliffs, and contemplate those stirring events of long ago, and look down on the harbour and read of Whitby's great seafaring history. Next to the Abbey ruins stands the Church of St Mary, with the remains of many a mariner in its graveyard, although not those of Whitby's most famous — albeit adopted — son. Captain James Cook served his apprenticeship with a Quaker family, learning mathematics and astronomy in a little house in Grape Street, overlooking the harbour from which the ships that were to take him to undreamed of shores first sailed.

Like the lady Goth, and the visitors who peer into the room where Cook slung his hammock and climb the 199 steps to the Abbey to inspect Caedmon's Cross, I had come to Whitby in search of some history. Most of what I was looking for was contained in some dusty volumes left long undisturbed on the shelves of the Whitby Literary and Philosophical Society's library. They documented the genesis, creation and poignant fate of perhaps the most peculiar of the many ingenious devices inspired by meteorology, Doctor George Merryweather's Tempest Prognosticator.

My first thought when I came upon the reference was that this must be a joke. Doctor Merryweather! The Tempest Prognosticator! It sounded like one of those bogus Victorian peepshows on display in seaside amusement halls. But no one, it turned out, could have been more in earnest than Dr Merryweather. His motives were not commercial but altruistic: to save lives and assist the sea trade on which the prosperity of his town and his country depended. And it was not for want of energy or persistence that his efforts should have gone so unappreciated.

He was born in Yorkshire in 1793, studied medicine at Edinburgh University and came to Whitby to take up a position as a junior partner in an established medical practice. In time he married his senior partner's daughter and set up on his own. Of his medical career and his personal life, I was able to discover little, beyond that he was a member of the Literary and Philosophical Society for many years, that he twice served as curator of the Whitby Museum and that he died at his home near the Abbey on 1 November 1870. It is also safe to say of Dr Merryweather that few people can have had so close and affectionate a relationship with that humble bloodsucker, the leech.

The inspiration for his great project came from a letter written by the eighteenth-century poet William Cowper to his cousin Lady Hesketh in which he referred to the prophetic powers of his pet leech. 'I have a leech in a bottle that foretells all these prodigies and convulsions of Nature,' wrote Cowper fondly. 'No change in the weather surprises him . . . he is worth all the barometers in the world.'

Dr Merryweather was moved to wonder if the well-documented inclination of the leech to become restless at the approach of wind and rain might be exploited in a regulated, scientific manner. His first step was to confine several of them in bottles and monitor their movements. He found that Cowper had not exaggerated. On 7 August 1849, Doctor Merryweather recorded, the sun was shining benignly on Whitby, but his leeches were restless, foretelling stormy weather. Later that same day he was obliged to travel fifteen miles inland to Darby Beacon, where – lo and behold! – a furious tempest burst on him, fully vindicating his captives' misgivings about the beauty of the day. 'I took it into my head,' he wrote, 'to surround myself with a jury of philosophical counsellors, which consisted of twelve leeches, each placed in a separate pint pot of white glass . . . I placed these in a circle in order that the leeches might see one another and not endure the affliction of solitary confinement.'

The twelve bottles were arranged by the tender-hearted Merryweather around the outside of a circular stand. Into the top of each bottle was inserted a narrow brass tube. Above the stand, rising like the dome of a Byzantine church, was a bell surrounded by twelve little hammers, each of which was attached by a gilt cord, via a pulley, to a piece of whalebone placed across the neck of the brass tube. 'Into each bottle,' the proud inventor explained, 'was poured rainwater to the height of an inch, and a leech placed in every bottle, which was to be its future residence; and when influenced by the electro-magnetic state of the atmosphere, a number of the leeches ascended into the tubes; in doing which they dislodged the whalebone and caused the bell to ring.'

Throughout 1850 the Tempest Prognosticator — or the Atmospheric Electromagnetic Telegraph Conducted By Animal Instinct, to give it its full title — was subjected to exhaustive tests. These were described in considerable detail by Dr Merryweather in a series of letters to the President of the Whitby Literary and Philosophical Society, Henry Belcher, which were evidently intended to serve as documentary proof of the Prognosticator's efficacy. Dr Merryweather would post Mr Belcher a timed and dated prediction, thus: 'Whitby, April 3rd, 1030pm. I beg you to prepare for another storm, which I have reason to suppose will take place in a short time. George Merryweather M.D.' Subsequently Mr Belcher would be informed of the outcome: 'Whitby, April 16th, 8 am. On Wednesday the 3rd instant, 10.30 pm, I intimated to you an approaching storm, which commenced

235

from the N.W. on the Thursday night following and wrecked a ship between the piers.'

Occasionally Dr Merryweather had to acknowledge a lack of geographical precision in his leeches' predictions. In that same letter of 16 April he gave notice of another approaching 'gale or storm', adding apologetically 'although this morning is so mild and beautiful, I must do my duty'. A fortnight later, referring to the fact that the weather had remained settled in Whitby, he alluded to events in Dublin where 'on the afternoon of Thursday the 18th a great storm took place . . . 235 miles distant from this place in a straight line'. On 23 October Dr Merryweather warned Mr Belcher of 'a storm of an extensive kind'. On that occasion Whitby escaped with a minor gale and much rain, but at Dover – also on a straight line – a breakwater was damaged; while along a different straight line, leading to a point off the coast of Denmark, the Emperor of Russia's steam yacht 'Peterhoff' was lost 'in a perfect hurricane'.

Early in 1851 the fully realised Prognosticator was ready to be shown off to the public. It was introduced by its inventor to the Literary and Philosophical Society on the night of 27 February, in the course of a lecture lasting almost three hours. Amid considerable local excitement, it was taken to London to be shown at the Great Exhibition, where its exotic appearance – by now it resembled a cross between an Indian prince's palace and a fairground ride – aroused interest. The *Weekly Dispatch* reported the doctor's boast that 'the apparatus will communicate at all times the processes that are taking place in the higher regions of the atmosphere, and for hundreds of miles in extent will foretell with unerring certainty any storm that is about to take place'. Lloyd's of London carried out tests which – so the *Dispatch* stated – showed the Prognosticator's prognostications to be 'perfectly accurate'.

It must have seemed to the Whitby GP that the contraption's success, and his own reputation, were assured. He told his friends at the Literary and Philosophical Society of his hopes that 'our Whitby pygmy temples would be distributed all over the world'. He arranged for a nationwide tour to promote the temples, and urged the powers in London to make haste in equipping all coastal stations with one. 'It is impossible,' Dr Merryweather asserted, 'to estimate the advantages and blessings that would be obtained to the British people.' But, alas, to the sober professionals at the Board of Trade the idea of committing resources to a bell rung by leeches was unappealing. Dr Merryweather's exhortations were ignored and his enthusiasm waned. The original Prognosticator did not survive, and it never went into production. There is, however, a model in the Whitby Museum, and enthusiasts at the Barometer Museum in Devon have recreated a working version, complete with leeches, which they say is extremely reliable.

I learned as much as I could of Dr Merryweather's achievements and disappointments and bid farewell to the lady Goth. I spent a little time in the museum, admiring the glassy-eyed stuffed birds and fish, and the narwhal tusks and harpoons and other relics of Whitby's whale-hunting past. Then I made my way down the hill into the town spread out either side of the mouth of the River Esk. I passed a fish and chip shop that had been recommended to me and went in to ask how late they stayed open. 'Last serving's at seven o'clock,' a youth in an apron informed me. Noticing my look of surprise, a female customer paused in the act of thrusting a forkful of batter and white flakes of cod into her mouth, and said: 'Nothing in Whitby's open after seven.'

An insistent whiff of kipper hung around several of the narrow alleys on the Abbey side of the river, emanating from little blackened smokeries tucked behind some of the old cottages. Whitby is celebrated for its kippers, as it is for jet, a form of lignite which has long been mined in these parts to be carved and polished into jewellery and ornaments as black or blacker than the lady Goth's eyebrows. I passed several shops in the tourist part of town specialising in jet trinkets, then crossed the swing bridge back to the west side of the river and made my way out to the harbour walls. Somewhere out and off to the right, a Russian schooner, the *Demeter*, had come to grief in a storm in the 1880s, releasing a cargo of coffins containing bodies which were later washed up along the shore – an event which inspired an imaginative young Irishman, Bram Stoker, to bring his thirsty Goth of an earlier era, Count Dracula, ashore at Whitby. I passed a shack advertising the Dracula Experience, but it was shut; as were Nobles Winkles, assorted fudge and ice cream kiosks, the booth in which Esther Anita Lee, true-born Romany, revolved her crystal sphere, and every other amenity and attraction. Nevertheless, there were still pleasure-seekers about: not just Goths preparing for their outlandish rituals, but couples there for a spring break beside the sea, marching beside the steely water, hands thrust deep into pockets, hoods pulled around ears.

I took a turn around one side of the outer harbour walls, which are arranged like a pair of pincers, opened slightly for the waves to come in and the boats to go whichever way. Two or three hardy anglers stood guard, muffled against the wind, waiting for a codling or a plaice to extract a nod from the end of their rods. Turned against the wind, I looked back at the storm-shattered cliffs and the wind-whipped khaki beach, and at the handsome town tumbled down the steep slopes, with the Abbey keeping vigil on one side and the cracked and peeling walls of the Royal Hotel on the other. Dark cloud scudded in over the darkening water. Was there a storm brewing somewhere, I wondered? What would Doctor Merryweather's little friends have had to say?

Dr Merryweather's motives were clearly honourable; those of Patrick Murphy MNS (his own joke: Member of No Society) more dubious. Yet it is Murphy who warrants an entry in the *Dictionary of National Biography* and George Merryweather who is ignored. Such is the lottery of fame.

Towards the end of 1837, Murphy – who may have been an Englishman or may have been an Irishman from Cork – published his *Weather Almanac on Scientific Principles Showing the State of the Weather for Every Day of the Year of 1838*. Murphy stated that, according to his scientific principles, the weather in January would be exceptionally severe, and that the 20th would be 'fair and probably the lowest degree of winter temperature'. He struck gold. The average temperature for the month in London was 29.6 degrees Fahrenheit, and on the 20th itself the thermometer maintained by the Royal Humane Society at Hyde Park registered minus 3 degrees Fahrenheit at 6.30 a.m., 9 degrees at noon and a maximum of 18 degrees – 14 degrees below freezing. All was as Patrick Murphy had foretold and suddenly he was famous. As the word spread, the offices of his publishers, Whittaker and Co., were besieged by customers. Edition after edition of the almanac was rushed out, forty-five in all. Murphy himself is said to have made £3000, an enormous sum in those days, which he promptly lost in speculating on the price of corn, an aspect of the future evidently not as amenable to his scientific principles as the weather.

That winter lingered in the collective memory on account of

its severity and was known for many years as Murphy's Winter. But for Murphy himself, whether he knew it or not, his moment had come and gone, and his bolt was shot. If, at the end of 1838, he had reviewed his predictions for the year as a whole, he would have found that he had been near the mark on 168 days and thoroughly wide of it on 197, and he might have concluded that weather prophecy was a chancy business. But Murphy was not one for looking back. He stuck to his principles, and was working on his forecasts for 1848 when he died at his lodgings in St Bride's, London, on 1 December 1847. The news prompted this epitaph in *The Times*:

> When Murphy says 'frost', then it will snow,
> The wind's fast asleep when he tells us 'twill blow,
> For his rain we get sunshine, for high we have low,
> Yet he swears he's infallible — weather or no!

It would have been interesting to know what went on in Murphy's mind: whether he was merely a charlatan, or whether he genuinely believed that it was possible to predict the weather for a particular day up to a year ahead. Did he ever suspect that such a degree of foreknowledge was unattainable and that, compared with the weather, fluctuations in corn prices were almost tediously predictable? I suspect that he did believe and continued to believe in his scientific principles. These were expounded at length in a book which Murphy entitled *Observations on the Laws and Cosmical Dispositions of Nature in the Solar System*. The thesis — that our weather was determined by the movements of the planets — was not that far removed from Zadkiel's astrological pseudo-science. While other heaven-watchers identified the moon as the chief influence, Murphy clearly believed that the whole planetary system was involved. This, in his view, explained why weather forecasting was so tricky: 'The chief obstacle which prevents more than a qualified approach to exactitude . . . is the principle of *perturbation* to which the great meteoric tides of the atmosphere, similar to those of the ocean (and to which they bear a much closer analogy than may be supposed) are exposed . . . The fact that the approach of comets, particularly those of the superior class, should be set down as the principal.'

In other words, if the weather turns out different from that promised by the prophet, it does not mean that the prophecy was defective, but merely that forces and circumstances over which the prophet has no control – probably a comet of the superior class – has intervened to change everything. It's a neat escape route from blame and censure. It also anticipates, in a curious way, the acceptance of science's limitations in the matter of forecasting which is at the heart of what has become known in our time as chaos theory.

Orlando Whistlecraft! The Thwaite Weather Prophet! I had assumed that the one was a pseudonym and the other a self-bestowed honorific. But I was wrong on both accounts, as I discovered from the edition of the *East Anglian Daily Times* of 15 September 1892.

The editor of the paper had received a letter from a reader in Ipswich reporting that Orlando Whistlecraft, now in his eighty-second year, was living in straitened circumstances, and calling for a public fund to help him. Recalling Whistlecraft's former fame, the editor dispatched one of his staff to the village of Thwaite, on the main road between Ipswich and Norwich, to interview the sage.

The reporter entered a 'roomy and somewhat rambling

edifice', whose door was open to reveal 'a picture full of homely pathos'. 'Sitting upright under the canopy of a four-poster bed was a venerable man who had on his knees a large manuscript book in which he was writing in his left hand.' The sage, attended by his 'faithful spouse . . . a woman of good-humoured shrewdness', spoke at length about his life and work: how as an infant he had been crippled down his right side by rheumatic fever and had learned to write left-handed; how, as a boy, he had begun to study 'the look of the heavens and the actions of the glass', and to forecast the weather; how, little by little, people had got to hear of his predictions, prompting the approach from an Ipswich bookseller which led to the appearance in 1856 of the first *Whistlecraft Almanac*. It did well, selling four thousand copies; and twenty-five years and twenty-five almanacs later sales were still healthy. In the meantime, Whistlecraft contributed regular forecasts and weather reports to the *Ipswich Journal*, and wrote numerous papers and pamphlets as well as one full-length study, *The Climate of England*.

Orlando Whistlecraft's enduring success can be explained by contrasting his methods with those of Patrick Murphy. Neither man had any formal scientific qualifications. But unlike Murphy, the Thwaite prophet knew a great deal about the weather, did not rely on theories about planetary influences and had the wit to realise that a forecaster's surest route to failure was precision.

'Of course,' he replied to a question from the man from the *East Anglian Daily Times*, 'I didn't propose to say exactly what would happen on certain dates. My forecasts related only to the general character of the weather each month.' And what was his system? The prophet was vague: 'I took daily observations of wind, sunshine and temperature and in time I got to know that from certain signs in the sky and the clouds, a certain kind of weather might be expected – just as a doctor would see that some diseases would follow particular symptoms.'

In fact, his method was founded on close observation and methodical record-keeping, allied to an impregnable confidence in divine omnipotence. Whistlecraft had begun keeping a weather register at the age of nine. In 1827, aged seventeen, he introduced a much expanded version thus: 'Highly interesting and sublime is the science of meteorology which gives us so noble an idea of the Infinity of the Almighty, and which strikes the Creature with great amazement at the incomparable power of the Creator.'

From then on, the pattern of Orlando Whistlecraft's day was set. He read the thermometer at least three times a day, normally at 6 a.m., noon and 3 p.m, and the barometer twice. He recorded the nature of the clouds, the direction and force of the wind, the incidence of rain, snow, hail, frost and sunshine, and wrote a commentary on the character of the day. This he did every day of his life. Here, for a taste of Whistlecraft, is the entry for 26 May 1841, my birthday 110 years early:

Bright and very hot morning, no dew, some cirrus and cirro-cumulus, a very bright day and extremely hot; no clouds after 11, blue haze over the landscape after 5 pm. The thermometer above 80 degrees for an hour, and at 4pm only down to 76. Evening perfectly clear, except for the haze below – sunset in golden splendour and quite red. 9pm thermometer 63 degrees. A great number of immense mushrooms brought me this evening – one weighing 18 ounces and above one foot in diameter.

Fifty-nine years before the day of my birth, he was still at it: 'May 26th 1892. Thunder and rain 7am to 9am. Hot and bright from 11am. Close night, electric. The barometer stood at 30.09, the temperature between 57 and 75, there was 0.64 of an inch of rain.' The writing, though by now somewhat shaky, is perfectly legible.

When I came across the Whistlecraft weather journals in the Met Office's archives, I was awestruck. For more than six decades this simple Christian man had never wavered in his dedication to his calling. Twenty-six volumes, millions of words and figures, a million inspections of barometer and thermometer, a lifetime spent staring at the skies over that flat Suffolk coun-tryside. How could anyone be that driven? By the weather? He tried to explain it, referring to 'the endless amusement the science of meteorology yields to us and the elevation of soul it produces, drawing us nearer in mental converse to Him who rules the storm, guides the spheres and bids the waves be still'. He believed that his studies had given him an insight into the operations of what he called 'the great chemical laboratory, the grand wonder-working machinery of an infinite establishment, unerring in its performance and never out of order'.

In a talk to the Ipswich Farmers' Club published later as a pamphlet, the Thwaite Weather Prophet revealed a little more about his system. It was based, he said, on patterns which recurred regularly and thus predictably through the sequence of the months. Thus, whatever was the 'prominent feature' of the weather near 7 April would generally be repeated around 7 July and 7 November. The finest period in June would 'most commonly' be the finest in each of the following three months. The 23rd of each month was 'usually' a time for marked change, 'more especially in April, June, September and November'. Whatever the predominant character of May, 'the following September will generally prove the reverse'.

He claimed to the *East Anglian Daily Times* that his success rate was 'four, certainly and very often five' out of six predictions. The Whistlecraft strategy to shorten the odds was to give the impression of precision, while actually − through the deployment of adverbs such as generally, commonly, usually and so on − being anything but, thereby providing himself with a defence should the patterns let him down. He was canny enough to admit the occasional error, pointing ruefully to the presumption of a mere human in poking his nose inside the Almighty's chemical laboratory. Just as important, he could generally rely on his public's ignorance and defective memories, and a high degree of probability that none of them would trouble themselves with a thorough review of his performance.

When I first came across the name of Whistlecraft, I condescendingly assumed that he belonged to the tradition of the rural seer. I pictured him as a gnarled descendant of the Shepherd of Banbury, in close communion with the rhythms of earth and air as divined by the beasts and the birds, with a nugget of folkloric wisdom for every shift in the skies and a withering contempt for 'them with their new-fangled, fancy-dan instruments as thinks THEY knows'. In fact he was a thoroughgoing enthusiast for technology and reliant on his barometer and thermometer. Far from being inclined to park himself on the bench by the village pond and predict the weather for the next few days from the behaviour of tadpoles and newts, Orlando Whistlecraft stated firmly that he had little faith in the old weather saws, and none whatever in the memories of old-timers and their talk of the hotter summers and icier winters of long ago. He put his confidence in scientific instruments, his vast experience of the weather over Thwaite, and God.

*   *   *

I met my latter-day weather prophet, Philip Eden, on a summer's morning so blissful that even the wastelands of White City and the vast, jerry-built palace that is the BBC's Television Centre seemed a delightful place to be. A few dabs and smudges of cirrus and cumulus drifted across a sky of perfect pale blue, and I felt the sun warm on my back as I crossed the road from the tube station. Through the windows I could see the BBC worker ants scurrying about their business. For several years I had been a member of this colony, exiled to this soulless agglomeration of modern building materials from the congenial locality of Broadcasting House in central London. Normally, just a glimpse of the place was enough to rekindle old resentment at being expelled to such a dump. But on a day like this, even TV Centre extended a smiling welcome.

Had I but known it, this was the start of the great heat of 2003, and I rather kick myself for not having thought to ask Philip Eden, the Luton weather guru, what sort of a summer we were in for. I suspect that, being a modest man with a proper appreciation of the weather forecaster's limitations, he would have politely declined to commit himself. But it would have been amusing to accost him three months later and say: 'Ha! Never saw that coming, did you? Call meteorology a science, eh?' Which is the kind of thing weather forecasters have to put up with.

I had known Philip for a number of years, literally as a passing acquaintance. I used to come upon him when I was delivering news summaries to the studios used by Five Live, the BBC's cheerful chat 'n' sport radio network which employed him as its resident weather man. Sometimes he was in the studio, thrusting his fingers through an unkempt thatch of hair as he waited to pronounce on the likelihood of showers in the south-west or of sunny intervals with a brisk wind over

Orkney; sometimes outside the door, keeping vigil over his computer screen, tracking fronts and checking barometric pressure. In summer I would ask him about the prospects for my Sunday cricket match. Being a fanatic about the game himself, with a statistician's hunger for accumulating useless information, he took such matters with proper seriousness. 'Should be all right,' he'd say, 'though you might just catch a shower after tea.'

From as early as he can remember, Eden wanted to be a weather man. 'Classic anorak' he says of his nine-year-old self, the age at which his first meteorological paper was published in the school magazine. He took an M.Sc. in meteorology at Birmingham University, a sure step into forecasting as a career, which in those days meant the Met Office. But there was something of the maverick in him, and instead of following the conventional path up to and through the doors of Met Office's headquarters in Bracknell, he stayed outside, in the private sector. For a time he was in Aberdeen, preparing forecasts for the North Sea oil industry; it is a matter of lasting regret to him that, as a result, he was not in the Home Counties on 26 June 1976 for the hottest June day ever recorded, when he could have watched in trembling excitement as his thermometer climbed to the dizzying height of 35 degrees Celsius.

In 1983, Eden was hired as weather presenter by the independent London radio station LBC, and he found his vocation. 'Of course, I was terrified in the beginning,' he told me, 'but I found out straightaway that I could do it, and that I enjoyed it.' His way of doing it was, and remains, highly individual – not in any mannered, studied way, but in his awareness of the medium of broadcasting and his understanding of the way in which ordinary people listen to the radio and get information from it.

Having always been outside the mainstream, he did not fall into the forecasting orthodoxy. He did not talk about belts of rain and prolonged spells of sunshine, he said it would rain or the sun would shine; and he was happy to own up when he got it wrong. None of this endeared him to the Met Office apparatchiks, who, in his early days, used to telephone his employers to protest against their use of an 'unauthorised' source.

Eden began contributing weather reports to the *Sunday Telegraph*, where he found a complementary niche. His distinctive broadcasting style had already won him a loyal band of listeners. Now he was able to deploy his vast knowledge of weather history, with all its quirks and curious characters, and his grasp of climatology, to establish a bond with the host of like-minded enthusiasts among the *Telegraph* readership. He was happy, and clearly remains so, even though he has now reined back on his Five Live work to avoid the disablingly early starts which he endured for so long.

What sustains Philip Eden's pleasure and enthusiasm is not the modest measure of public recognition meteorology has brought him but the subject itself. As we sat on a standard grey BBC sofa sipping our standard BBC *caffè latte* next to a staircase up and down which BBC legs appeared and disappeared on their way to outposts of the great BBC news empire, he spoke rather touchingly about the obsession. 'I'll never lose it,' he said, 'even when all this' – he waved around him – 'is finished. I still do my records every day, I always will.' Why, I asked him. He smiled, tugged at his hair and rasped a hand over his heavy, bristly features (it's easy to tell why he never made the leap to television). 'I told you, I'm an anorak.'

He said he still maintained a rain gauge at his mother's house in Luton, as well as a computerised weather station at his own home not far away, and another at his holiday house near Limoges. At some point every day he logs on to record another footnote to the weather history of Bedfordshire and Limousin. 'I was lucky,' he says gratefully, 'to be around when climatology became politicised by the global warming issue. Suddenly it was the sexy science. Climatologists, who had always been dusty old fossils, came blinking out into the sunshine.'

Television and radio weather forecasters are like television and radio news readers and correspondents. As long as we see and hear them regularly, they are familiar to us and their faces and voices become a part of our lives. But hardly have they gone than they are forgotten.

There was Bill Giles, with that wink and the friendly tilt of the big head. There was Suzanne Charlton, Bobby's girl, with the teeth (who's now back again). Remember Ian McCaskill, with his weird, mangled accents, jerking around like a puppet with St Vitus's dance? For a time he was a national institution, until retirement came and he faded away like the tail end of a passing low-pressure system. Michael Fish, the affable uncle with his cardigans and stock of woolly socks for those chilly winter days, seemed an institution as permanent as Big Ben until he, too, hung up his bag of homely wisdom and joined the after-dinner speaking circuit. John Ketley had a song written about him and is still spouting weather wisdom somewhere with that chirpy-chappy grin in his voice. On the radio the voices, without faces, come and go. Is it Darren Bett, or Philip Avery? No, it's Rob McElwee — you can tell him from those strange pauses and the swooping delivery, like gulls diving for bread. Is it Isobel Lang, or Helen Young? Who are these people, and what is our relationship with them?

We are the customers, the punters — necessary, ignorant, incapable of sustained attention or concentration. They are the providers, the carriers of the Met Office message, paid to officiate according to the Met Office liturgy in one of the ritualistic pillars of our national life. They exist, not primarily to interpret weather data and pass it on in clear, colloquial English, but to minister to the people's need for the comfort and sense of safety offered by routine.

Speaking for myself, I readily confess that I am a man of routine, in need of routine, in thrall to routine. I get up at pretty much the same time every day, and follow the same pattern of behaviour. I prepare my breakfast according to a rigid procedure, so that when I return from the newsagents with my newspaper — the *Guardian* Monday to Friday, the *Henley Standard* on Friday, *The Times* on Saturday, the *Sunday Telegraph* or *Observer* on Sunday — my coffee is close to bubbling through and my two slices of toast are already cooling to the point at which butter may be spread on them without melting. After breakfast, I . . . well, perhaps there is no need for me to continue. I am welded to the repetitive patterns on which my life is constructed, I am content in my enslavement, I view the prospect of my routines being demolished with horror, and I care not a jot if people think me a dull dog.

The weather forecast on Radio Four is one of the pillars of my daily routine. I generally listen at three minutes to seven and again at three minutes to one. Other behavioural patterns tend to prevent me from catching it at three minutes to six, but I know it is there if I need it. The term 'listen' needs qualifying. I have the weather forecast on, and if it is drowned out by noisy children I am apt to demand silence. But I do not listen in the dictionary sense of 'attentively exercising the sense of hearing'. Why should I? Very rarely do I actually NEED information about the weather coming my way. I am observing a ritual; and ritual does not require or warrant full mental engagement. Indeed, that is one of the points about it: to provide reassurance to the participant that the world this morning is, in its essentials, the same as the world yesterday, and that the same will apply tomorrow.

Although there are circumstances in which I listen more attentively – generally when I am due to go fishing or play cricket – in general, the weather forecast does not matter to me in a practical sense. The same is true for almost all of the people, all of the time. Of course, there is the very rare exception. It may be that, had not Michael Fish on that notorious day in October 1987 been so blithe in his assurance that a hurricane was not brewing, some of those who were crushed to death by falling trees or fatally wounded by flying slates would have stayed at home and been alive today. But it is equally likely that – even if he had prophesied the tempest as it turned out – they would not have had their televisions on when he was performing, that they would not have been paying attention, or that they would have chosen to ignore his warnings. What is sure is that nothing could have dissuaded the storm from arriving, nor have diminished the number of trees that toppled over that night, or the quantity of roofing material and masonry that flew through the air with such lethal effect.

It follows that the issue of the accuracy or otherwise of weather forecasts is unimportant, except insofar as it provides essential grist for the grinding mill of collective griping, and an occasional helping hand to the great legion of newspaper and magazine columnists forever casting about for subjects on which to bellyache. I came upon an example in the *Spectator* not long ago, written by Ross Clark, normally an intelligent and amusing chronicler of contemporary absurdities. It consisted of a prolonged grumble about the inability of the Met Office to predict with any useful degree of precision the weather in Mr Clark's corner of Cambridgeshire during a changeable week in early June 2003, combined with some unkind reflections about the cost to the taxpayer of the Met Office's operations. As usually happens in such exercises, Mr Clark invoked the aid of a scientific expert to back his contention that weather forecasts and forecasters are useless. Almost inevitably, the expert in question turned out to be Dr John Thornes, Reader in Applied Meteorology at Birmingham University and self-appointed chief scourge of the Met Office.

Periodically Dr Thornes and his helpers subject a selection of Met Office forecasts from a certain period to close critical analysis. I have the fruits of one of these exercises before me as I write, published a few years ago in the journal *Weather*. It is entitled 'Persisting with Persistence − the Verification of Radio Four Weather Forecasts', and is an intimidatingly dense piece of research, crammed with charts and tables and peppered with inscrutable algebraic equations. The main conclusion is clear: the Met Office's claim of 86 per cent accuracy is bunkum. In fact, says Dr Thornes, if you take out those days − around three-quarters of the total − when the weather one day is essentially the same as the next, and concentrate on times of significant change, the accuracy level falls to less than 40 per cent. His verdict is that this large and lavishly funded government agency consistently exaggerates its efficiency; that its performance should be regularly monitored and assessed by 'an independent organisation'; and, inevitably, that much more research needs to be done on this important matter.

I'm afraid that the work of Dr Thornes and his colleagues carries with it a high 'so what?' factor. What do he and Mr Clark want? Do they believe that the forecasters are incompetent at interpreting the data collected by the Met Office computers? Or that the computers themselves are not up to the job? Or is it their contention that the whole business of trying to divine what the weather is up to is a waste of time and money? And if that is their belief, the only conclusion must be that the Met Office should be wound up and its new headquarters in Exeter disposed of, Peter Gibbs, Penny Tranter, Helen Young and the rest of them made redundant and the weather forecasts either abolished or handed over to the contemporary equivalents of the Shepherd of Banbury. In that case, Dr Thornes might find himself out of a job, and I suspect that even Mr Clark might regret the disappearance of such a reliable outlet for his peevishness.

The value of weather forecasts has very little to do with the quality of the information they provide. It is, rather, that – like cat's-eyes on a dark night – they help meet our need for the reassurance of the familiar as well as offering an outlet for our appetite for grumbling. The weather itself is another outlet: satisfactory in that it so often warrants complaint, but less so in that it lacks the desirable element of human fallibility. With the forecast, there is someone to blame when it is wrong, and, by a process of transference, someone to blame for the weather itself.

I do not blame the forecasters for the weather or the forecasts. But that is not to say that I don't have grievances against them. I have, plenty. One concerns geography. I live near Reading, in Berkshire, which is a long way from the west coast and a long way from the east coast. That puts it, to my way of thinking, in the middle of southern England. Therefore when the forecasters, as they usually do, divide the country into east and west, I have no idea where I am to be found. This is very annoying.

Worse is the addiction to witless value judgements and inane clichés. Why should spells of sunshine be 'good', and showers 'nasty'? Why should rainfall after a long dry spell be welcomed by gardeners, but not by those 'out and about'? Why should it be thought necessary, whenever a late frost threatens, to alert the same green-fingered mob to see to their 'tender plants'? Why should a mild few days in mid-December be hailed as congenial to 'the Christmas shopping'? Why should we be exhorted not to 'put away those brollies just yet', or to keep our windscreen scrapers handy? Why should driving conditions in frosty weather invariably be 'treacherous'? What is meant by 'a few drops of rain' – a hundred drops? A million? Fifty million? Fifty billion? Why should cloud always 'bubble up' and thunder come in 'odd rumbles'? Why should . . . ?

But that's probably enough of that. The Met Office forecasters – with their regional accents, their jaunty ways and sunny smiles and roguish winks and chummy wags of the head, their little asides and eagerness for a spot of badinage with presenters, their ceaseless plundering of the stock of platitudes and banalities, their pathological reluctance to own up when they have got it all wrong – are easy targets. As such they perform an indispensable function, and we would all be the poorer without them.

Enormous strides have been taken over the past thirty years to improve the accuracy of short-range forecasts, thanks – in the main – to a corresponding increase in computer power. Seventy-two-hour forecasts are now markedly more reliable than twenty-four-hour forecasts were in 1970. But medium-range predictions – for up to six days ahead – are still accurate in their detail less than half the time. And even in the short term, significant errors regularly occur. One example was highlighted by Philip Eden in the *Sunday Telegraph* in November 2003. For several days the Met Office forecasters had been assuming solemn voices to deliver warnings about an approaching Atlantic depression whose genesis in the atmosphere had been detected some considerable time before it organised itself. Northern Scotland was identified as the target landfall, and people there were advised to brace themselves for severe gales and lashings of rain. In the event the centre of the low slipped, without warning, four hundred miles south, tracked across the middle of Ireland to north-east England, and inflicted a severe pounding on south and west Wales. Why? No one knew. It just changed direction, as if it had changed its mind.

There is a growing suspicion within the international community of meteorologists that − however powerful the computers, however intricate the models, however comprehensive the data from the atmosphere − it will never be possible to forecast the weather with any precision more than two weeks ahead. It goes without saying that these doubts do little to restrain the desire to acquire new computers, recruit additional staff, carry out new programmes of research and extend existing ones. But philosophically, the idea that the science of forecasting may be approaching the buffers is receiving sober consideration.

The explanation for this worrying possibility is derived from the chaos theory whose shadowy outline may or may not have been glimpsed by that one-prophecy wonder, Patrick Murphy. Chaos theory was formulated by an American meteorologist, Edward Lorenz, and famously illustrated by him using a golf ball and a piece of paper. Lorenz would twice hold the ball at a fixed point and drop it, and each time it would hit the floor at the same spot. Then he would do the same with the piece of paper, and each time it would float down and land in a different place. Lorenz, who had spent many years studying convection in the atmosphere, hypothesised that the weather did not belong in the group of Newtonian linear systems, in which very small variations in starting conditions led to correspondingly small variations in the final state. The weather was non-linear, disordered, irregular: thus chaotic. Minute differences at the starting point could lead to enormous fluctuations in the final results. While the weather followed broadly similar patterns over years – defining what we call climate – within those patterns its behaviour was non-periodic, and therefore inherently unstable and unpredictable. The system never returned to the same starting point, and never repeated itself exactly. Lorenz believed that the dream of long-range forecasting was just that, a dream. Nothing that has happened in meteorology in the forty years since he first presented his theory has significantly challenged that view.

This is a serious matter for the professional meteorologist deep into the study of the atmosphere – particularly one trying to secure a renewal of funding for whichever research programme is paying his or her wages. But the rest of us can afford to take a more relaxed view. Mercifully, efforts to develop ways of deliberately changing the weather have progressed little further than the extremely expensive and rather pointless exercise of persuading clouds to drop rain by 'seeding' them with condensation nuclei. But even if we were able to do more than tinker at the margins, what reason is there to believe that our organisation of the weather would be superior to the system provided? Would we in Britain, for instance, be capable of devising a climate which suited us better than the one we have, and a system of delivering it more reliable, subtle and beautiful than the interaction between ocean and air currents that unfolds far to the west of us? Is there actually anything seriously wrong with our weather?

Chapter 12

Best in the World?

IN 1480 A CRIME WAS COMMITTED IN THE WILD AND RUGGED COUNTRY of Wester Ross that was atrocious even by the bloodthirsty standards of the Highland clan chiefs in those vengeful times. The lands between Loch Ewe and Loch Torridon, looking west towards Lewis and Harris, and south-west towards Skye, were held by Allan MacLeod, who lived with his wife and two small sons on an island in a smaller loch, Loch Tollaidh. She was a Mackenzie, daughter of Alexander Mackenzie, laird of Kintail, and sister to Hector Roy Mackenzie. Although Allan MacLeod was a peaceful man, there was a history of hatred between these two branches of two powerful clans, and the brothers of MacLeod had vowed that no drop of Mackenzie blood should contaminate their line.

According to the old story, the brothers went forth one day to search for Allan, who had gone for a day's fishing on the River Ewe, which flows from the northern end of Loch Maree into the tidal waters of Loch Ewe. They found him asleep in the sunshine on a little hill called, after the events of that day, Cnoc na Miochomailie, the Mound of Evil Council. They murdered him and cut off his head, then made their way to Loch Tollaidh. They took the boat which their brother had left on the shore and rowed to the island, where they told Allan's wife what they had done, and seized her sons from her. They took the boys to a house called An Tigh Dighe, the Moat House, beside Loch Gairloch, and slaughtered them. A servant found the blood-soaked clothes and brought them to the mother. She fled to her father and showed him the garments to convince him of what had happened. Mackenzie dispatched his son, Hector Roy, to Edinburgh, where he successfully petitioned King James III for a commission of fire and sword against the MacLeods. This the Mackenzies prosecuted until all the lands of the MacLeods of Gairloch became theirs.

Four centuries later, the age of feuding and raiding and blood-letting had long since lapsed (even if the memories had not). The Gairloch estate had passed to Sir Kenneth Mackenzie, while the adjoining lands of Kernsary and Inverewe − 12,000 acres of treeless land in the shape of a thumb thrust north-west into The Minch between Loch Ewe and Gruinard Bay – had been presented to his half-brother, Osgood Mackenzie, on the occasion of his twentieth birthday. The mind of Osgood Mackenzie − shaped by extensive travels through Europe − turned to creating a garden. It was an unpromising place to pursue what Bacon defined as 'the purest of human pleasures'. But Mackenzie was a determined man, and he decided to build his house and make his garden on a promontory jutting out into Loch Ewe from the eastern shore which was known by the name of the high point overlooking the water, Am Ploc Ard, the High Lump.

The land was red sandstone overlaid with a layer of black peat covered by heather and crowberry. 'There was,' Mackenzie wrote in his classic autobiography *100 Years in the Highlands*, 'nothing approaching good soil in any part of the peninsula, hardly even any gravel or sand; but in a few places the rotten rock and the peat had somehow got jumbled up together, and when we came across some of this we thought it grand stuff in comparison with the rest.' Not merely was there no soil, but the place was exposed to frequent batterings from the salt-laced storms that have shaped this wild coastline over the ages. These were obstacles that could, with tenacity and patience, be overcome. The one factor over which Osgood Mackenzie had no control was the one most in his favour: the climate.

The one fact that every schoolchild knows about the climate of Britain is that it is controlled by the warm waters of the Gulf Stream, 'the river in the ocean', as Robert Fitzroy's American colleague Matthew Maury famously labelled it. The chief characteristics of our weather — its moistness, its mildness, its changeability — are maintained by the Gulf Stream's child, the North Atlantic Current or Drift. Geographically, Britain lies in the convergence between the cold polar airflow and air currents heated in the tropics and kept warm by contact with the Gulf Stream and North Atlantic Current. That position ensures that our weather is 'constant in nothing but inconstancy'. For gardeners, it makes — as Osgood Mackenzie demonstrated — remarkable things possible.

On the afternoon that I came to Inverewe, the temperature was around 30 degrees Celsius. The sun burned from a cloudless sky, and the High Lump shimmered in the haze of the heat. Once within the great belt of conifers that Mackenzie organised as his first line of defence against the gales and the salt spray, I could have imagined myself almost anywhere other than north-western Scotland. The perfume of Brazil filled the still, damp air around the spikes and enormous green leaves of the *Gunnera manicata* in the Wet Valley. From South America I wandered north to Mexico, and further north still, until I was standing beside the banks of North American ostrich fern that hug the sides of the Small Pond. Then I took a slow boat to Australia and hiked through a Tasmanian eucalyptus grove, from where I made my way to China, through Tibet to Bhutan and Sikkim. Quite suddenly, I emerged from the shade of the avenues of oriental rhododendrons on to the lookout above the cliffs of the High Lump. I looked across the dazzling blue waters of Loch Ewe to the low hills of ancient Lewissian gneiss beyond the mouth of the River Ewe, with the blue Torridon hills behind, and the Hebrides somewhere out in the sea. Then, taking in the barrenness of the distant scene, I remembered where I was, and what it would have been like before Osgood Mackenzie's imagination took flight.

He made a place of utter enchantment, and eighty years after his death that enchantment endures, despite the place having been taken into the embrace of the National Trust for Scotland, with all that entails. I stretched out on the soft turf beneath the outreaching branches of one of the most wonderful trees I have ever seen, a variegated Turkey oak planted by Mackenzie's daughter Mairi Sawyer to the north-east of the white manse which replaced her father's grander mansion after it was burned down in 1914. Over my head dry, pale lichen clung to the immense branches like wisps of green candyfloss. The foliage whispered drily in the breeze, the leaves light green around their edges, darker within, the variegation lit by the sun. Over the lawn and the rock garden and past a wind-twisted eucalyptus I could see the sparkling sea. Soothed by the rustling overhead, and scents of pine and salt, I nodded off.

After a time I roused myself and forced my steps to 'The Garden'. 'As is the case with us Highlanders,' Mackenzie explained, 'I possess only the one garden for fruit, flowers and vegetables', although he was always careful to refer to it as 'the kitchen garden' when in the company of English friends. It was cut with an infinity of labour into the side of the promontory at the only point where there was a slope down to the shore. 'Thousands upon thousands of barrowloads of small stones had to be wheeled into the sea,' Mackenzie related, and in their place were dumped cartloads of 'red soil from long distances . . . peaty stuff from old turf ditches . . . and a blue marl from the sea, full of decayed oyster shells and crabs and other good things'. The garden, one acre in extent, was enclosed in high walls, the one along the top being surmounted by a great rampart of rhododendron hedge. It was planted with vegetables, soft fruits and fans and cordons of fruit trees, and with great masses of agapanthus, scarlet lobelias, dahlias, 'tea roses almost as good as on the Riviera', and other showy blooms arranged to be appreciated from a boat in the bay.

The garden faces south, taking all the sun and the nourishing rains brought in by the winds off the warm water currents. The display of fruit and vegetables was astounding, making my own raised beds, created and cherished with such loving care far away in the tame south of England look like an impoverished patch hacked out of a parched hillside in Palestine. Blackcurrant bushes sagged under the weight of lustrous berries as big as marbles. Raspberry canes dripped with fruit. Gigantic Red Grant carrots strained to lift their cloches off the dark soil. Leeks as wide as spade handles stood flanked by turnips and beetroot like lilac and purple tennis balls, and forests of swaying sea kale and Swiss chard with deep crimson and buttery yellow stalks. The espaliers of apples and pears burst with swelling fruit, and the branches of the plum trees were bent to the ground under the burden of the crop. 'There is one thing I may mention,' wrote Mackenzie, 'which I hardly suppose my friends on the south coast can boast of — viz. that I have never yet, in over forty years, failed to get a crop of apples, and, I might almost add, pears and plums as well . . . Really our difficulty is that we have not force enough to get them thinned, so thickly do they set, a fact which I suppose must be credited to our good Gulf Stream.'

It is down the western seaboard of Britain — from Wester Ross to Cornwall — that the influence of the warm flow is most powerfully felt. At Inverewe, Osgood Mackenzie could grow tender plants in the open that, to survive in London, required cosseting in one of the glasshouses at Kew. At Tresco Abbey, in the Scilly Isles, exotics from all over the southern hemisphere which would soon wither and perish on the mainland flourish in a humid, frost-free micro-climate. The further east the colder it becomes in winter, the hotter in summer and the drier all the year round. Inverewe receives about 55 inches of rain a year. Barely a third of that falls down the other side of the country, at Elmstead Market in Essex, where Beth Chatto created her celebrated Dry Garden on what had previously been sun-baked, gravelly mud, thereby transforming a wasteland into a tapestry of lavenders, sages, grasses, poppies, alliums and other plants conspicuous for their modest need for water. Despite the sharp regional variations, there is nowhere in these islands that a garden cannot be made. Nor can much of a case be made for a peculiar British genius in the art. As Jane Brown points out briskly in her social history of gardening, *The Pursuit of Paradise*, 'it is the British climate that encouraged gardens, rather than any native tendency to green fingers or nonsense about "love of plants" — at which the Dutch beat us hands down'.

The gardener generally has the sense to acknowledge the debt he or she owes to our weather, in the sense that without it there would be no garden and no recreation. But the relationship is not a tranquil one. It is characterised on one side (we will never know what the clouds think of us) by a watchful, neurotic impatience born from the need for constant vigilance, and an exasperation that so little of what the elements deliver comes in the right measure and at convenient times. Serious gardeners can never relax. Dangers constantly threaten: a late frost to nip and burn new buds and shoots, a gale whipped up to wrench the honeysuckle from its moorings, a day or two of windless damp to send the mildew leaping through the gooseberries and stimulate the full reproductive powers of aphids and slugs. Gardeners can fret endlessly about their gardens, but their opportunity to tend to them is dictated by a force over which they have no influence: the weather. As the necessary rain tips down throughout their one free afternoon of the week, they stare from the window wondering why some means cannot be devised to make it fall at night or when they are at work, and what the slugs are up to. Their attitude is more suspicious than appreciative, but their weather awareness is generally well developed, even intense. They have the 'weather eye'.

The same is true of those enthralled by gardening's only rival as a mass recreation: angling. But the angler's perspective on the weather is different, not so much sceptical as fundamentally antagonistic. Gardeners complain, but they do not rage and shake their fists. In contrast, it is almost unheard of for a fisherman to declare that the weather has been entirely favourable to his sport, still less to give it credit for any success he may have had. He may be aware that without it there would be no water in his river or lake, and no fish to fish for. But he is not grateful to it, for one of the principles in his philosophy is that there is always too much or too little of water, warmth, sunshine, cloud, or wind.

Wind is the angler's chief adversary. If it is his intention to fish with flies for trout on a great sheet of still water – say, Lough Corrib in the west of Ireland, or Rutland Water in the middle of England – the sight of flat calm will fill him with the deepest gloom, since boat fishing demands a decent breeze to keep the boat drifting and to obscure the trout's view of those conspiring after its downfall. But then again, if the wind is too boisterous, the boat charges over the best places, the flies are whirled into tangles, and the angler is buffeted into a state of morose discomfort. Moreover, the wind must be from the right quarter. The north wind, with its Arctic edge, is plain bad, while an east wind is imbued – in the words of James Cheetham's *Angler's Vade Mecum* of 1681 – with 'a secret malignity . . . that generally abates fishes' appetites and desire of baits'.

On the river, the fly fisherman generally prefers no wind, unless he happens to be after salmon or sea trout in midge-infested regions of Scotland or Ireland, where no wind means torment verging on madness. If he is fishing a floating fly – known as the dry fly – he will want to cast upstream, in which case a wind blowing downstream will be hateful to him. But, of course, rivers flow in all sorts of different directions, so that the wind which makes the fisherman happy on one stretch will provoke protests on another. It is little wonder that, from the fisherman's point of view, the ideal day is a rare event indeed, nor that so much fishing talk and writing revolves around this matter of the weather. There is a whole book on the subject, *Fishermen's Weather*, which was compiled a century ago by F. G. Aflalo, and very dull it is, since all it does is to bring together an incoherent mass of subjective and contradictory theories about the effects of the elements on fish and the chances of catching them. Its one conclusion, a cliché in itself, is that the weather is almost never so bad as to make fishing impossible, and that since any fishing is better than no fishing, the fisherman should keep swearing and get on with it.

My favourite fishing writer, Hugh Tempest Sheringham — the atheist, socialist son of the vicar of Tewkesbury — captured the essence of the matter in a droll piece entitled *Three Wild Days in Wessex*. After being repeatedly battered by storms and threatened by bolts of lightning, Sheringham's friend — 'the indomitable one' — lays down his rod and refuses to pick it up again. 'It was not that his heart quailed before our English summer,' Sheringham wrote, 'but that it was filled with righteous indignation. A refusal to fish seemed to him the only way in which he could mark his disapproval of the weather.' Sheringham himself persists, cheering himself one morning with 'the old adage which promises sunshine before eleven if it is raining before seven'. In the event, the rain which is falling 'nicely' at half past six begins 'in real earnest' at half past ten, and continues 'vigorously' the rest of the day. But the angler — despite sodden sandwiches and the searching out by the rain of the inevitable gap between mackintosh and waders — angles on, and is rewarded by a basket of three dozen dace ('nice little fish') and one fat trout whose capture, Sheringham reflects, 'formed a curious conclusion to a curious experience of weather and fishing'.

Because their playground is close at hand, gardeners are usually able to garden around the weather, whereas fishermen pursue their pleasure in spite of it. That pleasure is diminished by wind and rain, which is one of the reasons fishermen tend to become irritable at a favourite comment of the ignorant — 'Oh, I always thought fish bite better in the rain' — which is often accompanied by references to sitting under green umbrellas. In general, adverse weather makes outdoor sports and pastimes more uncomfortable than they would be in fine weather, but not impossible. But there are summer games — such as tennis, crocquet and bowls — which cannot cope with a sustained downpour; and one which, because of the length of time it takes to play — anything up to five days — is especially vulnerable to the capriciousness of the British climate.

Broadhalfpenny Down, a long lump of chalk smoothly topped with thin soil and turf, rises like a surfacing whale in the downland of southern Hampshire a mile and more from the village of Hambledon. It was a Saturday in mid-June, as perfect an English early summer's day as the mind could picture. The film of milky cirrus of the morning had been burned off by the sun. There was a freshness in the blue of the sky that was answered in the fields of green corn stretching away from the lower slopes of Broadhalfpenny. A soft breeze came from the south, enough to stir the tops of the stand of beeches blocking the view towards the village. In short, it was an afternoon for cricket. And this, of all the places in the world for it, was the one to be. The drawback was that there was, and would be, no cricket that day.

So instead, as I leaned against a fence-post on the boundary, I had to settle for echoes of history. Opposite me, to jog the memory, stood a pub of famous name, the Bat and Ball; no matter that the name and the situation are about all it shares with the hostelry where Richard Nyren once catered for the visitors who flocked from far and wide to see the finest cricket team in the land, before himself hurrying across in flannels and top hat to take his place in its ranks. Nyren's advertisement promised beef, ham, chickens and tarts 'for those with good appetites', disdaining 'Marbres, Aspiques, Blancmanges' or any other fancy foreign delicacy here in the heart of England.

For the great multitude of the lovers of cricket's past spread across the civilised world, Hambledon is, was, and ever will be 'The Cradle of Cricket'. In the sense of being the game's birthplace, this is nonsense. Two hundred years before Nyren was drawing ale at the Bat and Ball, youthful shepherds on the Weald of west Kent and east Sussex were amusing themselves at idle moments by hurling a ball of compressed wool at the narrow gate of the sheep pen – the wicket – and defending it with a cut-down crook. By the mid-1740s Kent, Sussex, Surrey and Gloucestershire were fielding representative sides, and in 1744 the first Laws of Cricket were formally drawn up at the Artillery Ground in Finsbury, north London. The occasion was a match between Kent and All England which inspired a well-known stage performer and versifier, James Love, to compose his 'Cricket: An Heroic Poem'.

> Hail cricket! Glorious, manly British game!
> First of all sports! Be first alike in Fame . . .

But it was on top of Broadhalfpenny Down, in the course of one decade – the 1770s – that the game was raised to the level of an art by the men of Hambledon under the proud eye of the club's presiding genius and chief patron, the vicar of Itchen Abbas, the Reverend Charles Powlett. Powlett's father was the Duke of Bolton, a notorious buck and man about town until he was smitten by the charms of the darling of the London stage, the irresistible Lavinia Fenton, who forsook her career – she was the original Polly Peachum in Gay's *The Beggar's Opera* – to become the Duke's mistress, and bore him three children, of whom one was the cricket-loving Charles.

Powlett and his aristocratic friends were determined that this Hambledon team should be champions. Craftsmen were recruited in the village, and farmers from around, and notable talents from further afield. In September 1768, Hambledon played Kent, and John Small – a Petersfield man who sang in the church choir there for seventy-five years – 'fetched above seven score notches off his own bat'. When the best bowler in England, the Kentish ace Lumpy Stevens, got Small out in 1772, it was the first time he had been dismissed in years. Between 1771 and 1780 Hambledon played All-England fifty-one times, and on twenty-nine of those occasions victory went to the Hampshire men. The greatest of these great days was 17 June 1777. A purse of 1000 guineas was at stake, and enormous crowds gathered to watch the Duke of Dorset and Lumpy Stevens open the batting for England. But they were no match for Hambledon, for whom the left-hander James Aylward batted for two days and made 169. At the Bat and Ball the celebrations were prolonged. 'Little Hambledon pitted against All-England was a proud thought,' reflected Richard Nyren's son John. 'Defeat was a glory in such a struggle, Victory indeed made us little lower than ANGELS.'

A few years later the club moved their ground to Windmill Down, which was closer to the village, where they enjoyed several more years of glory. The springy turf of Broadhalfpenny was left to the sheep, and would see no more of the great occasions. Indeed it saw no more cricket at all until the 1920s, when it came into the possession of Winchester College. These days it is used by a club called the Broadhalfpenny Brigands, who have links with the Royal Navy and play only on Sunday afternoons – hence the ground's deserted condition the afternoon of my visit. The pitch, so the landlord of the Bat and Ball informed me, is distinctly dodgy, the thin soil over the chalk making it low, slow, excessively helpful to bowling of a rather mean-spirited type, and way below the standard required for league cricket.

I left the ground and the whispering of its departed spirits: the impregnable John Small; Richard Nyren with his cunning left arm; David Harris, the Elvetham potter, wheeling in from the south-west end; Billy Beldham, for forty years the finest batsman in England, 'safer than the Bank', according to young Nyren. I found their successors perspiring freely at Hambledon CC's current ground, on the outskirts of the village, playing against their local rivals, Whitchurch. The grass was green velvet compared with the threadbare rug on the down. On the front of the pavilion, rather overshadowed by a sign advertising the sponsorship of a local carpet firm, were a clock and a plaque dedicated to the memory of Edward Whalley-Tooker, club captain for no less than thirty-seven years. Dogs panted in the shade while the tea ladies chattered. Out on the square, under a sun which was now fierce, Whitchurch's opening bowler was hard at work. He had thick grey hair, carefully brushed, and a neat grey moustache, and hurried in off five paces. 'Come on, Jonno,' exhorted the slips after each ball. 'Keep it up, fella.' As he walked back to the start of his run-up, Jonno polished the ball against his right thigh as he had done a million times before. Hambledon's number three batsman, lean and upright with an obvious touch of class, drove him easily through the covers to the boundary. The next ball struck the front pad. 'Whaaaooorrhhhh,' yelled Jonno, whirling round to face a little elderly umpire in a white cap, white coat, white shoes and black trousers. A shake of the white cap and Jonno walked briskly back to his mark. The next ball flashed across the grass to the boundary again.

On such a day as this the game would undoubtedly be fought to the finish, by which time the sun would be sinking over the Downs and the shadow cast by the Whalley-Tooker pavilion would be stretching towards the pitch. There is a particular happiness that settles upon the club cricketer with the certainty that the weather is set fair, and the match on which his heart has been set all week will take place. Of course, his happiness may well be clouded at some point by misfortune or misjudgement, but unless the disaster is exceptionally severe, by the time stumps are drawn, the sweaty body showered, the gear stowed away and the first pint of beer addressed, it will have reasserted itself. The cricketers will stand together, ruddy faces aglow, united in their confidence that no better way to spend a summer's afternoon and evening has ever been devised, that no place more pleasing to the eye than a cricket field in the English countryside can be imagined, that of all the blessings that England has shared with the rest of the world, none is more blessed than this game.

This happiness is all the more acute because of the cricketer's awareness of the rarity and preciousness of the perfect day. It used to be the case, when 'the typical British summer' still held sway, that whole seasons could come and go without such days occurring at all; and anyone whose career goes back a decade or more will have had much to endure at the hands of our climate. On the basic theme – of low spirits caused by the annihilation of his fun – a number of variations are possible. The mid-morning cancellation on a Sunday which dawns with the insistent hiss of rain and continues that way until tea and beyond is bad, but bearable, since everyone's spirits are affected in the same way, if not to the same degree. More trying are those occasions when, having driven some distance to an away fixture, the cricketer arrives to be confronted by a mass of purple and black marching across the sky towards the ground to the accompaniment of drumrolls of thunder. The first fat drops of rain plop on to the windscreen as he pulls up, and he is swept by the dismal certainty of impending washout. Almost as bad are games which start promisingly enough, only to be torpedoed by a downpour conjured like magic from a sky which, a mere hour or two before, was innocence itself.

But these are minor troubles compared with the anguish of the day which begins wet enough to warrant a decision at, say, eleven o'clock to cancel the match, and then — twenty minutes after the teams have been given the tidings and the man doing the tea has been told his egg mayonnaise and tuna salad sandwiches will not be needed — decides to mend its ways. The clouds are chased away and a warm sun rolls up its sleeves. Gardeners look up, fetch out their boots and gloves and forks and step forth to tackle the weeding. The angler, picturing the river sparkling, its surface dimpled by rising trout, gathers rod, bag and waders. Families make ready for the park or a walk in the woods. The world smiles, except that part of it where the cricketer is slumped in his misery, the taste of ashes in his mouth.

That is very bad. But there is worse: those mercifully rare days on which the weather seems to be not so much indifferent to the cricketer's plight, but actively intent on making him wretched. One such day occurred a week before my visit to Hambledon. It was a special Sunday for the village team for which I have played for thirty-five years. We were coming home after three summers of playing all our fixtures away as a result of the destruction of our pavilion at the hands of a teenaged, female arsonist. Now we had a new ground and a new pavilion, and our new beginning was to be marked with a game against our oldest rivals. Players from our distant past had been invited. Members of the parish council would be there, possibly even our local MP. There was a beer tent and a barbecue, and a photographer from the local paper was coming to record the dedication of a bench to the memory of a club stalwart who had not lived long enough to witness our rebirth. For us, it was an event.

The weather had been temperamental for some days and the forecast that morning was equivocal. It rained at breakfast time, then stopped. The sun came out, then it rained again. Then the sun reappeared, long enough for the tents to be put up and the pitch to be rolled once more. Everything looked splendid, it was agreed: the close-shorn turf of the outfield almost emerald in its verdancy, the white lines of the boundary and the pitch markings standing out with precision, the smell of grass and summer. Hope and expectation soared. Guests arrived, then the visiting team. The beer began to flow, and one or two impatient souls put on their whites and knocked a ball about.

All the time we watched the sky, like men waiting for bad news. Suddenly it darkened in the west. The darkness rushed our way at amazing speed. Within minutes a curtain of rain swept across the village. The tents flapped and strained at their moorings as if possessed by devils. As we watched the deluge from under cover, heads were wagging. 'Half an hour of this and we'll have to call it off' was the consensus. After twenty minutes the storm dashed off to attend to urgent business elsewhere. The sun came out. The scoreboard was put back on its legs. The pitch was inspected. It was soggy, undeniably so, but there were no puddles. With a drying wind and sunshine, a start might be made in − say − forty minutes. Hope was reborn. The photographer arrived and we put on our white flannels and stood behind Stan's bench, while he darted around, clucking and snapping. The stumps were put in, the two captains stood on the pitch while a coin was tossed to decide who should bat. More beer was drunk, and smoke from the sausages and burgers whirled into the air. Tales of the old days were swapped, and hopes for the new. But the atmosphere was not relaxed. There was too much staring at the sky.

Enemy forces were again gathering in the west like Thordor's armies, filling the sky from one side to the other. There was no escape, and we waited to receive our fate. The storm flung itself at us. We had to grab the tent poles to stop the canvas being torn away. The barbecue was doused, the salads were drenched, the paper plates turned dark with the rain and blew away. All was confusion and wretchedness. The tempest lingered, like a raiding party intent on finishing the job, then galloped off. We gathered sorrowfully beside our pitch, now half submerged in standing water. The visiting team departed with sympathetic waves and mutters of 'better luck next time'. A few of my team-mates, more resilient than me, smiled bravely and went back to the beer. I felt too drained by the protracted duet between hope and despair to do anything other than go home. I was dejected, but also filled with that futile rage that unusually malign weather induces; and the childish and absurd suspicion that such an intricate sequence of weather events must have been organised to an end, to provide amusement. I am slightly ashamed to confess that, recalling it all now, I feel angry again.

Chapter 13

Harmless Idiots

EVERY DAY SINCE 1 JANUARY 1946 CEDRIC ROBERTS[*] HAS RECORDED THE weather in Halesowen. There is nothing in the least remarkable about Halesowen, which was once a market town surrounded by Worcestershire countryside but is now hardly distinguishable from its neighbours in the system of satellite settlements around Birmingham. Nor is there anything remarkable about its weather, which is no different from that anywhere else across the middle of England. But I would suggest that — even by the standards of dedicated weather-watchers — Mr Roberts' devotion to his self-appointed mission is remarkable.

He has not missed a day. On the very rare occasions he has left Halesowen, he has ensured that the record has been maintained. Not a drop of rain, nor a flake of snow nor a stone of hail has fallen on his home town, nor has a ray of sunshine illuminated it, nor a cloud rolled over it in well over half a century without Mr Roberts knowing about it and noting it down. As a teenager he had to pester his aunts and uncles to raise the £5 2s 6d to buy a standard rain gauge and fix it into a patch of grass

---

[*] Cedric Roberts died in November 2004. When I wrote this chapter he was still alive, and was still maintaining his records, which he continued to do until a few weeks before his death. I have decided to leave it as I wrote it then.

in the garden. These days he has every technological aid the amateur meteorologist could dream of. But his purpose remains unchanged: to keep a close eye on the skies above the place where he was born, where he has lived all his life and where he will surely die. Meteorologically, the day I visited Mr Roberts — 25 July 2003 — was not without interest, as meteorologists are wont to say. Following several weeks of drought, and before several more weeks of drought, it rained. It was raining when I left Reading by train at mid-morning and still raining when I got to Birmingham at lunchtime. The city, which I had never been to before, did not look its best. Down the road at Edgbaston, the entire day's play in the Test match against South Africa was rained off, an extraordinary event in that summer of summers. It took me some time to locate the bus stop for Halesowen, and I was damp and steaming by the time I took my seat. Condensation on the inside of the windows and the rain on the outside made it impossible for me to follow our progress. I asked an elderly lady in a rain hat for help. She at once formed a committee with two others to discuss my situation. 'Don't worry, dear,' the youngest of the three said in a strong West Midlands accent. 'I'm gowing to 'Alesowen meself. I'll see yer roit.' I thanked the committee. 'Ow, we're famous for ower 'ospitalitee, we Brummagens,' she answered with the warmest of welcoming smiles. And she was as good as her word, shepherding me out at Halesowen bus station and propelling me to the stop where I could catch another bus to Mr Roberts' part of town.

By now the rain had stopped. There was some ragged blue sky above, though the urgency with which swollen black clouds were racing in from the west suggested the streets of Halesowen would not be dry for long. I got off the bus outside a large and unappealing Harvester Inn, and found Mr Roberts' maisonette without difficulty. This was partly due to the fact that I had his address. But even if I hadn't, the roof of the maisonette – which in other respects is just like any other maisonette in a part of the world where there are many – would have provided a strong clue. Outlined against the shifting sky was a clutter of apparatuses, fixed there – as I discovered later from their owner – to measure and record sunshine, radiation, wind speed and direction, and other vital matters. On another, lower roof was a second sunshine recorder, next to a hedge kept assiduously clipped to ensure that every sunbeam got through.

'The Weather Man', as he is known around Halesowen, was waiting for me. He is in his seventies and moves slowly and with difficulty. Mr Roberts has suffered from bone marrow cancer for some years, a disease which – apart from the inconvenience of removing him at regular intervals from his weather station to hospital – is the cause of continual discomfort and often worse. But he suffers it with resilient good spirits. 'I've had a very good life,' he says, beaming, then stops to show me the photograph of him meeting Prince Charles to receive his MBE for services to the British weather. He appears on local radio and TV whenever a weather event occurs, to place it in its historical context. He grinned with evident delight when I asked him if he enjoyed his status as a Halesowen celebrity. And why shouldn't he?

Geographically, Mr Roberts has not moved far in his life's journey. His maisonette stands on part of what was once the garden of his family home. His parents, and their parents, were Halesowen people, and it was to Halesowen Grammar School that young Cedric, a bright lad and an only child, went in 1943. Most of the male teachers had left to fight, and the geography teacher was a Mrs Brash, who had the idea of establishing a weather station on the school roof. The class was divided into pairs, boys with boys, girls with girls – 'it was very strict in those days,' Mr Roberts explained – with each pair taking charge of the rain gauge, barometer and thermometer for a week. Cedric's partner was Edgar Brown, and in the course of their week they became thoroughly infected by the bug. They made themselves a 5-inch rain gauge out of a varnished flower pot, and acquired a wind vane and a thermometer.

By 1944 Cedric was recording his readings in neat columns in an exercise book. The following year he happened to see an advertisement placed by the Met Office. With the war now over, it was time to get back to the important things in life and the Met Office was looking for volunteers to maintain a network of weather stations all over the land. Young Cedric applied, much to his mother's disapproval. 'She went berserk,' he told me. 'She used to say "Where's the weather going to get you, going out and getting soaked all the time?" She wanted me to follow my father and become a welder.'

A buff-coloured envelope arrived, stamped On His Majesty's Service. It was followed not long after by a Met Office man, to inspect Cedric's setup. By the end of 1945, thanks to the aunties and uncles, he had equipped himself with all the prescribed instruments, and on 1 January 1946 he started upon his duties as a member of the British Rainfall Organisation, engaged on work of national importance. 'I was completely fascinated from the word go,' Mr Roberts recalls without a trace of self-consciousness. 'When there was a really good downpour I got excited, I could hardly wait to get hold of the gauge and find out how much had fallen.'

The following winter, between January and March 1947, Halesowen – together with the rest of the country – was assailed by the most prolonged and disruptive freeze of the century. While

Britain shivered and shuddered and slipped and went hungry and lamented, Cedric Roberts was in his element. By 7 February the depth of the level snow in the Roberts' garden was 19 centimetres, and there were drifts 12 feet deep in the lanes and fields around. The wind blew constantly at 30 to 40 kilometres an hour, and between the 1st and the 15th of that month there was one hour of sunshine. By the end of February the depth of snow had reached 27 centimetres, and further blizzards on 4 and 5 March raised it to 42 centimetres. On 12 March a fall of freezing rain deposited a 6-centimetre layer of ice on top of the snow, and people were able to walk over buried hedges and signposts. The thaw came amid gales and days of torrential rain, and enormous areas along the Severn were flooded. As Mr Roberts noted in an article published in the Royal Meteorological Society's monthly journal *Weather*, in March 2003, it had been 'a spell of quite amazing weather'.

It confirmed him in the vocation he had chosen for himself: to be Halesowen's modern counterpart of William Merle of Driby, Thomas Barker of Lyndon, Orlando Whistlecraft of Thwaite and the other weather chroniclers of the past. The idea of leaving Halesowen and seeing the world has never occurred to Cedric Roberts. Why should he, when all the world he wanted to see was there? As a young man he found the ideal job, teaching maths and science at a local school. As soon as he could afford to, he expanded the scale of his weather station, adding more thermometers, a sunshine recorder and an automatic recording rain gauge. After retiring from teaching in 1987, he bought himself a BBC computer on to which he laboriously transcribed his records — only to be told by his Met Office masters that he really needed a PC. It took him a further three and a half years to transfer his thirty-six years' worth of data on to his PC.

He told me something of his life story as we sat at the back

279

of the maisonette, looking out on to the garden. It is not the cosiest of rooms, crowded as it is with computer gear and screens, on one of which Mr Roberts monitors the images beamed to him by two satellites: the Meteosat Second Generation, 24,000 miles up but still able to focus on cloud movements over Halesowen; and the American NOAA, or National Oceanic and Atmosphere Agency, a mere five hundred miles overhead. The garden is even further removed from the Halesowen norm. It is rectangular, and in the centre – raised above a patch of grass – is a white, slatted box containing the wet and dry bulb thermometers. Other thermometers poke up from the turf, measuring the temperature at ground level, and at the heights of 1, 2 and 3 metres above it. A battery of rain gauges bristles from a gravel rectangle: six in all, including one with an infra-red beam which registers automatically when it is broken by a single drop.

At the far end is a Campbell-Stokes sunshine recorder, and on one side is the satellite dish and a junction box, through which is fed the underground cabling which transmits the daily flood of information from the instruments to the computer in the kitchen. At least, that is the theory. But there is no accounting for fate, or the weather, even in Halesowen. A couple of months before my visit, a storm had dispatched a thunderbolt horizontally along the rooftops which eventually struck a house a mile away and largely destroyed it. As the bolt passed over Mr Roberts' home it blew all his electrical circuitry and wiped his specially designed software. This was now being restored, and in the meantime he was being compelled to do all the readings manually, an exhausting task for someone in his condition. 'It is a struggle when it is pouring with rain and I'm not feeling well,' he told me. 'But, no, I've never been tempted to give it a miss. And I just pray that I will be able to continue.'

He says this very simply, in the manner of someone with deep religious convictions talking about his faith. I had the impression that it would take more than incurable cancer and a mere thunderbolt to deflect Cedric Roberts from his chosen path. Of course I asked him what it was about the subject which exercised such a grip on his inner self; and of course he could give no adequate reply. 'Our weather is so much more interesting than what they have in other countries,' he said with the authoritative air of someone who had travelled widely to investigate the matter. 'All right, we don't have hurricanes and all that. But it's so changeable, so full of surprises. How could you ever lose interest in it?' So I asked him if he thought there was a point in collecting this enormous mass of information about the weather in one small place in one small country, beyond satisfying his hunger to do it. He thought there was, simply in its existence, which he intended to safeguard by depositing it with the local archives.

As I left, some large raindrops fell on to my head from a large black cloud suspended over Halesowen. It struck me later that – despite his sickness and solitariness – Mr Roberts was a fortunate fellow. At a time of life when a purpose to that life often seems elusive, he was still driven by his mission, his obsession, his ruling passion – call it what you will – and would be to the end of his days. But there was a sadness as he told it to me. He could not find anyone to carry on his work after he was gone. He had sounded out various contacts infected to a degree by the bug, but no one had shown any readiness to replace the man who put Halesowen on the weather map.

The Royal Meteorological Society has a little over three thousand members, of whom fewer than four hundred are women.

Actually, the proportion is higher than I had expected. But I probably had that expectation because I am a man and find it difficult to imagine anyone who isn't a man becoming sufficiently roused by the subject of the weather to join an organisation devoted to its study. Even so, the fact remains that weather-watching as a pastime — as distinct from meteorology as a profession — is a male domain. I am aware that the way in which our society is organised carries an inherent bias favouring male outside interests over female. But I would still risk the assertion that there is something about the close observation and punctilious recording of our daily weather that is, in itself, peculiarly congenial to a certain kind of man, but wholly uncongenial to all types of the female temperament. But what is that something? And why should this be?

The subject of gender types and stereotypes is a quagmire of conflicting views and prejudices. Is it, for instance, true that women are naturally — whatever that means — more passive, submissive, emotional, neurotic, frightened of success, dependent, verbal, nurturing, intuitive, more concerned with and about intimacy, personal relationships, social issues and perceived injustices than men? And, conversely, is it true that men are inherently more aggressive, vigorous, exploratory, group-oriented, and more inclined towards ideology, theory and politics than women? For each of these assumptions there is a challenge — either on the grounds that it is not true, or that any validity it has is derived from the conditioning imposed by the way we live rather than a chromosome in the genes.

It would clearly be untrue to suggest that women are not interested in the weather, or that whatever interest they have is generally related to concerns about what clothes they should be wearing. In the Met Office archive there are several weather journals by women, maintained with great care and attention to detail over many years. But these records emphatically do not exhibit the delight in statistical data so characteristic of the epic registers compiled by Barker, Whistlecraft and others. This – the rigid routine of examining instruments at the same time every day of every week of every month of every year, the recording of those readings, the transcription of those readings into columns, the distillation of the information in those pages of columns into averages and trends – this is a male thing.

It isn't for all of us, of course. Although I consult the little weather station outside my office two or three times a day, it would not occur to me to keep a record of the readings it supplies. On the other hand, I approve of the concept of the routine that conscientious weather-watchers must observe, because routine offers discipline and structure in a world where chaos threatens from all sides. As I have already admitted, I am attached to my own routine, but not – I like to think – fanatical about it. I do not fly into fits of rage if I am prevented from following it. I would say – some might disagree – that I am its master, rather than the other way round. On occasions I introduce variations into it that are quite radical, like having honey on my second slice of breakfast toast instead of jam. My point is that the notion of structuring the day by reading the barometer at 6 a.m. noon and 6 p.m., noting the maximum and minimum temperatures, measuring the contents of a rain gauge, and recording the amount of sunshine and the strength and direction of the wind, does not strike me as sad or futile, even though, in practice, I would not care to do it.

An earlier book of mine dealt with lawns and lawnmowers and obsessive attitudes to the care of turf. The cutting and cherishing of grass and the warfare against its numerous enemies are even more of a male preserve than watching the weather. When researching the book, I telephoned the eminent social psychologist Doctor Halla Beloff to ask if she could shed any light on the gender issue in lawn care. She could and did, explaining that men tended to see the garden as separate from the house, as an arena of challenge in which they were required to impose and maintain control by mowing the grass, lopping off branches, trimming hedges, chopping down trees and so on, and then by destroying the casualties by fire. Women, in contrast, saw the house and garden as complementary to each other, together forming home, both enhanced by the exercise of the creative, rather than the destructive, impulse. Doctor Beloff also suggested that the mower was invested with a subliminal role as a penis substitute, which gave me food for thought and still does.

I telephoned her again to pick her brains about weather-watchers, and she was just as amiable and forthright as she had been on the subject of lawn fanatics. She said she herself had no interest whatever in the weather beyond its influence on her decisions about what clothes to wear, and that she would regard anyone who made it a central part of their lives as a 'harmless idiot'. She thought the fondness for exhaustive and meticulous record-keeping was probably related to a common male desire to fix, and in a sense capture, reality as a means of challenging its amorphousness and unpredictability. She argued that, rather than being a strategy to achieve control, as in the case of mowing the lawn, this was more an impulse to drop an anchor, to establish and hold on to a position, and a sense of permanence. I pointed out that these were assertions about the male character rather than accepted facts. Doctor Beloff cheerfully agreed, adding that they were, nonetheless, true. Women, she maintained, were much more preoccupied with human relationships to wish to establish close and regular contacts with a collection of meteorological instruments. 'Men like that,' she said. 'It doesn't ask too much of them.'

Perhaps I should have asked Dr Charles Briscoe if he found it easier to keep up a harmonious relationship with his automatic weather station than with members of his own species. However, he was much too pleasant, too courteous, too patient with my other inquiries for me to abuse his hospitality with such an insolent question. He was tall, slim, diffident, softly spoken, and immensely well mannered in that old-fashioned, gentlemanly, public school way. But it would be a mistake to confuse the reserve with lack of passion.

Dr Briscoe is keeper of the weather in Buxton, a straggly, nondescript village in a rather nondescript stretch of country-side a few miles north of Norwich. I came to see him on what would have been regarded, by the standards of what we used to think of as the typical British summer, as a pretty nondescript sort of day: a bit of blue, a lot of grey, a bit of wind, temperature in the mid-60s. But the fact that, an hour or so before my arrival, there had been a light shower producing 0.2 millimetres of rain in Dr Briscoe's gauge made it worthy of notice. It was the first day of September 2003, and came after an August which had been the hottest and one of the driest in living memory. So, after a long drive across a country the colour of a digestive biscuit, a shower of rain was something to be talked about. And we did.

At the age of nine, Charles Briscoe wrote to the Met Office to report a rare sighting of a blue moon, believed to have been caused by ash blown from a forest fire in Canada. Aged twelve, he was the only boy in his class at prep school who knew what freezing point was on the Fahrenheit scale, a fact he had first stored when he was five. For as long as he can remember, the state of the weather has been a matter of consuming interest for him. He was sent to Eton, where he acquired an illicit radio so that he could keep abreast of the forecasts. After Cambridge, he went to medical school in London, and then – in the early 1970s – he took a position as an anaesthetist at a hospital in Norwich. This enabled him to live again in the village where the Briscoes farmed and belonged, and to embark upon his study of its climate. He's still there, retired now from hospital work, but continuing to supervise the weather over Buxton.

Unlike Cedric Roberts, Charles Briscoe does not regard the immense wealth of data he has collected about the weather in his home village as having great historical value. For him, the collection and the recording are what matter; it is as much as any man could hope for from his hobby that it should still hold his attention, and that the daily round of examining his instruments and recording their readings should still provide nourishment for his spirit. He is quietly amused by his reputation as the Buxton Weather Guru, and happy to pop up every now and then on Anglia TV and the local radio station. But his status as a local fount of weather wisdom is beside the point. Nor, in further contrast to Mr Roberts, is he entirely content with the object of his affections. To put it crudely, Dr Briscoe wishes that Buxton could, more often than it does, come up with something out of the ordinary.

There was one unforgettable night, some time ago – 1 December 1975 – when East Anglia was invaded by a succession of tornadoes, six in Norfolk and one in Cambridgeshire, which Dr Briscoe and the Anglia TV weather presenter Michael Hunt tracked on their various paths of destruction and subsequently wrote up for the *Journal of Meteorology*. But since then things have been pretty quiet, apart from a hailstorm in '85 and a couple more tornadoes a few years later. 'I do sometimes wish for more exciting weather than we have here,' Dr Briscoe said wistfully. 'For instance, the fact that we haven't had any real snow since 1987 rather takes the fun out of it. I'd love to go to Alaska, just for the snow.'

His wife came in from her toils in the garden. I asked her if she shared anything of her husband's meteorological passion. She looked at me as if I were mad. When he talked about the subject, she looked at him in a way that was familiar to me from having met the wives of lawn mowing enthusiasts. It is a look in which incomprehension is mixed with a kind of impatient fondness and an awareness that the situation could be a lot worse. It says: I don't understand, and I never will, how a grown-up person could be so possessed by something so trivial, particularly when you think of the useful things he could be doing. But at least it's harmless. He could be down the pub every lunchtime, instead of peering at his bloody instruments.

Dr Briscoe's records of Buxton's weather go back thirty years. The detailed figures for the past five years can now be inspected through the village website, along with the history of Buxton's notable buildings, the opening hours of the fish and chip shop, news of parish council meetings and much else. For each and every day back to November 2001, there is a record of the maximum air temperature, minimum air temperature, the minimum temperature at grass level, the temperature 30 centimetres down in the earth, the amount of sunshine, rain, snow, sleet or hail, the highest wind speed and dominant direction, the barometric pressure and a summary for each month.

Take the August which had ended the day before my visit. There was no frost, hail, sleet or snow. There were two days on which thunder was heard, one of which – the 10th – saw the highest temperature of this roasting month, 33.2 degrees Celsius. There were four days on which the sun shone for more than thirteen hours, and one – 1 August – when it didn't shine at all. Rainfall totalled 4.9 millimetres, making it the driest August since 1983. Everything bar the number of raindrops and the average weight of the dewdrops is there. The thought of the effort, the concentration, the attention to detail required to bring this mountain of information into the public domain is enough to make the casual inspector shake his or her head incredulously. And that is but one month of the year, and there are twelve months in the year, and year succeeds to year.

Charles Briscoe may be unusual in his devotion to his duties but he is by no means alone. He is a member of an organisation called the Climatological Observers' Link, which might be characterised as the hard core of zealots within the broad church of meteorology. It has more than four hundred members, of whom no more than half a dozen are women. I do not know if they are all as thorough in documenting the weather in their areas as Dr Briscoe is in Buxton, but certainly some are, including Dr Roger Brugge. Dr Brugge is a scientific researcher at Reading University and lives in Maidenhead, whose recent climatic history he has recorded in formidable detail. He also compiles the Link's monthly bulletin, which synthesises into a national picture the data supplied by the members. The Link's website keeps an issue available for inspection. It is an awesome document so densely crammed with information that no man, no matter how fanatical, could possibly absorb more than a small fraction.

The Climatological Observers' Link is a club, a word defined by Johnson in his *Dictionary* as 'an assembly of good fellows meeting under certain conditions'. Johnson probably had in mind his own Literary Club which met at the Turk's Head in Gerrard Street, where the other verbal jousters included Gibbon, Sheridan, Burke, Goldsmith, Joshua Reynolds and Boswell. But the essence of the concept of the club lies in the fellowship rather than the venue, and although Roger Brugge does organise outings to places of high meteorological interest, most of the members of his Link never meet each other. The development of information technology has allowed the fellowship aspect to flourish, and there are other advantages to the disembodied state. For instance, the club bore can be permanently avoided and members can hold forth at whatever length they wish without fear of being interrupted or shouted down, and without any obligation to attend to what anybody else is saying.

None of this, however, begins to answer the question which may perplex the outsider: what is the purpose of accumulating this great reservoir of information about what the weather has been doing in various parts of the land? Philosophically, the point is that there is no point beyond the act, the doing. It is rather like catching a fish and putting it back alive in the water.

However, the existence of the knowledge can serve a subsidiary purpose by acting as a guarantee against uncertainty and as a means to settle arguments. A curious example was given in one of the multitude of columns on weather matters contributed for many years by the Irish meteorologist Brendan McWilliams to the *Irish Times*. On 4 July 1862 the Reverend Charles Dodgson, better known as Lewis Carroll, took his three nieces for a boat trip on the River Isis near Oxford and related to them the story that became *Alice's Adventures in Wonderland*. One of the nieces, Alice

Liddell, recalled much later that the afternoon had been so hot that the party had taken refuge in the shade of a hayrick, where the tale was told. Not so, piped up some nit-picking fact-checker, having looked up the meteorological records, which appeared to show that it had been a rainy day. Alice Liddell and Dodgson himself – who recorded the event in his diary – were chided for letting their memories play them false. It was only much later that the records were more rigorously investigated, and it was shown that two weather fronts had indeed passed over Oxford on that day – but that between them a ridge of high pressure had brought sunshine and warmth for the afternoon.

Another illustration, even more inconsequential, is provided by my own fiftieth birthday, 26 May 2001. I can remember that the evening was warm enough to induce abundant sweating during the livelier numbers in my celebratory barn dance at the village hall, requiring the swallowing of much beer, but nothing else. Now, having consulted Dr Briscoe and the Climatological Observers' Link, I have learned that a south-west airflow delivered warm air from the Azores that day, giving a maximum temperature of 23.8 degrees Centigrade at Buxton, and maximums of 22.6 in Maidenhead, 22.7 in Wokingham, 22.6 in Bedford, 20.00 at Cromdale in Strathspey and 19.1 at Brampton in Cumbria. There were 10.5 hours of hazy sunshine in Buxton, 8.8 hours in Maidenhead and half an hour less in Wokingham. Barometric pressure varied between 1014 and 1020 millibars (or hectopascals, as we are supposed to have learned to call them). Everywhere was dry, except Brampton, where there was 0.7 millimetres of rain.

In other words, I was lucky with the weather on my fiftieth birthday, and I can prove it!

Chapter 14

The Crack of Doom

FOR MID-NOVEMBER IT WAS AN EXCEPTIONALLY BALMY EVENING, PERHAPS ominously so. London's Piccadilly seethed with people, late-shopping, crowding into pubs and bars, hastening home, all apparently oblivious to their fate. Those who were concerned about the impending end of the world — few in number, I thought, considering the urgency of the matter — were making their way into Wren's handsomely light and airy church of St James's.

Inside, the harbingers of doom were taking their seats on the platform, smiling at each other and shaking hands. The Rector, the Reverend Charles Hadley, called the meeting to order. The matter under discussion, he said solemnly, was a grave one. You might call it global warming, you might prefer something more dramatic. He introduced the first speaker: Aubrey Meyer, of the Global Commons Institute, a tall man, broad-chested under his white T-shirt, his dark hair gathered into a ponytail. Mr Meyer told us in a deep, musical voice, tinged with a South African accent, that he was a musician, and that his mission was to end emissions, so we could all sing from the same hymn sheet. He had a computer linked to a screen, and quickly conjured images to show the incremental loading of carbon into the atmosphere since 1970. He clicked on one to illustrate the contribution of Texas – 'the greatest polluting entity on the planet', he observed, adding after a little pause: 'That's where George Bush is from.' The audience laughed, pleased that the demon should have been identified.

'How do we make music out of what is noise?' Mr Meyer mused. His answer was his brainchild, the doctrine of contraction and convergence, which envisages a global limit on the production of greenhouse gases at a level tolerable to the planet, to be achieved by the rich nations reducing their share until they and the developing nations come together and every one of God's children has the same, safe, share. All that was needed, Mr Meyer said, was the will to forge the necessary international agreement. He accepted that this presented an obstacle. It would mean the taking of some difficult decisions, decisions that were in the hands – not of those, like himself, who knew what was at stake – but of political leaders. 'Intelligence' was the way, he said gnomically, conceding that this commodity was in short supply among the breed. Fortunately, however, there were exceptions, one of whom was sitting to Mr Meyer's left, nodding enthusiastic agreement with every word. This was the former Environment Minister, Michael Meacher.

Like many Labour MPs of a certain vintage, Mr Meacher had waited long for the chance to be in office, to change things for the better. The government he joined had loudly proclaimed its deep concern for the environment and for the planet. Had not its leader, the man who appointed him, identified climate warming as 'the issue that threatens global disaster'? As if to press home Mr Blair's message, towards the end of 2000 an unusual amount of rain fell in a brief period on various parts of England, producing floods which caused considerable damage to property in low-lying areas, and a good deal of inconvenience. The floods were interpreted by Mr Meacher, among others, as a portent. This was hard evidence that the threat posed by global warming was not some airy scientific hypothesis. It was real, here in England, lapping in liquid form at the foundations of the venerable town of Lewes in Sussex. But although Mr Meacher toured the flood-stricken areas proclaiming that something must and would be done to 'tackle' the crisis, very little was.

It is not surprising that Mr Meacher should have wearied of crying in the wilderness. Or perhaps it was the other way round, and it was Mr Blair who wearied of someone else's preachifying. Either way, Mr Meacher threw off the chains of office, and with them the irksome need to pay attention to the electorate's sordid aspirations. He was born again, as a prophet, a role which – to judge from his appearance beneath the gilded ceiling of St James's, Piccadilly – he finds congenial. His cheeks glowed with health and his eyes glistened with vitality behind his glinting spectacles as he rose to deliver his vision of world destruction. It was, he said, not merely the single biggest challenge facing mankind now, but the biggest mankind had ever faced. He trotted through a familiar recitation of warning signs: mud slides in Venezuela, inundations in Bangladesh, seven thousand people in the West Midlands 'severely affected' by floods – each of them in such a way as to suggest that such horrors had never been known until George Bush and his gang of eco-criminals got to work. 'People in the tropics will literally burn,' Mr Meacher stated; then apologised in case anyone found his depiction of equatorial incineration uncomfortable.

What might be done, he asked, beyond the obvious necessity of completely transforming society. He saw no hope in

America, and precious little in Russia. Let the EU take the lead, with Britain at the helm, opening its arms to the more enlightened nations: China, for instance, which — so Mr Meacher asserted trustingly — had cut coal production and subsidies; and India, which had more wind power than the US. Let the developing nations be helped to turn aside from the evil path of fossil fuels. Let Ethiopia be encouraged to seek compensation from the polluting nations for the millions of deaths in successive droughts caused by CO_2 emissions. Let contraction and convergence be our watchwords. Mr Meyer smiled approvingly. Mr Meacher sat down to warm applause. 'Meacher for Prime Minister' someone in the audience cried out. There was more applause.

Mr Meacher was succeeded by a small, clever man, Professor Michael Grubb, who provoked a perceptible growl of dissent by calling for renewed efforts to persuade the Americans to join the Kyoto Agreement on limiting greenhouse gas emissions, and suggesting mildly that it would be unrealistic to believe the problem could be addressed without having the world's biggest economic power on board. Us? Lacking in realism? They didn't like that at all.

The speakers having spoken, contributions were invited from the floor. The microphone was immediately seized by a bearded fanatic from Friends of the Earth who ranted about the melting icecaps being a bomb that would destroy us all, and sooner rather than later. Others wanted to know what they could do, in practical terms, to help avert catastrophe. One idea was to 'engage with the American electorate' by writing to all of them to tell them what a menace Mr Bush was. Another was to switch to an electricity supplier that was investing in wind power. Mr Meyer said we had to stay sensible and overcome separateness.

I asked Mr Meacher if he agreed with me that the notion of urging either rich or poor countries to commit themselves to emissions cuts on a scale requiring the dismantling and rebuilding of the world economic order might strike some people as unrealistic to the point of futility. He did not agree; or if he did, he kept it to himself. In fact he did not answer my question at all. Instead, he said he had to hasten to Westminster to meet two American friends with – as he put it with a conspiratorial smirk – 'interesting information' about intelligence to do with the war in Iraq.

I left and went to a pub. The street outside was thronged with drinkers laughing and conversing vivaciously in the warm night air. As I drained my pint I thought of alerting them to their peril. But, being a coward, I held my peace.

A year earlier I had attended another public meeting on global warming at the Institute of Contemporary Art in London. This was a rather more illuminating event, partly because there was more science on offer and less pious hot air, partly because the orthodoxy that extinction beckons was rigorously challenged, and partly because of the clarity with which the limits of knowledge were exposed. There were two principal combatants. First into the ring was an academic called Julian Morris, blue-chinned, black-haired, saturnine and brimming with the certainty and impatience of youth. Doctor Morris is director of the International Policy Network, a research organisation characterised – or caricatured – by his opponents as a mouthpiece for the right-wing, multinational-funded, global-warming denial conspiracy. He did not disappoint. He stated, as fact, that most of the warming of the twentieth century had taken place before 1940; that Europe was warmer in the tenth century than now; that temperature fluctuations correlated more closely with sunspot activity than with CO_2 loading; that the Antarctic icecap, far from melting, was actually increasing in size. Glowering sternly through black-rimmed spectacles, he warned us that we were the victims of an unholy alliance between governments trying to justify higher taxes, scaremongering environmentalists, climate scientists seeking funding for ever-more expensive computers, an insurance industry up against it because of natural disasters, and a renewables industry hoping for enormous subsidies to develop alternative technologies.

Having done his bit to blacken the reputation of the community of climatologists, Doctor Morris slumped in his chair, his chin sunk on to his chest. His adversary was Professor Mike Hulme, once a pupil and subsequently a colleague of Hubert Lamb, and now executive director of the Tyndall Centre for Climate Research, which has a world-wide reputation – clearly undeserved, in Doctor Morris's view – for sound science and independent thinking. Professor Hulme certainly did not look or sound like a fanatic as he aligned himself with the consensus on likely global temperature rises, while refraining from conjuring visions of flood, pestilence and apocalypse. 'The future is uncertain,' he commented mildly, 'the challenge is to manage the risk.'

Doctor Morris rose to demand menacingly whether Professor Hulme believed the precautionary principle should be applied to the possibility of the earth being struck by a giant meteor or engulfed in the aftermath of an unprecedented volcanic eruption. The atmosphere between the two men was briefly charged with antagonism. 'You cannot wish it away,' responded Professor Hulme disdainfully.

★   ★   ★

For anyone still clinging to a belief in the will of political leaders to engage seriously with global warming, the G8 summit at Gleneagles in July 2005 must have blown away the last shreds of illusion. The event itself – dedicated by the Prime Minister to the 'hard choices' of poverty in Africa and climate change – was not so much overshadowed by the series of bomb attacks carried out in London on the morning it was due to start, 7 July, as exposed for what it was: a sideshow. In particular, the communiqué on climate, bereft of targets, commitments or any acceptance of awkward truths, represented a masterpiece of empty phrase-turning. To fulfil the greater purpose of avoiding a split with the United States, substance and purpose were jettisoned, all for a meaningless recognition from George Bush of human activity as a factor in the process.

The wonder is that any intelligent observer of the climate debate could have expected more. Long, long ago, when in opposition, Mr Blair committed a future Labour government to reducing Britain's carbon emissions by a fifth by 2010. It was a promise he repeated when in office: not merely will we achieve the targets set for us in the Kyoto Protocol of 1998, we will do better, for we care for this planet of ours and for our children's future. In September 2004 Mr Blair made a speech rededicating himself to his climate crusade. 'No one,' commented the *Guardian* in response to his words, 'could doubt his sincerity in this vital area.' Yet two months later his Environment Secretary, Margaret Beckett, disclosed that the 20 per cent cut would not be achieved, and that the volume of emissions was the same as when Labour came to power.

One of the measures suggested by the Prime Minister to address the problem was to press within the EU for the aviation industry to be included in the arrangements under which governments will be able to trade in carbon emissions. 'I am advised that by 2030 emissions from aircraft could represent a quarter of the UK's total contribution to global warming,' Mr Blair said in the surprised tone of someone who'd previously been under the impression that aeroplanes were powered by recycled glass. Is it possible that he could have been unaware that his government has presided over and energetically promoted the biggest expansion in air travel in our history, in doing so resolutely ignoring a clamour of warnings about the consequent pollution of the skies? Or is it possible that the sincerity observed and lauded by the *Guardian* might not be all it seems?

In the event, because of the blanket coverage of the London bombings, the complete failure of the Gleneagles summit to address the reality of the warming of the planet attracted comparatively little media attention. Anyway, speaking for myself, I'm not sure we have any right to be hard on Mr Blair and his colleagues. It is true that when they boast of their tenderness for the environment and all they have done for it, they are deceivers and hypocrites. But their falseness is no more than a reflection of our own. The reason our government will not take the actions necessary to cut emissions of greenhouse gases by an amount that would have any meaningful impact is simply that to do so would require the abandonment of the goal of ever-increasing affluence, and the complete reordering of the way we live. It would demand revolutions in public transport, private car use, the energy industry, what is left of manufacturing industry, the building industry, the food industry – to name but a few. It would require us to accept not merely radical changes in our habits but a fall in our living standards which would slash thick slices off the loaf of tax revenues, which would in turn sabotage spending on health, education, the police and all other cherished public services. Any party that committed itself to such a programme would be annihilated at the polls and consign itself to outer darkness.

Therefore it will not happen. Or if it does, it will not be as a consequence of government policy.

It suits us to swallow the dubious proposition that we can, simultaneously, continue to become more comfortable and prosperous, care for others less fortunate than ourselves and save the planet. Politicians are fully conscious of this. They know that to tell us unpleasant truths and to attempt to force those truths on us is a sure route to electoral oblivion. We become conspirators together, and there is no room in our cocoon of make-believe for a possibility so unpleasant as the destruction of our planet through overheating. As a tribe, our dominant impulse is not altruistic but competitive: to establish advantage, to maintain and defend advantage, to extend advantage. Everything else is secondary to that.

In 1995 the International Panel on Climate Change – a large group of specialists brought together under the aegis of the World Meteorological Organisation and the United Nations – declared that 'the balance of evidence suggests a discernible human influence on global climate'. Seven years later it went much further: 'There is new and stronger evidence that MOST OF THE WARMING OVER THE PAST FIFTY YEARS IS ATTRIB-UTABLE TO HUMAN ACTIVITY' (my capitals). The IPCC endorsed the prediction that temperatures would rise by between 1.4 and 5.8 Celsius by 2100, and that sea levels would rise by between 17 and 49 centimetres.

This is a statement of the majority view among climate

experts. Global warming is happening, and we are making it happen. There are, of course, those – like Julian Morris and the Danish academic Bjørn Lomborg – who argue that the case has not been made and any impact has been grossly exaggerated for sinister political reasons. There is very little point in a rank amateur such as myself attempting to wrestle with the riddles of the troposphere or to address the science of global warming when men as familiar with these matters as Doctor Morris and Professor Hulme can reach such opposing views. I am content to go along with the IPCC declaration, while bearing in mind that something does not become true simply because a majority of those who have considered the matter believe it to be true, any more than something cannot be true simply because only one in a thousand experts believes it to be true.

So I am prepared to be acquiescent about the science. But I believe that even the rankest of amateurs is obliged to be sceptical about the prophecy industry that has been created on the back of the science. To question the scientists' qualifications as fortune-tellers is not to doubt their intelligence, their dedication, the rigour of their methods of inquiry or their worthiness to hold their doctorates and professorships. It is to propose that there are limits to human competence in the field of prediction, and that a little more humility in acknowledging those limits would not go amiss. It is also a means to register protest at the way in which the debate has come to be dominated by the shrill voices of those who take the top of the predicted temperature increase as a given fact, and look forward with apocalyptic excitement to the end of everything.

One example to illustrate the constraints on scientific competence must suffice: the study of the mighty system of ocean currents that shapes the weather on both sides of the North

Atlantic. It is well known that the warm-water Gulf Stream flows north up the coast of the United States until it reaches the Flemish Cap off Newfoundland, where one branch – the West Greenland Current – turns up towards Labrador, and the other – the North Atlantic Current or Drift – flows north-east towards the British Isles. It is further known that the system is powered, in the manner of a conveyor beld, by a countervailing current of much colder, saltier water running beneath the warm flow. At two northerly points, the circulation drive is given a vital thrust by influxes of cooled, dense, saline water. One of these so-called pumps is off Labrador, the other east of Greenland. Over the past ten years evidence has accumulated that the volumes being discharged sourthwards past Greenland have been diminishing at an accelerating rate, raising the possibility that the pump itself might be failing. The reason was not hard to identify: the melting of the Arctic icecap was pushing unprecedented quantities of freshwater into the top of the pump, drastically reducing the salinity which thrusts the cold water down.

So far, so good. The knowledge represented a great leap in understanding of an immensely important, subtle and intricate influence on the climate of the northern hemisphere. But there are limits to the knowledge. The scientists are in no position to assess accurately what impact the reduction in cold water output from the Greenland pump is having. They cannot say if the whole North Atlantic current system is running slower and more erratically – but still at a self-sustaining rate – or if it is moving towards a complete shutdown. They have their suspicions, they make their guesses. But they do not know.

One of the wiser judges of the condition of knowledge about global warming is the British climatologist, Bill Burroughs. He belongs in the orthodox camp, in that he accepts the IPCC warming projections, and agrees that the situation is serious and that action to curb greenhouse gas emissions should be taken as a matter of urgency. But he is also keenly aware of the ways in which the ability to work out what is going on is circumscribed. For instance, he accepts that the use of computer-driven simulation models – known as General Circulation Models – is 'the only physically realistic way to predict the impact of human activities on the climate'. But he is also prepared to acknowledge openly that the models have their limitations, and that they cannot take into account and calculate the effect of each and every potential factor.

Burroughs identifies other areas of profound uncertainty. For instance there is no firm evidence (but try telling this to Mr Meacher) that global warming is causing a greater incidence of extreme weather events; or that it is causing hurricanes to occur more frequently and become more powerful. 'The cosy notion', Burroughs wrote in his book *Climate Change*, 'that warming will simply produce a gradual displacement of climatic zones to higher latitudes, so England would have a climate like southern France, is probably a gross over-simplification'. His conclusion – 'it does not help to gloss over the limitations in our current understanding of climate change' – should flash up each day on the computer screen of every environment correspondent, every eco-activist, every Michael Meacher and Aubrey Meyer, and every other self-appointed harbinger of doom.

'Excessively damp, thick, gloomy . . . barometer high, but two-thirds of days wet . . . the air has been singularly mild, almost to oppression . . . unnatural warmth and extreme humidity . . . The public prints are rife with accounts of precocious vegetation

. . . apple trees in blossom, carnations, wallflowers, primroses in full bloom. We are told of bees looking for material for honey, of strawberries being found ruddy ripe under the hedges . . .' These words were written by the Whitehaven rain investigator John Fletcher Miller in December 1843, and one may be reasonably sure that – had the notion of a progressive, man-made heating of the planet been current then – the appearance of blossoming fruit trees and blooming primroses before Christmas would have been seized upon as conclusive proof that we were heading for disaster.

The fact is that extreme and extraordinary weather has occurred throughout history, and has been noticed, noted and subjected to speculative interpretation. Doctor Short's *General Chronological History of the Air* is an enormous catalogue of such episodes: droughts, floods, earthquakes, plagues, famines, hailstones the size of grapefruit, comets, dragons, horses in the sky and so forth. In his day, interpretation was easy. Anything unusual, particularly if it caused death and destruction, was a symptom of divine displeasure at human wickedness, and a sure sign that there would be worse to come if sinful ways were not mended. In our time we have retained the fascination with the abnormal, but dispensed with the religious convictions that explained it. Alternative explanations have been sought to satisfy our deep-rooted need to experience alarm, while having the appearance of scientific plausibility. Global warming, with the infinite scope it offers for prophecy of the doom-laden variety, fits the bill perfectly.

Responsible climatologists concede that single weather events – whether they be scorching summers, sodden or warm winters, hurricanes in the Gulf of Mexico, cyclones in Bangladesh, mud slides in Venezuela – do not, of themselves, demonstrate anything about the climate. Yet for some of them, the need to get their voices heard in the hubbub of scaremongering that passes for scientific debate is a stronger imperative than preserving their virtue. They feed the journalistic appetite, then protest in the tones of outraged virgins that their work has been sensationalised, taken out of context, abused.

It took Isaac Newton more than twenty years before he was ready to sit down and distil his observations of the motions of the planets into written form, and a further three years before his *Principia* was completed. Darwin spent five years sailing around the southern seas collecting specimens and information, and took another twenty to ponder it all and compose his *The Origin of Species*. These days there is more urgency to scientific research, and less time for reflection. This urgency is often represented as a necessary response to the growing awareness of the dangers pressing in on humankind. But more mundane factors play their part, among them the need of researchers to get attention for their work. One way and another, they are under pressure to produce results; and since it is the nature of their business that firm and final conclusions are very rarely reached, often the best they can manage is projections, scenarios, which you or I might call informed guesses.

The projections are projected. In their original form, usually in a paper for a specialist scientific journal, they are expressed in impenetrable jargon and hedged around with qualification. But a projection is of little use in this competitive field unless it attracts attention. Research bodies need profile, journals seek it, some scientists come to enjoy it. Profile is acquired through publicity, which is bestowed by journalists who are not interested in possible scenarios festooned with provisos and weighed down with verbs in the conditional tense. If they cannot have facts – which, in the context of climate change, are few and generally somewhat stale – they will make do with the next best thing. So projections become predictions, and scenarios forecasts, and science is corrupted into sensation.

In general, the media do not see their role as being to present an accurate synopsis of scientific research, but to make news from it. And news is not made by encouraging the affluent middle classes to think that everything in the garden is rosy, but by warning them loudly and insistently that behind the perfume of the petals is the smell of war and flames.

During the evening of the second day of August 2003, I was helping – not at all effectually – put up a tent in a field half a mile of so from the coast of south Devon. It may not sound much of an adventure, but for me it was. I had never been camping before. It had always been my view that among the minimum requirements for a holiday were a solid roof and four walls of brick. However, a swelling family and shrinking financial resources had compelled a reappraisal; and here we were in a field in Devon. There was one large tent for myself, my wife, and our two infant daughters, and one small one for my teenage son and my ten-year-old nephew. The potential for disaster in this arrangement appeared to me almost infinite. How would I deal with the close proximity of strangers, the intimacies of the communal washing facilities, being permanently bent double, sleeping on the ground, eating off plastic plates? Above all, what would we do if – when – it rained? This was England, Devon, county of sea fogs and winds and moisture, the English summer.

It did not rain. Each morning before breakfast, while the campsite was still quiet and the unruly youth still snug in their smelly sleeping bags, I would sit outside on a surprisingly comfortable collapsible chair and marvel. A few tendrils of mist would be clinging to the meadows rising to the left. Dew sparkled across the grass and beaded the tents. Overhead the sky was a delicate blue, yellowing towards the sea where the sun was rising in a halo of pale fire. The air was still, soft and sweet, the promise of the day utterly beguiling. In my mind's eye I would see the beach at the end of the lane, the bright sand clasped between rocks with grass-topped cliffs behind, the water clear and blue and inviting. I had never imagined that a swim in the sea in England could be anything other than a gasp-inducing trial of will; yet now I could feel the blissful warmth of it around me, and the wish to be held in it for hours. Was this really Devon, I wondered, or − recalling palmier days − Corsica?

I cannot remember ever in my life having felt more purely content than when watching those mornings unfold in their glory. And − for all the innumerable irritations that spring from having small children around, and from the unavoidable company of guitar-strumming adults, teenagers intent on drunkenness and fornication, and noisy urchins whose idea of fun was to fire bags of frozen peas over and occasionally on to the tents from a giant catapult − the days that followed those mornings were pretty good as well. We were happy, everyone was happy, and the most significant factor in our happiness was that wonderful weather.

For a great many people in Britain, the heat, the sunshine and the blue skies of that summer were a source of enormous, memorable pleasure. Day after day it was possible to enjoy simple delights inconceivable in the cool, rain-laced British summer as it used to be: lazing in the garden, strolling to the shops in shorts and sandals, swimming in lakes and rivers and the sea, eating outside in the evening, picnicking, watching and playing cricket in ideal conditions, eating strawberries and raspberries and plums and figs ripened to a state of sweet perfection. If it were possible to measure enjoyment quantitatively, this was surely a record-breaker among summers.

Yet this is not the way the media saw it. A few days after I pitched our tent in Devon, the *Guardian* reported a suggestion made by the German climate expert Hans Joachim Schnellnhuber that the heat wave over Europe might signal an acceleration in global warming. Across the top of the page was a map of the earth's northern hemisphere, studded with panels recording a variety of calamities – the worst fire season in Canada in fifty years, the deaths of 569 people from flood and heat in China 'so far', billions of euros of drought-related crop damage in Italy, tea harvests in Sri Lanka down 20–30 per cent because of drought and flood, swathes of Siberia and the Russian Far East incinerated in forest fires; and so on. To the right was placed a further selection of bullet points under the headline 'Europe battles drought and fire', reporting deaths in Portugal and Spain, the feeding of iced fruit to chimpanzees at Amsterdam Zoo, power cuts in Italy and forest fires in Poland and Bosnia.

The next weekend the *Observer* took up the theme. 'Britain braced for a Sunday roasting' the paper proclaimed over a compendium of familiar heat-related horrors. 'As climate extremes become normal, the country – and the planet – will pay a high price.' The head of the Met Office's Climate Prediction Unit was wheeled on to warn us that even if the emission of greenhouse gases stopped at once, global warming – or roasting – would continue for at least another forty years. The analysis of the planet's future was rounded off with a selection of other possible catastrophes waiting in the wings should the heat fail to finish the job: the sinking of south-east England 'for separate geological reasons', a switch by the soil from absorbing carbon dioxide to discharging it, the release from beneath the ocean floor of 'tens of thousands of tonnes' of methane currently frozen, and the triggering of a repeat of 'the end of the Permian era when 90 per cent of all animals and plants were eradicated'. Against such a background, the *Observer*'s editorial – headlined 'Mankind is on a path to meltdown' – seemed no more than a sober statement of fact.

In the doom-monger's world view, there are no winners, only losers. As the 2003 heat wave reached its scorching climax in continental Europe, the people of France surrendered themselves to a frenzy of breast-beating and self-flagellation after it was reported that as many as 13,000 people had died because of the summer heat – mainly the elderly, many of whom had been abandoned in their oven-like flats by children and grand-children too intent on hastening to the blue Mediterranean to spare them a thought. Although this 'final death toll' is open to all kinds of statistical challenge, it is certainly true that the deaths of a large number of old, infirm people occurred earlier than would have been the case in a cooler summer. It is equally true, however, that the advent of milder winters has meant that many of the large number of elderly, infirm people who used to perish in the cold winters of old now survive into the spring, and longer. Some of them, of course, will then expire in the heat of the summer that follows the warm spring that follows the mild winter. But according to the apocalyptic perspective, they remain victims, not survivors.

One tricky dilemma for the apocalyptists is how the necessary replacement of the economic order can be engineered in an ethical manner. Some are less troubled by this than others, because they believe that, when confronted by the wickedness of our leaders, the corruption of our institutions and the inertia of the brainwashed masses, it is legitimate for the minority able to recognise the truth to take 'direct action' to bring about its implementation. But for others, the prospect of enforcing cuts of up to 80 or even 90 per cent in emissions of greenhouse gases across the world carries with it troubling practical and moral implications. They are aware that the primary impulse of every society is to secure and protect the prosperity that it believes – rightly or wrongly – guarantees a better life; and that to believe this impulse could be crushed or redirected by force exercised by small groups of extremists is fantasist rubbish. But, even assuming for a moment that a way could be found for the enlightened to compel the wilfully ignorant to adopt the measures necessary to save the planet, would it be ethically justified? Is it right to save people who do not want, for a variety of selfish reasons, to be saved?

Faced by this moral quicksand, the majority of the doom-mongers – who retain a lingering aversion to the idea of waging global warfare, even in a just cause – tend to retreat within the laager of their own rightness. Their choice is to give up the struggle and resign themselves to the inevitable, or to persist in the prophecy business in the hope that, one day, the light will dawn.

How forlorn that hope must sometimes seem! The Kyoto Protocol of 1998 set down some modest objectives for curbing greenhouse gas emissions. Even though Russia belatedly signed the Protocol in 2004, the United States has not and will not. Nor have the leaders in charge of the burgeoning economies of the world's two most populous nations – China and India – displayed a jot of interest in the proposition that they should restrain growth in the interests of a greener planet. As a species, we show no inclination to rouse ourselves from the course characterised by one doom-monger as our 'sleepwalk to extinction'.

Faced by this collective denial of the impending reality, the warning cries of the prophets grow ever-more shrill and despairing, while the admonitions of the newspapers and magazines that employ them are invested with an impotent, querulous futility. The *Guardian*, reflecting on a report in the scientific journal *Nature* which forecast that global warming COULD wipe out a quarter of the world's species of land animals and plants over the next fifty years, addressed the eternal question: what is the something that must be done? The paper castigated the usual villains – the government, the 'scandalous' behaviour of the United States, etc – and urged the citizen to assume responsibility. 'There are plenty of things that individuals can do that would make a dramatic difference,' it declared. 'If every driver took one fewer car journey a week averaging nine miles, it would cut carbon emissions from traffic by 13 per cent. Is that too much to ask?'

Well, is it? The answer is: of course it is. I should like to know, as a matter of interest, if the editor of the *Guardian* has reduced his own motoring in line with his newspaper's appeal (to be fair to Alan Rusbridger, he is the proud owner and driver of a non-polluting G-Wiz electric car). And is he taking a short shower, rather than a bath? And has he put a brick in all the household's lavatory cisterns? Is he recycling waste, composting vegetable cuttings, disposing of chemicals carefully and encouraging wildlife in his garden? And, assuming that he is observing all the sixty actions recommended by the Environment Agency to enhance the world about us 'with minimum effort', has he exhorted, and does he continue to exhort, his staff to do the same? Has he considered making adherence to a code of good environmental conduct a condition of employment on the *Guardian*? And if he hasn't, why hasn't he? Could it be that he is more like the rest of us than he might care to admit?

So, what of the charge that we are imprisoned in our dream world of denial? Will we awaken from our slumbers, or will we stumble over the edge of the cliff?

It is in our natures to be suspicious of other people's certainties. That may be why no one religion or political ideology has conquered the world. It may also be that a reluctance to embrace other people's convictions has helped keep parts of the world free from tyranny and oppression. It is standard for those with the convictions to assert that everyone else is blind, deaf, stupid, wicked or locked in a dream, and that all the evidence supports their case. The prophets of climatic doom declare that the science proves their case, and that the inability of their fellows to accept this must therefore be a symptom of denial. But, as I have tried to indicate, they have chosen the science that supports them and discarded the rest, and their opponents have done exactly the same. We, the alleged dreamers, are left with very few certainties and a great many possibilities.

In April 1815, the top four thousand feet of Mount Tambora in eastern Indonesia disappeared in an eruption considerably more violent than that of Krakatoa in 1883. The dust and ash expelled into the atmosphere circled the earth, reflecting the sun's rays back into space and reducing global sunshine by at least a quarter. Zonal air circulation was weakened over the northern hemisphere, pushing the Atlantic storm track south; 1816 became known as 'the year without a summer'. Red and yellow snow fell in southern Italy. Brown, blue and red snow fell in Maryland. The weather everywhere was atrocious.

Lord Byron was in Switzerland that summer, where he wrote a poem which he called 'Darkness':

I had a dream, which was not a dream
The bright sun was extinguished, and the stars
Did wander darkling in the eternal space,
Rayless and pathless, and the icy earth
Swung blind and blackening in the moonless air;
Morn came and went – and came, and brought no day,
And men forgot their passions in the dread
Of this desolation.

In Byron's nightmare, the familiar world is turned into a hideous parody of itself, before being consumed. Palaces and thrones and houses are burned to make heat and light. The birds fall to the ground, snakes lose their venom, dogs eat their masters. War is succeeded by famine, the world is made void:

The winds were wither'd in the stagnant air,
And the clouds perish'd! Darkness had no need
Of and from them – she was the Universe!

Byron's vision finds its contemporary equivalent in the over-heated world pictured by the apocalypse brigade. Of course, it is possible that they are right, and that rising temperatures and sea levels will progressively make the planet uninhabitable; that a relentless shrinking of the space and resources which make life possible will trigger war, starvation and final extinction; that the situation is beyond the power of human ingenuity and will to correct; that our tenure on earth is finite.

But there are other possibilities. It may be that the species' ingenuity and adaptability will meet the challenge, that new technologies and sources of energy will be developed in time to preserve the economic order from collapse, and that the reductions in gas emissions necessary to stall the warming effect will be achieved. It's even possible that we might mend our ways, that we might throw off our enslavement to the motor car, learn to shop and work locally and to consume only renewable energy. It could happen.

It could be that global temperatures will not rise by as much as the majority of climatologists think they will (possible, too, that they might rise more); that the equation will be suddenly upset by factors that have been entirely overlooked – for instance, a volcanic eruption of a magnitude not seen since before the evolution of humankind which could halt global warming in its tracks, or destroy the human race. It's also possible – assuming warming does proceed according to the projections, and that global temperatures rise over this century by 3.6 Celsius degrees (the mean between the upper and lower limits) – that the effects have been exaggerated or miscalculated. It may be that sea levels will rise less than the forecast 27 centimetres, or more. It may be that higher temperatures will make it possible to cultivate land currently unviable, and thus partially compensate for the loss of agricultural land to flooding. It could be that James Lovelock's Gaia hypothesis – that life on earth, and its environment, are two parts of a single system in which physical, chemical and biological processes interact to maintain the conditions necessary for life – is true.

It's also possible that we may devise a way of destroying ourselves long before climate change does its work. That, after all, was the conviction shared by many right-minded activists in the period between the end of the Second World War and the disintegration of the Soviet empire. They could not know what the future would hold, and nor can we.

There is but one certainty. It is that no one knows. I don't. You don't. They don't.

A summer's day as English summer's days used to be. The barometer is at 997 and falling, but the sun is shining benignly between tall billows of white and black clouds treading purposefully across the sky. The air feels unstable, promising change.

Outside my window, the grass on my lawn is rich green, glowing with vigour. The raspberry canes are heavy with fruit and the courgettes and carrots in the raised beds are swelling by the moment. The earth is dark with moisture, the air sweet with scents. The scorched world of 2003 is a distant memory.

Over the past three years the British summer has reverted to something like its familiar form. 2004 and 2005 were thoroughly mixed; 2006 saw deluges of rain in May, a record heat wave in July, and a typically inconstant August. The warnings about the future of the planet still come thick and fast, as do politicians' promises of 'tough action' to tackle global warming. In the meantime most of us have gone back to what we are most comfortable with, which is griping about the weather.

The mad astronomer in Johnson's *Rasselas* claimed that he could control the weather and alter the seasons. The difficulty he faced, insuperable as it turned out, was to devise a way to use his powers for the benefit of all. The idea of fixing the weather has superficial attractions. Imagine being able to plan the summer holiday in the knowledge that the government had negotiated a two-week spell in the middle of August with constant sunshine and temperatures in the high twenties Celsius; or being informed in April that the third Tuesday of the following October was on the list of days that would see heavy rain crossing the country from the south-west with a mixture of sunshine and showers to come. Then think again, how impoverished we would be by the loss of our chief source of harmless uncertainty from lives already quite full enough of monotony and repetition.

Outside, the breeze is tugging at the branches of the big cherry that stands guard over our garden. One moment the shifting foliage glows golden in sunlight, then darkens. Rain is coming, but when? What will tomorrow bring?

Select Bibliography

Banfield, Edwin, *The Italian Influence on English Barometers from 1780*, Baros, 1993

Barker, Thomas (ed. John Kington), *The Weather Journals of a Rutland Squire*, Rutland Record Society, 1988

Boia, Lucian, *Weather in the Imagination*, Reaktion Books, 2005

Boutmy, Emile, *The English People: A Study of their Political Psychology*, Unwin, 1904

Brown, Neville, *History and Climate Change*, Routledge, 2001

Burroughs, William J., *Climate Change: A Multidisciplinary Approach*, Cambridge University Press, 2001

Castellani, Aldo, *Climate and Acclimatization*, J. Bale & Co., 1938

Cathcart, Brian, *Rain*, Granta Books, 2002

Cox, John D., *The Storm Watchers*, John Wiley, 2002

Currie, Ian, *Frosts, Freezes and Fairs*, Frosted Earth, 1996

Eden, Philip, *The Daily Telegraph Book of the Weather*, Continuum, 2003

Fagan, Brian, *The Little Ice Age: How Climate Made History, 1300–1850*, Basic Books, 2000

Fleming, James Rodger, *Historical Perspectives on Climate Change*, Oxford University Press 1998

Golinski, Jan, *Barometers of Change from the Sciences in Enlightened Europe*, Chicago University Press, 1999

Goodison, Nicholas, *English Barometers 1680–1860: A History of Domestic Barometers and Their Makers and Retailers*, Antique Collectors' Club, 1977

Heninger, S. K., *A Handbook of Renaissance Meteorology with Particular Reference to Elizabethan and Jacobean Literature*, Duke University Press, 1960

Hulme, Mike, and Barrow, Elaine (eds), *Climates of the British Isles: Present, Past and Future*, Routledge, 1997

Inwards, Richard, *Weather Lore*, Rider and Co., 1950

Inwood, Stephen, *The Man Who Knew Too Much: The Inventive Life of Robert Hooke*, Macmillan, 2002

Jankovic, Vladimir, *Reading the Skies: A Cultural History of the English Weather 1650–1820*, Manchester University Press, 2000

Jeffrey, Reginald W., 'Was It Wet or Was It Dry', unpublished MS, 1933

Johnson, Samuel, *Discourses on the Weather from The Idler*, 1758

Johnson, Walter, *Gilbert White: Pioneer, Poet and Stylist*, John Murray, 1928

Kimble, George, *The Weather*, Penguin Books, 1951

Kington, John, *The Weather of the 1780s Over Europe*, Cambridge University Press, 1988

Lamb, Hubert, *The English Climate*, English Universities Press, 1964

— *Weather, Climate and Human Affairs*, Routledge, 1987

— *Climate, History and the Modern World*, Routledge, 1995

Langford, Paul, *Englishness Identified: Manners and Character 1650–1850*, Oxford University Press, 2000

Lynn, Richard, *Personality and National Character*, Pergamon Press, 1971

Mabey, Richard, *Cold Comforts*, Hutchinson, 1983

McWilliams, Brendan, *Weather Eye*, Lilliput Press, 1994

Manley, Gordon, *Climate and the British Scene*, Collins, 1971

Middleton, W. E. Knowles, *The History of the Barometer*, Johns Hopkins Press, 1964

— *A History of the Theories of Rain and Other Forms of Precipitation*, Oldbourne, 1965

Mills, John, *An Essay on the Weather*, 1773

Monmonier, Mark, *Air Apparent: How Meteorologists Learned to Map, Predict and Dramatize the Weather*, University of Chicago Press, 1999

Nevin, Charles, *Lancashire: Where Women Die of Love*, Mainstream, 2004

Page, Robin, *Weather Forecasting the Country Way*, Penguin Books, 1981

Parry, M. L., *Climate Change, Agriculture and Settlement*, Dawson, 1978

Pevsner, Nikolaus, *The Englishness of English Art*, Penguin Books, 1964

Pointer, Revd John, *A Rational Account of the Weather*, 1723

Reed, Arden, *Romantic Weather: The Climates of Coleridge and Baudelaire*, University Press of New England, 1983

Richardson, Lewis Fry, *Weather Prediction by Numerical Process*, Cambridge University Press, 1922

Ross, Sinclair, *The Culbin Sands: Fact and Fiction*, Centre of Scottish Studies, University of Aberdeen, 1992

Sargent, Frederick, *The Hippocratic Heritage: A History of Ideas About the Weather and Human Health*, Pergamon Press, 1982

Tooley, Michael, and Sheail, Gillian (eds), *The Climatic Scene*, Allen & Unwin, 1985

Uttley, David, *The Anatomy of the Helm Wind*, Bookcase, 2000

White, Gilbert, *The Natural History of Selborne*, The World's Classics, 1965

Willis, Douglas, *Sand and Silence: Lost Villages of the North*, University of Aberdeen, 1986

Index

suicide: weather's effect, 188–9
summers
  14th century, 19–20
  17th century, 102
  18th century, 72, 79–80,
    107, 109
  1976, 6–7, 247
  2003, 165–8, 285, 305–8
Sunday Telegraph, 248
Swaffham Bulbeck, 215–16
Swift, Jonathan, 8, 110–11, 182
Switzerland, 189
Sydenham, Thomas, 181–2
Symons, George James, 21,
  210–12

Tacitus, 153
Taine, Henri, 157–8
Tao-Tze *see* Morrison, Richard
Taoism, 180–1
Taylor, Joseph, 35–6
telegraph, 220
television forecasts, 246–54
Tempest Prognosticators,
  233–7
Thames freezings, 6, 104–5,
  111, 112
Thanet, 112
theology and science, 24–5, 47
Theophrastus, 23–4, 30, 34
thermometers, 29
Thetford Forest, 90
Thomson, David, 127
Thoresby, Ralph, 20
Thornes, Dr John, 252–3

thunder: early theories, 25
thunderbolts *see* lightning
Thwaite Weather Prophet *see*
  Whistlecraft, Orlando
Tokyo, 138
Tollaidh, Loch, 258
Tompion, Thomas, 54–5
tornadoes, 286–7
Torricelli, Evangelista, 47–8
Torridon, Loch, 258
Tostig, Earl, 128
Towneley, Richard, 67, 197
Towneley Hall, 197
Towton, Battle of (1461), 128–9
Travelling Sands of Santon
  Downham, 92–5
trees: afforestation, 90–1, 125–6
Tresco Abbey, 263
tropics: effect on health, 172–4
Twain, Mark, 15
Twyne, Thomas, 26–7
Tyndall Centre for Climate
  Research, 296

Ubley, 103–4
Uckfield, 113
Ullswater, 111
umbrellas, 96
University of East Anglia:
  Climate Research Unit, 132
Upminster, 197
Upton-upon-Severn, 29
USA, and global warming,
  294, 309
Uttley, David, 148–9

THE POWER OF READING

Visit the Random House website and get connected with information on all our books and authors

EXTRACTS from our recently published books and selected backlist titles

COMPETITIONS AND PRIZE DRAWS Win signed books, audiobooks and more

AUTHOR EVENTS Find out which of our authors are on tour and where you can meet them

LATEST NEWS on bestsellers, awards and new publications

MINISITES with exclusive special features dedicated to our authors and their titles

READING GROUPS Reading guides, special features and all the information you need for your reading group

LISTEN to extracts from the latest audiobook publications

WATCH video clips of interviews and readings with our authors

RANDOM HOUSE INFORMATION including advice for writers, job vacancies and all your general queries answered

Come home to Random House

www.randomhouse.co.uk

ALSO AVAILABLE IN ARROW

Underwater to Get Out of the Rain

Trevor Norton

This is the beautifully told tale of Norton's growing love of the sea, from family holidays in Whitley Bay as a boy, to his first over zealous attempts at diving.

All that we know and love of the British seaside weaves throughout this funny, nostalgic and richly told memoir. Fortune telling gypsies found on crumbling promenades, lighthouses standing to attention, fishing villages giving way to arcades and brass bands and sand-playing in the bracing chill of a British summer.

This is both a history and a memoir of an enduring, if at times perplexing, love of the sea that won't fail to resonate with all who have felt the pull of the shores.

'A wonderfully readable memoir, full of amazing facts and funny stories, but ultimately an elegy for a fast-disappearing world' *Daily Mail*

'To plunge into this book is to experience a glorious drenching. it is erudite, funny, weird and endearing. the deeps will never seem the same again' John Banville, author of *The Sea*

arrow books

ALSO AVAILABLE IN ARROW

Reflections on a Summer Sea

Trevor Norton

This is the funny and touching story of a menagerie of eccentric and talented ecologists who, mainly as a hobby, spent forty summers at Lough Ine, a stunning marine lough in a corner of Ireland, where myths seep from the ground like will o' the wisps and, in one of the most unlikely projects in the history of science, were responsible for the reinvention of marine biology.

Among the stars of the book are the marine creatures that occupy the lake: sea urchins that won't dine unless they wear a hat, otters that steal experiments, and worms that will only mate by order of the moon. The creatures' eccentric behaviour is matched only by that of the ecologists themselves, whose antics and interactions with their Irish neighbours are all lovingly described with Norton's keen eye for both the wonderful and the absurd.

But for all its humour, the book is also a moving account of two ecologists who collaborated for forty years until their friendship came to a tragic end. The book brings together all the rich flavours of Ireland, the wonders of natural history and the magic of being a marine biologist just for the fun of it.

'A lovely book – Norton writes beautifully' *Sunday Express*

'Reflections on a Summer Sea stands apart, a thoughtful, funny look at life as it was' *Home & Country*

arrow books

ALSO AVAILABLE IN ARROW

Stars Beneath the Sea

Trevor Norton

This is a story of some of the brave, brilliant and often barmy men that invented diving. It is a story of explosive tempers and exploding teeth, of how to juggle live hand grenades and steer a giant rubber octopus.

A series of vivid portraits reveal the eccentric exploits of these pioneers. They include Guy who held a world altitude record when only sixteen, wrote a film for Humphrey Bogart, invented snorkelling and loved his wife enough to shoot her. Roy wore a backet over his head and stole a coral reef. Bill wearied of fishing with dynamite and wrestling deadly snakes, so he sealed himself in a metal coffin to dangle half a mile beneath the ocean. Cameron, testing the bouncing bomb for dam busters, made a plastic ear for a dog, a false testicle for a stallion and invented a mantrap disguised as a lavatory. He ascended from a depth of 200 feet without breathing equipment to see if his lungs would burst, then studied the effects of underwater explosions by standing closer and closer until shattered by the blast.

The book also traces the evolution from spear fishermen to conservationists, from treasure hunters to archaeologists, from photographers to philosophers. The sea is a secretive and seductive place and the author describes the magic and mystery of being beneath the waves.

'Norton writes with wit and a fine eye for the poetry in the scientific work' *Guardian*

arrow books

**Order further Trevor Norton titles
from your local bookshop, or have them delivered
direct to your door by Bookpost**

☐ **Underwater to Get out of the Rain**	9780099446583	£7.99
☐ **Reflections on a Summer Sea**	9780099416166	£8.99
☐ **Stars Beneath the Sea**	9780099405092	£8.99

Free post and packing
Overseas customers allow £2 per paperback

Phone: 01624 677237

Post: Random House Books
c/o Bookpost, PO Box 29, Douglas, Isle of Man IM99 1BQ

Fax: 01624 670923

email: bookshop@enterprise.net

Cheques (payable to Bookpost) and credit cards accepted

Prices and availability subject to change without notice.
Allow 28 days for delivery.
When placing your order, please state if you do not wish to receive any
additional information.

www.randomhouse.co.uk/arrowbooks

arrow books